Case Study
Research

This book is dedicated to Hans-Lukas Teuber,
who made research a lifelong goal for
all who studied with him.

Case Study Research
Design and Methods

Robert K. Yin

COSMOS Corporation

Los Angeles | London | New Delhi
Singapore | Washington DC

Los Angeles | London | New Delhi
Singapore | Washington DC

FOR INFORMATION:

SAGE Publications, Inc.
2455 Teller Road
Thousand Oaks, California 91320
E-mail: order@sagepub.com

SAGE Publications Ltd.
1 Oliver's Yard
55 City Road
London EC1Y 1SP
United Kingdom

SAGE Publications India Pvt. Ltd.
B 1/I 1 Mohan Cooperative Industrial Area
Mathura Road, New Delhi 110 044
India

SAGE Publications Asia-Pacific Pte. Ltd.
3 Church Street
#10-04 Samsung Hub
Singapore 049483

Acquisitions Editor: Vicki Knight
Editorial Assistant: Jessica Young
Assistant Editor: Kalie Koscielak
Production Editor: Brittany Bauhaus
Copy Editor: Gillian Dickens
Typesetter: C&M Digitals (P) Ltd.
Proofreader: Theresa Kay
Indexer: Rick Hurd
Cover Designer: Edgar Abarca
Marketing Manager: Nicole Elliott
Permissions Editor: Karen Ehrmann

Copyright © 2014 by SAGE Publications, Inc.

Printed in the United States of America

Library of Congress Cataloging-in-Publication Data

Yin, Robert K.
Case study research : design and methods / Robert K. Yin. — Fifth edition.

pages cm.
Includes bibliographical references and index.

ISBN 978-1-4522-4256-9 (pbk.: alk. paper) —
ISBN 978-1-4833-0200-3 (web pdf) 1. Case method.
2. Social sciences—Research--Methodology. I. Title.

H62.Y56 2014
300.72′2—dc23   2013008876

This book is printed on acid-free paper.

14 15 16 17 10 9 8 7 6 5 4 3

Brief Contents

Detailed Contents

ABOUT THE AUTHOR

Robert K. Yin is President of COSMOS Corporation, an applied research and social science firm. Over the years, COSMOS has successfully completed hundreds of projects for federal agencies, state and local agencies, and private foundations, and most of this book's applications come from these projects.

Outside of COSMOS, Dr. Yin has assisted numerous other research groups, helping to train their field teams or to design research studies. Recent engagements have been with evaluation teams at The World Bank and the United Nations Development Programme. Another assignment has been to provide guidance to assist doctoral students at the University of Copenhagen. Currently, Dr. Yin holds the position of distinguished scholar-in-residence at American University's School of International Service (Washington, D.C.). Earlier, he served as Visiting Scholar at the U.S. Government Accountability Office's research methodology division.

Dr. Yin has authored over 100 journal articles, reports, and books. His first book on the case study method, *Case Study Research: Design and Methods* (2014), is in its fifth edition. A companion book, *Applications of Case Study Research* (2012), is in its third edition. He has edited two case study anthologies (Yin, 2004, 2005) and has most recently authored a new text on qualitative research methods (Yin, 2011). Dr. Yin received his B.A. in history from Harvard College (magna cum laude) and his Ph.D. in brain and cognitive sciences from MIT.

FOREWORD

It is a privilege to provide the foreword for this fine book. It epitomizes a research method for attempting valid inferences from events outside the laboratory while at the same time retaining the goals of knowledge shared with laboratory science.

More and more I have come to the conclusion that the core of the scientific method is not experimentation per se but rather the strategy connoted by the phrase "plausible rival hypotheses." This strategy may start its puzzle solving with evidence, or it may start with hypothesis. Rather than presenting this hypothesis or evidence in the context-independent manner of positivistic confirmation (or even of postpositivistic corroboration), it is presented instead in extended networks of implications that (although never complete) are nonetheless crucial to its scientific evaluation.

This strategy includes making explicit other implications of the hypotheses for other available data and reporting how these fit. It also includes seeking out rival explanations of the focal evidence and examining their plausibility. The plausibility of these rivals is usually reduced by ramification extinction, that is, by looking at their other implications on other data sets and seeing how well these fit. How far these two potentially endless tasks are carried depends on the scientific community of the time and what implications and plausible rival hypotheses have been made explicit. It is on such bases that successful scientific communities achieve effective consensus and cumulative achievements, without ever reaching foundational proof. Yet, these characteristics of the successful sciences were grossly neglected by the logical positivists and are underpracticed by the social sciences, quantitative or qualitative.

Such checking by other implications and the ramification-extinction of rival hypotheses also characterizes validity-seeking research in the humanities, including the hermeneutics of Schleiermacher, Dilthey, Hirst, Habermas, and current scholarship on the interpretation of ancient texts. Similarly, the strategy is as available for a historian's conjectures about a specific event as for a scientist's assertion of a causal law. It is tragic that major movements in the social sciences are using the term *hermeneutics* to connote giving up on the goal of validity and abandoning disputation as to who has got it right. Thus, in addition to the quantitative and quasi-experimental case study approach that Yin teaches, our social science methodological armamentarium also needs a humanistic validity-seeking case study methodology that, although making no use of quantification or tests of significance, would still work on the same questions and share the same goals of knowledge.

As versions of this plausible rival hypotheses strategy, there are two paradigms of the experimental method that social scientists may emulate. By training, we are apt to think first of the randomized-assignment-to-treatments model coming to us from agricultural experimentation stations, psychological laboratories, randomized trials of medical and pharmaceutical research, and the statistician's mathematical models. Randomization purports to control an infinite number of rival hypotheses *without specifying what any of them are.* Randomized assignment never completely controls these rivals but renders them implausible to a degree estimated by the statistical model.

The other and older paradigm comes from physical science laboratories and is epitomized by experimental isolation and laboratory control. Here are the insulated and lead-shielded walls; the controls for pressure, temperature, and moisture; the achievement of vacuums; and so on. This older tradition controls for a relatively few but explicitly specified rival hypotheses. These are never controlled perfectly, but well enough to render them implausible. Which rival hypotheses are controlled for is a function of the disputations current in the scientific community at the time. Later, in retrospect, it may be seen that other controls were needed.

The case study approach as presented here, and quasi-experimentation more generally, is more similar to the experimental isolation paradigm than to the randomized-assignment-to-treatments model in that each rival hypothesis must be specified and specifically controlled for. The degree of certainty or consensus that the scientific community is able to achieve will usually be less in out-of-doors social science, due to the lesser degree of plausibility-reduction of rival hypotheses that is likely to be achieved. The inability to replicate at will (and with variations designed to rule out specific rivals) is part of the problem. We should use those singular-event case studies (which can never be replicated) to their fullest, but we should also be alert for opportunities to do intentionally replicated case studies.

Given Robert Yin's background (Ph.D. in experimental psychology, with a dozen publications in that field), his insistence that the case study method be done in conformity with science's goals and methods is perhaps not surprising. But such training and career choice are usually accompanied by an intolerance of the ambiguities of nonlaboratory settings. I like to believe that this shift was facilitated by his laboratory research on that most hard-to-specify stimulus, the human face, and that this experience provided awareness of the crucial role of pattern and context in achieving knowledge.

This valuable background has not kept him from thoroughly immersing himself in the classic social science case studies and becoming in the process a leader of nonlaboratory social science methodology. I know of no comparable text. It meets a longstanding need. I am confident that it will become a standard text in social science research methods courses.

—Donald T. Campbell
Bethlehem, Pennsylvania

PREFACE

Ever since this book's first edition (1984), you and many others have increasingly recognized case study research as a valuable research method. More broadly, the rising recognition has taken at least three readily observed forms.

Rising Recognition for Case Study Research

One sign has been the sheer frequency with which the term *case study research* appears in publications. Although far from providing a definitive estimate, Google's *Ngram Viewer* counts such frequencies in published books (Michel et al., 2010).[1] The figure below shows the *Ngram Viewer*'s findings for the period 1980 to 2008, comparing the citations to "case study research" with those for three competing terms: "survey research," "experimental designs," and "random assignment." During these years—roughly coinciding with the 30 years between the first and fifth editions of this book—the frequency for "case study research" shows a distinct upward trend in contrast to the other three terms, even though the absolute level is still lower than those of the other terms. The trend may surprise you (as it did me), because of the decade-long hullabaloo over random assignment designs as the preferred "gold standard" in doing any social science research.[2] Clearly, as evidenced by the frequency trends, case study research may be having an increasingly prominent place in everyone's portfolio.

A second form of recognition occurs when comprehensive reference works, documenting a research method in some formal way, emerge. For case study research, two such hefty works have now appeared, just since 2006: a four-volume, 1,580-page compilation of the seminal articles on case study research, reprinted from academic journals (David, 2006a), and a two-volume encyclopedia of case study research (Mills, Durepos, & Wiebe, 2010a).

The compilation of seminal works covers "the most important articles on the subject of case study research" published during "the entire span of the 20th century" (David, 2006b, p. xxiii). The volumes contain 86 articles reprinted from their original journals and covering a "wide spectrum of disciplines and fields" (David, 2006b, p. xxiii). Given that a good bunch of these articles was first published in the 1920s and 1930s, the

Figure   Frequency of Four Methodological Terms Appearing in Published Books, 1980–2008

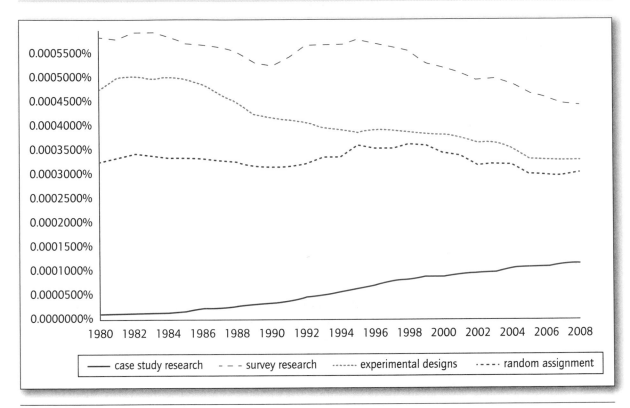

SOURCE: *Google Ngram Viewer* (http://books.google.com/ngrams), March 2012.

four-volume work now makes the case study research legacy readily accessible to you and other contemporary readers.

The encyclopedia of case study research contains 357 entries and more than 1,100 pages across its two separate, 8½" × 11" volumes (Mills, Durepos, & Wiebe, 2010b, p. xxxiii). The entries reflect the features of case study research as well as its place "within and alongside other research strategies" (Mills et al., 2010b, p. xxxiii). In producing the encyclopedia, the editors' expressed goal has been for the encyclopedia to serve as a valuable resource to "encourage new and renewed interest in case study research" (Mills et al., 2010b, p. xxxiii). Thus, the encyclopedia provides another rich resource for learning about case study research.

A third and more general form of recognition comes as a result of publications that focus on case study research methods in a particular field. Figure 1.1 in this book (see Chapter 1) contains a sampler of illustrative publications in 12 different fields. The works reflect the presence of case study research and its contributions to numerous research topics across a broad range of social science fields (disciplines and professions). The numerosity and diversity of these works appear to have increased and give scholars yet additional access to case study research.

The various editions of this book have possibly contributed to the growing recognition of case study research. More important, and as stated in earlier prefaces, the book's enduring objective is to guide you and other researchers and students to do case study research rigorously.

Distinctiveness of This Book

The book claims to be distinctive in several ways. First, it presents the breadth of case study research and its scholarly heritage, but also at a detailed and practical level. Other works do not offer as comprehensive a combination. Thus, the earlier versions of this book have been used as a complete portal to the world of case study research. Among its most distinctive features, the book provides

- a workable technical definition of the case study as a research method and its differentiation from other social science research methods (Chapter 1),
- an extensive discussion of case study designs (Chapter 2), and
- a continually expanding presentation of case study analysis techniques (Chapter 5).

These features are important because case study design and analysis tend to create the greatest challenges for people doing case study research. Sandwiched between the design and analysis chapters, the book has two extensive and important chapters pertaining to the preparation for (Chapter 3) and then collection of (Chapter 4) case study evidence. Chapter 6 then concludes the main text with a thorough discussion on composing case study reports, both written and oral.

Second, the book briefly depicts numerous case studies, deliberately drawing from different academic and professional fields. The depictions are found in the BOXES sprinkled throughout the text. Each BOX contains one or more concrete examples of published case studies, to illustrate points made in the text. The citations will increase your access to existing and (often) exemplary case studies. Most of the citations are contemporary, making the works easy to retrieve. However, to avoid losing connectivity with "roots," the citations also include older works that might be out of print but that still deserve to be recognized. The contents of these BOXES have changed over the various editions of this book, with some works having been replaced and other works having been added. The main text of this fifth edition now has 50 BOXES, covering more than 50 separately published case studies. Appendices A and B contain case studies presented in another 8 BOXES, and Appendix C has an index to the case studies in all these BOXES.

Third, the book has several distinctive technical features. These have been present since the first edition in 1984 and appear as themes across the chapters. One theme emphasizes the importance of defining the appropriate research question(s) when choosing to do case study research. The framing of the question(s) can directly influence the choice of research methods, with an essential goal being to avoid mismatches between the type of question and the type of method selected. Equally important, the framing of the questions can affect both the design of a case study and your ability to generalize from its findings. An excellently written article by Mario Small (2009) discusses these latter issues and is well worth reading.

Another theme derives from a seeming paradox: a parallel between case studies and experiments. One part of the parallel involves the pursuit of a replication strategy when conducting multiple experiments—a strategy that also applies to multiple case studies. The other part involves the pursuit of analytic generalizations when trying to generalize from experiments—but that also applies to case study research. Since its inception, this book has pointed out this parallel and its usefulness in designing case study research, though other works hardly mention the topic (the just-cited article by Small, 2009, being an exception).

Yet another theme is the importance of identifying and considering rival explanations throughout the case study research process, whether during the design, data collection, data analysis, or interpretation phases of the research. The attention to rivals—and especially knowing how to identify substantive rivals that go beyond those commonly associated with methodological artifacts (see Yin, 2000b)—is central to the research process. Donald Campbell points to the centrality in the Foreword to this book, and other key works, such as Paul Rosenbaum's (2002) work on *non*experimental research designs, also give prominent attention to rivals. However, most methodological works are only slowly beginning to attend to this aspect of social science research.

Using This Book

Aside from its technical aspects, this book contains several features aimed at making the book more practical and accessible. First, an overarching, *six-circled visual display* initially appears right after the dedication page and then at the outset of each of the six chapters. Each circle represents one of the six chapters of the main text. The visual display, showing the research process as a "linear but iterative process," serves as a basic roadmap for the entire process of doing case study research, helping to keep your bearings as you deal with any individual chapter. The beginnings of each chapter also start with an *abstract* as well as a *tip*. The tip poses key questions and answers for the core material in the entire chapter. The tips will quickly enable you to know how hard you might want to focus on any given chapter. An easily understood tip might suggest that the chapter only needs brief perusal. Conversely, a tip that appears confusing or obscure might suggest the need for a close reading.

Second, the book has a large number of *practical exercises*. Each exercise appears next to the chapter section that is most pertinent to the exercise. The exercises present a methodological situation or pose a methodological query worthy of being addressed. Whether the exercise is then used as part of an actual classroom or formal assignment is less important than the sufficient level of comfort you should ideally have with the situation or query.

Third, Appendix C consists of a cross-referencing index to specific case studies cited throughout the text. These include the case studies in the 50 BOXES as well as additional case studies cited in the text—and whose whole or excerpted versions appear in two books related to the present one (Yin, 2004, 2012). The index sorts the case studies according to 15 topics, so that you can more readily identify the case studies on a topic that might be of interest to you.

Finally—and in part reflecting the helpful suggestions of the reviewers of the fourth edition of this book—each chapter's headings and subheadings have been enhanced and also printed to be more friendly, to help you follow the flow and structure of the chapter. Likewise, to see the flow of the entire book and to find topics more readily, the Table of Contents lists the headings in greater detail than before.

New Features in This Edition

The challenge in composing this fifth edition has been twofold: to retain the book's key features and organization from earlier editions because of the warm reception given to those earlier editions, but to expand and enhance the presentation because of the advances in case study research since the fourth edition. Hopefully, the result also is twofold: Those familiar with the fourth edition should feel that the fifth edition has not changed all that much, but the new material and more detailed coverage of certain topics should nevertheless be readily apparent.

Added breadth and depth. Large portions of the new material now appear apart from the main text—to avoid disrupting the original organization from earlier editions—but also to make the new material easy to find. The material in Appendices A and B add breadth by covering brief notes about the role of case study research in two fields: psychology and evaluation. Although the main text, as with earlier editions, still gives scattered reference to these two topics, the growing use of case study research in psychology and in evaluation suggested the need for highlighting the two topics in separate places at the end of the book.

The added depth comes in the form of seven *tutorials,* located at the end of relevant chapters. Each tutorial provides a more detailed if not slightly more advanced discussion on a central topic already covered by the main text. The tutorials respond to reviewers who asked that the text provide more information on selected topics, to aid the more ambitious case study researchers. The tutorials explore the complexity of these central topics—but still in roughly vignette length—and also provide a few key references for further inquiry. At the same time, the main reason for separating the tutorials from the main text is because the main text already conveys the essential ideas on the central topic. As a result, the tutorials can be easily skipped if a researcher already has command of the topic or wants to avoid the greater complexity. Hopefully, this use of the tutorials also poses less of a threat to the compactness of the original book—which reviewers considered one of the book's main virtues.

Additional changes in the fifth edition. In addition to the new material just discussed, the fifth edition has benefited from an extensive amount of editing and rewriting (every sentence was revisited). All of the changes have been aimed at keeping the book as crisp as possible—despite the presence of the new materials—to help budding social scientists feel comfortable as they become acquainted with case study research. Aside from the sheer editing and copyediting, the more substantive clarifications are as follows:

- Greater attention to doing case studies under *relativist* (or *interpretivist*) as well as *realist* epistemologies:
  - An introductory discussion (Chapter 1)
  - Clarification that field interviews can be motivated by either epistemology (Chapter 3)
  - Change of terms from *facts* to *findings,* to accommodate the option of having field participants' multiple realities as the relevant findings (Chapter 4 and elsewhere)
  - Option for presenting participants' perspectives in case study reports (Chapter 6)
- A tightened definition of case study research (Chapter 1) and clearer definition of *the case* (Chapter 2)
- A more pointed discussion of the use of *analytic generalization* as the preferred strategy for generalizing case study findings (Chapter 2)
- The addition of other new terms:
  - For single-case studies, a change of terms from *unique* and *typical* to *unusual* and *common,* reinforcing the book's position that cases *not* be considered a sample of any larger universe or population (Chapter 2)
  - In the case study protocol, a change from *case study questions* (the original but inappropriate reference to the questions to be posed during data collection) to *data collection questions,* to reduce confusion because the former term has properly been used to refer to the questions of the full case study, not just of the data collection (Chapter 3)
- An expanded discussion of researchers' values and ethics, as well as of the procedures for protecting human subjects (Chapter 3)
- For data collection procedures (Chapter 4):

- An expanded discussion on the collection of interview data
- A new reference to *memo-writing* as an adjunct to data collection procedures
- New material on the care needed when collecting evidence from electronic sources and social media websites

- A greater emphasis on an inductive strategy for analyzing data, with a new discussion under the heading, *working your data from the ground up* (Chapter 5)
- An expanded discussion of the use of logic models, with new figures (Figs. 5.5 and 5.6)
- Enhancements in composing case study reports, noting that having a *flair* for composing does not hurt (Chapter 6):

    - A new discussion, as recommended by reviewers, on previously underemphasized portions of the case study report: the methodology section and the literature review section

    - A new reference to the parallel between case study reporting and *non*fiction writing

    - A reorganized sequence of sections in Chapter 6, making the flow more logical

- An expanded coverage and references to a broader set of case studies:

    - Case study methodological works in specific disciplines and professions (sampler found in Figure 1.1, Chapter 1)

    - Nine new case studies in the BOXES, five case studies covering a previously underemphasized topic—international affairs (see BOXES 4, 7D, 26, 37, and 49 and a sixth such case that appears in Tutorial 6-1)

- A brief glossary of terms directly related to case study research (but not social science research more generally)
- Updated and expanded citations throughout the text, with a large increase in the number of references listed at the end of the book

Given all these features in the fifth edition, one place where the book has not changed at all deserves repeated mention: Donald Campbell's insightful foreword. His succinct words, written nearly 30 years ago, still stand as a masterpiece about social science methods. Within the context of today's research dialogues, Campbell's work continues, remarkably, to speak with freshness and direct relevance. His foreword also positions well the role of case study research as portrayed in this book. I continue to be deeply honored by the inclusion of this foreword and have attempted to return but a modest contribution, now to his memory, in a subsequent publication (Yin, 2000b).

Overall, the continued advances in case study research have heavily influenced the revisions in the fifth edition. For instance, the new materials unhesitatingly add some more difficult concepts in doing case study research. As a result, readers should be forewarned that this edition may again be "harder" than the earlier ones. However, successful adoption of this edition's techniques and guidance also means that case study research will be better than in the past. The ultimate goal, as always, is to improve our social science methods and practices over those of previous generations of scholars. Only in this manner can every generation make its own mark, much less establish its own competitive niche.

Δ ACKNOWLEDGMENTS

Over the years, the initiation and continued evolution of this book have benefited from the advice and support of many people. I will resist creating a cumulative list acknowledging all these people from, in some cases, many years ago. However, Professor Leonard Bickman and Dr. Debra Rog invited me to submit the first manuscript of this book as part of their (then) new series on Applied Social Research Methods. Under their editorship, the series became a bellwether among all of Sage's publications for many years. I will be forever grateful to Leonard and Debra for providing the opportunity as well as the initial feedback and encouragement in completing the earlier versions of this book. Similarly, in relation to the book's still-early editions, colleagues such as Profs. Larry Susskind at the Department of Urban Studies and Planning (Massachusetts Institute of Technology), Nanette Levinson at the Department of Computer Sciences (The American University), and Eric Maaloe (the Aarhus School of Business in Denmark) all provided opportunities to teach and learn about case study research in different settings.

In a complementary manner, many research colleagues from a variety of universities and research organizations have participated in case study workshops as part of the projects undertaken at COSMOS Corporation. Whether posed at these workshops or in related e-mails, the continued questions about how to use case study research to address specific topics often have led serendipitously to new insights. Similarly, staff and consultants at COSMOS have struggled with numerous case study research projects, creating an exciting learning environment that seems to evolve endlessly and reach continually into as yet unexplored vistas, despite the passage of more than three decades. Among COSMOS's staff, Dr. Darnella Davis and (now) Professor Angela Ware have been the most active in recent years, and I thank them both for their stimulating questions and contributions to applied research processes.

The learning environment also has included collaborations outside of COSMOS. Among those of recent years has been work with Drs. Sukai Prom-Jackson and Fabrizio Felloni and their colleagues in doing evaluations at the United Nations Development Programme, as well as interactions with Professor Iben Nathan and her several cohorts of doctoral students at the University of Copenhagen. I thank you all for continuing to place case study research in such a variety of contemporary settings.

Fast-forwarding to this fifth edition, and as part of its preparation, Sage Publications invited reviewers to share their experience in using the fourth edition. I thank them for their invaluable remarks, and I hope they will see that their comments have influenced the new edition's enhancements and updates, although I could not respond to all of the suggestions: Lee Robbins, Ph.D., Golden Gate University; Dr. Jon Patterson, Chicago State University; Joy C. Phillips, East Carolina University; and Michael F. Ruff, Bentley University.

Research methods editors at Sage Publications also have, over the years, been extremely helpful in identifying ways of making the book more useful and usable for readers. For this most recent edition, I have had the pleasure of working first with Vicki Knight and Catherine Chilton. Vicki set the course for the revision, providing a vision and context based on her extensive knowledge gained as the acquisition editor for Sage's entire array of research methods books. Catherine then made sure that the final manuscript would be converted into a distinctive book. As you can guess, we all have worked hard to make the fifth edition have its own identity, beyond being a mere retread of earlier work. Nonetheless, as with the earlier versions, I alone bear the responsibility for this fifth edition.

At the same time, I conclude this preface by repeating a portion from the preface to the fourth edition. In it, I suggested that anyone's ideas about case studies—and about social science methods more generally—must have deeper roots. Mine go back to the two disciplines in which I was trained: history as an undergraduate and brain and cognitive sciences as a graduate. History and historiography first raised my consciousness regarding the importance (and challenge) of methodology in the social sciences. The unique brand of basic research in brain and cognitive science that I learned at MIT then taught me that empirical research advances only when it is accompanied by theory and logical inquiry, and not when treated as a mechanistic data collection endeavor. This lesson turns out to be a basic theme in doing case study research. I have therefore dedicated this book to the person at MIT who taught me this best and under whom I completed a dissertation on face recognition, though he might only barely recognize the resemblances between past and present, were he alive today.

NOTES △

1. The counts are based on the appearance of a given word or term in published books. Unfortunately, *Ngram Viewer* does not indicate the number of books covered during any particular period of time, so the website does not provide the number of books accessed from 1980 to 2008. Overall, *Ngram Viewer* claims that it has amassed about 4% of all books ever published (Michel et al., 2010).

2. Avid supporters of the gold standard have nevertheless published a research article using "case study" in its title (Cook & Foray, 2007). Readers should not take this as an example of how to do case study research, however. The article mainly contains the authors' rendition of a set of events at the outset of the decade in question (which apparently could not be told with quantitative methods) but does not present much actual evidence to support that rendition. (The rendition may be important, but whether it should be accepted as an example of case study research remains an open question.)

**Doing Case Study Research:
A linear but iterative process**

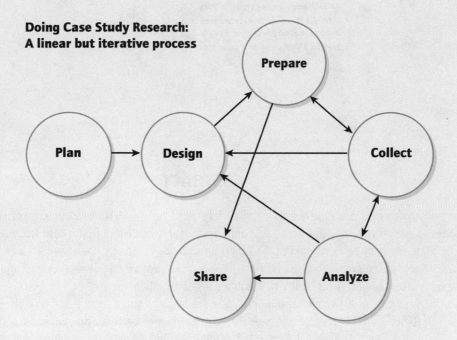

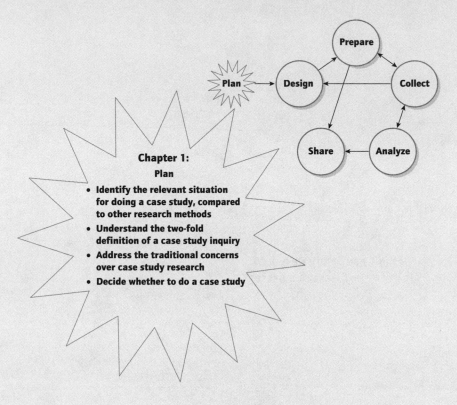

Chapter 1:
Plan

- Identify the relevant situation for doing a case study, compared to other research methods
- Understand the two-fold definition of a case study inquiry
- Address the traditional concerns over case study research
- Decide whether to do a case study

ABSTRACT

Case study research is one of several forms of social science research. Others include experiments, surveys, histories, and archival analyses such as economic or statistical modeling. Doing case study research would be the preferred method, compared to the others, in situations when (1) the main research questions are "how" or "why" questions; (2) a researcher has little or no control over behavioral events; and (3) the focus of study is a contemporary (as opposed to entirely historical) phenomenon.

As the first part of a twofold definition, a case study investigates a contemporary phenomenon (the "case") in its real-world context, especially when the boundaries between phenomenon and context may not be clearly evident. The second part of the definition points to case study design and data collection features, such as how data triangulation helps to address the distinctive technical condition whereby a case study will have more variables of interest than data points. Among the variations in case studies, a case study can include single or multiple cases, can be limited to quantitative evidence, and can be a useful method in doing an evaluation.

Properly doing case study research means addressing five traditional concerns about case studies—by conducting the research rigorously, avoiding confusion with teaching cases, knowing how to arrive at generalized conclusions if desired, carefully managing the level of effort, and understanding the comparative advantage of case study research. The overall challenge makes case study research "hard," although it has classically been considered a "soft" form of research.

1

GETTING STARTED

How to Know Whether and When to Use the Case Study as a Research Method

THE CASE STUDY AS A RESEARCH METHOD △

Doing Case Study Research

Doing case study research remains one of the most challenging of all social science endeavors. This book will help you—an experienced or budding social scientist—to deal with the challenge. Your goal is to design good case studies and to collect, present, and analyze data fairly. A further goal is to bring your case study to closure by composing a compelling article, report, book, or oral presentation.

Do not underestimate the extent of the challenge. Although you may be ready to focus on designing and doing case study research, others may espouse and advocate other research methods. Similarly, prevailing federal or other research funds may favor other methods, but not case study research. As a result, you may need to have ready responses to some inevitable questions.

First and foremost, you should explain and show how you are devoting yourself to following a rigorous methodological path. The path begins with a thorough literature review and the careful and thoughtful posing of research questions or objectives. Equally important will be a dedication to formal and explicit procedures when doing your research. Along these lines, this book offers much guidance. It shows how case study research includes procedures central to all types of research methods, such as protecting against threats to validity, maintaining a chain of evidence, and investigating and testing rival explanations. The successful experiences of scholars and students from using this book, for more than 30 years, may attest to the potential payoffs.

Second, you should understand and openly acknowledge the strengths and limitations of case study research. Such research, like any other, complements the strengths and limitations of other types of research. In the face of those who might only see the need for a single research method, this book believes that, just as different scientific methods prevail in the natural sciences, different social science research methods fill different needs and situations for investigating social science topics. For instance, in the natural sciences, astronomy is a science but does not rely on the experimental method; nor do engineering and geology (Scriven, 2009). Similarly, many studies in neurophysiology and neuroanatomy do not rely on statistical methods. In social science, later portions of this chapter will present more about the potential niches of different research methods.

> **Tip: *How do I know if I should use the case study method?***
>
> There's no formula, but your choice depends in large part on your research question(s). The more that your questions seek to explain some present circumstance (e.g., "how" or "why" some social phenomenon works), the more that case study research will be relevant. The method also is relevant the more that your questions require an extensive and "in-depth" description of some social phenomenon.
>
> **What are some other reasons you might cite for using or not using the case study method?**

Salience of Case Study Research in Different Fields

As a research method, the case study is used in many situations, to contribute to our knowledge of individual, group, organizational, social, political, and related phenomena. Not surprisingly, the case study has been a common research method in psychology, sociology, political science, anthropology, social work, business, education, nursing, and community planning. For instance, Appendix A describes the case study's lengthy but peculiar history in the field of psychology. Case studies are even found in economics, in investigations about the structure of a given industry or the economy of a city or a region.

Whatever the field of interest, the distinctive need for case study research arises out of the desire to understand complex social phenomena. In brief, a case study allows investigators to focus on a "case" and retain a holistic and real-world perspective—such as in studying individual life cycles, small group behavior, organizational and managerial processes, neighborhood change, school performance, international relations, and the maturation of industries.

This book covers the distinctive characteristics of the case study as a research method. The book will help you to deal with some of the more difficult questions still frequently neglected by available research texts. So often, for instance, the author has been confronted by a student or colleague who has asked (a) how to define the "case" being studied, (b) how to determine the relevant data to be collected, or (c) what to do with the data, once collected. This book answers these questions and more, by covering all phases of design, data collection, analysis, and composing.

At the same time, the book does not cover all uses of case studies. For example, it is not intended to help those who might use case studies as a teaching tool, popularized in the fields of law, business, medicine, or public policy (see Garvin, 2003; Llewellyn, 1948; Stein, 1952; Towl, 1969; Windsor & Greanias, 1983) but now prevalent in virtually every academic field, including the natural sciences. For teaching purposes, a case study need not contain a complete or accurate rendition of actual events. Rather, the purpose of the "teaching case" is to establish a framework for student discussion and debate. The criteria for developing good cases for teaching—usually of the single- and not multiple-case variety—are different from those for doing research (e.g., Caulley & Dowdy, 1987). Teaching case studies need not be concerned with the rigorous and fair presentation of empirical data; research case studies need to do exactly that.

Similarly, this book is not intended to cover those situations in which cases are used as a form of recordkeeping. Medical records, social work files, and other case records are used to facilitate some practice, such as medicine, law, or social work—or some case-based procedure such as conducting a child custody evaluation (e.g., Vertue, 2011). Although the creation of a case record or case evaluation may follow a similar procedure as if doing a case study for research purposes, in fact the criteria for developing good cases for practice differ from those for doing case study research (Bromley, 1986).

In contrast, the rationale for this book is that case study research is commonly found in both the social science disciplines and the practicing professions. For instance, Figure 1.1 lists 12 such fields, along with illustrative works that focus on the use of case study research in each specific field. (Not cited are either of two other kinds of works: general methodological texts that discuss various types of research, even if including case study research, and general texts on case study research that are not directed at any specific field.)

You as a social scientist would like to know how to design and conduct a single- or multiple-case study to investigate a research issue. You may only be doing a case study or you may be using it as part of a larger mixed methods study (see Chapter 2). Whichever, this book covers the entire range of issues in designing and doing case study research, including how to start and design a case study, collect case study evidence, analyze case study data, and compose a case study report.

COMPARING THE CASE STUDY WITH OTHER △ RESEARCH METHODS IN THE SOCIAL SCIENCES

When and why would you want to do case study research to examine some social science topic? Should you consider doing an experiment instead? A survey? A history? An

Figure 1.1   Sampler of Works Devoted to Case Study Methods in Specific Fields

FIELD	Illustrative Work(S)
DISCIPLINES:	
Anthropology and Ethnography	Burawoy, 1991
Political Science	George & Bennett, 2004; Gerring, 2004
Psychology	Bromley, 1986; Campbell, 1975
Sociology	Feagin, Orum, & Sjoberg, 1991; Hamel, 1992; Mitchell, 1983; Platt, 1992
PROFESSIONS:	
Accounting	Bruns, 1989
Business and International Business	Dul & Hak, 2008; Gibbert, Ruigrok, & Wicki, 2008; Johnston, Leach, & Liu, 2000; Meyer, 2001; Piekkari, Welch, & Paavilainen, 2009; Vissak, 2010
Education	Yin, 2006a
Evaluation	U.S. Government Accountability Office, 1990
Marketing	Beverland & Lindgreen, 2010
Nursing and Public Health	Baxter & Jack, 2008
Public Administration	Agranoff & Radin, 1991
Social Work	Gilgun, 1994; Lee, Mishna, & Brennenstuhl, 2010

analysis of archival records, such as the statistical modeling of economic trends or of student performance in schools?

These and other choices represent different research methods. Each is a different way of collecting and analyzing empirical evidence. Each follows its own logic and procedures. And each method has its own advantages and disadvantages. To get the most out of doing case study research, you need to appreciate these distinctions.

Relationships among the Methods: Not Hierarchical

A common misconception is that the various research methods should be arrayed hierarchically. Many social scientists still implicitly believe that case study research is only appropriate for the exploratory phase of an investigation, that surveys and histories are appropriate for the descriptive phase, and that experiments are the only way of pursuing explanatory or causal inquiries. The hierarchical view reinforces the idea that case study research is only a preliminary method and cannot be used to describe or test propositions.

This hierarchical view, however, may be questioned. Experiments with an exploratory motive have certainly always existed. In addition, the development of causal explanations has long been a serious concern of historians, reflected by the subfield known as historiography. Likewise, case study research is far from being only an exploratory strategy. Some of the best and most famous case studies have been explanatory case studies (e.g., see BOX 1 for a vignette on Allison and Zelikow's *Essence of Decision: Explaining the Cuban Missile Crisis,* 1999). Similarly, famous descriptive case studies are found in major disciplines such as sociology and political science (e.g., see BOX 2 for two vignettes). Additional examples of explanatory case studies, covering a university innovation, a drug prevention community organization, and small businesses, are presented in their entirety in a companion book to this text (Yin, 2012, chaps. 7–9). Examples of descriptive case studies, covering education leadership, residential crime prevention, and the development of a community organization, are similarly found there (Yin, 2012, chaps. 4–6). Thus, distinguishing among the various research methods and their advantages and disadvantages may require going beyond the hierarchical stereotype.

BOX 1
A Best-Selling, Explanatory, Single-Case Study

For more than 40 years, Graham Allison's (1971) original study of a single case, the 1962 Cuban missile crisis, has been a political science best seller. In this crisis, a U.S.–Soviet Union confrontation could have produced nuclear holocaust and doomed the entire world. The book posits three competing but also complementary theories to explain the crisis—that the United States and Soviets performed as (a) rationale actors, (b) complex bureaucracies, or (c) politically motivated groups of persons. Allison compares the ability of each theory to explain the actual course of events in the crisis: why the Soviet Union placed offensive (and not merely defensive) missiles in Cuba in the first place, why the United States responded to the missile deployment with a blockade (and not an air strike or invasion—the missiles already were in Cuba!), and why the Soviet Union eventually withdrew the missiles.

The case study shows the explanatory and not just descriptive or exploratory functions of single-case studies. Furthermore, the authors contrast the lessons from the case study with prevailing alternative explanations in post–Cold War studies of foreign policy and international politics. In this way, the book, even more thoughtfully presented in its second edition (Allison & Zelikow, 1999), forcefully demonstrates how a single case study can be the basis for significant generalizations.

BOX 2
Two Famous Descriptive Case Studies

2A. A Neighborhood Scene

Street Corner Society (1943/1993), by William F. Whyte, has for decades been recommended reading in community sociology. The book is a classic example of a descriptive case study. It traces the sequence of interpersonal events over time, describes a subculture that had rarely been the topic of previous study, and discovers key phenomena—such as the career advancement of lower income youths and their ability (or inability) to break neighborhood ties.

The study has been highly regarded despite its taking place in a small urban neighborhood (under the pseudonym of "Cornerville") and during a time period now nearly 100 years old. The value of the book is, paradoxically, its generalizability even to contemporary issues of individual performance, group structure, and the social structure of neighborhoods. Later investigators have repeatedly found remnants of Cornerville in their work, even though they have studied different neighborhoods and different time periods (also see BOX 20, Chapter 4, p. 114).

2B. A National Crisis

Neustadt and Fineberg's excellent analysis of a mass immunization campaign was issued originally as a government report in 1978, *The Swine Flu Affair: Decision-Making on a Slippery Disease,* and later published independently as *The Epidemic That Never Was* (1983). The case study describes the immunization of 40 million Americans that took place under President Gerald Ford's administration, when the United States was faced with a threat of epidemic proportions from a new and potentially lethal influenza strain. Because the case study has become known as an exceptionally well-researched case study, contemporary policy makers have continued to consult it for any generalizable lessons for understanding the quandaries of health crises and public actions in light of new threats by flu epidemics, such as the H1N1 strain of 2008–2010.

Exercise 1.1   Defining Different Types of Case Studies Used for Research Purposes

The more appropriate view may be an inclusive and pluralistic one: Every research method can be used for all three purposes—exploratory, descriptive, and explanatory studies. There may be exploratory case studies, descriptive case studies, or explanatory case studies. Similarly, there may be exploratory experiments, descriptive experiments, and explanatory experiments. What distinguishes the different methods is not a hierarchy but three important conditions discussed next. As an important caution, however, the clarification does not imply that the

(Continued)

(Continued)

boundaries between the methods—or the occasions when each is to be used—are always sharp. Even though each method has its distinct characteristics, there are large overlaps among them. The goal is to avoid gross misfits—that is, when you are planning to use one type of method but another is really more advantageous.

Define the three types of case studies used for research (but not teaching) purposes: (a) explanatory or causal case studies, (b) descriptive case studies, and (c) exploratory case studies. Compare the situations in which these different types of case studies would be most applicable. Now name a case study that you would like to conduct. Would it be explanatory, descriptive, or exploratory? Why?

When to Use Each Method

The three conditions consist of (a) the type of research question posed, (b) the extent of control a researcher has over actual behavioral events, and (c) the degree of focus on contemporary as opposed to entirely historical events. Figure 1.2 displays these three conditions and shows how each is related to five major research methods: experiments, surveys, archival analyses (e.g., economic modeling, or a statistical analysis in an epidemiological study), histories, and case studies. The importance of each condition, in distinguishing among the five methods, is as follows.

Figure 1.2 Relevant Situations for Different Research Methods

METHOD	(1) Form of Research Question	(2) Requires Control of Behavioral Events?	(3) Focuses on Contemporary Events?
Experiment	how, why?	yes	yes
Survey	who, what, where, how many, how much?	no	yes
Archival Analysis	who, what, where, how many, how much?	no	yes/no
History	how, why?	no	no
Case Study	how, why?	no	yes

SOURCE: COSMOS Corporation.

(a) *Types of research questions (see Figure 1.2, column 1)*. The first condition covers your research question(s) (Hedrick, Bickman, & Rog, 1993). A basic categorization scheme for the types of questions is the familiar series: "who," "what," "where," "how," and "why" questions.

If research questions focus mainly on "what" questions, either of two possibilities arises. First, some types of "what" questions are exploratory, such as "What can be learned from a study of a startup business?" This type of question is a justifiable rationale for conducting an exploratory study, the goal being to develop pertinent hypotheses and propositions for further inquiry. However, as an exploratory study, any of the five research methods can be used—for example, an exploratory survey (testing, for instance, the ability to survey startups in the first place), an exploratory experiment (testing, for instance, the potential benefits of different kinds of business incentives), or an exploratory case study (testing, for instance, the importance of differentiating "first-time" startups from startups by entrepreneurs who had previously started other firms).

The second type of "what" question is actually a form of a "how many" or "how much" line of inquiry—for example, "What have been the ways that communities have assimilated new immigrants?" Identifying such ways is more likely to favor survey or archival methods than others. For example, a survey can be readily designed to enumerate the "what," whereas a case study would not be an advantageous method in this situation.

Similarly, like this second type of "what" question, "who" and "where" questions (or their derivatives—"how many" and "how much") are likely to favor survey methods or the analysis of archival data, as in economic studies. These methods are advantageous when the research goal is to describe the incidence or prevalence of a phenomenon or when it is to be predictive about certain outcomes. The investigation of prevalent political attitudes (in which a survey or a poll might be the favored method) or of the spread of a disease like AIDS (in which an epidemiologic analysis of health statistics might be the favored method) would be typical examples.

In contrast, "how" and "why" questions are more explanatory and likely to lead to the use of a case study, history, or experiment as the preferred research method. This is because such questions deal with operational links needing to be traced over time, rather than mere frequencies or incidence. Thus, if you wanted to know how a community successfully overcame the negative impact of the closing of its largest employer—a military base (see Bradshaw, 1999, also presented in BOX 26, Chapter 5, p. 137)—you would be less likely to rely on a survey or an examination of archival records and might be better off doing a history or a case study. Similarly, if you wanted to know how research investigators may possibly (but unknowingly) bias their research, you could design and conduct a series of experiments (see Rosenthal, 1966).

Let us take two more examples. If you were studying "who" had suffered as a result of terrorist acts and "how much" damage had been done, you might survey residents, examine government records (an archival analysis), or conduct a "windshield survey" of the affected area. In contrast, if you wanted to know "why" the act had occurred, you would have to draw upon a wider array of documentary information, in addition to conducting interviews; if you focused on the "why" question in more than one terrorist act, you would probably be doing a multiple-case study.

Similarly, if you wanted to know "what" the outcomes associated with a new governmental program had been, you could answer this question by doing a survey or by examining economic data, depending on the type of program involved. Questions—such as "How many clients did the program serve?" "What kinds of benefits were received?" "How often were different benefits produced?"—all could be answered without doing a case study. But if you needed to know "how" or "why" the program had worked (or not), you would lean toward either a case study or a field experiment.

To summarize, the first and most important condition for differentiating among the various research methods is to classify the type of research question being asked. In general, "what" questions may either be exploratory (in which case, any of the methods could be used) or about prevalence (in which surveys or the analysis of archival records would be favored). "How" and "why" questions are likely to favor using a case study, experiment, or history.

Exercise 1.2   Defining a Case Study Research Question

Develop a "how" or "why" question that would be the rationale for a case study that you might conduct. Instead of doing a case study, now imagine that you only could do a history, a survey, or an experiment (but not a case study) to address this question. What would be the distinctive advantage of doing a case study, compared to these other methods, in order to address the question?

Defining your research question(s) is probably the most important step to be taken in a research study, so you should be patient and allow sufficient time for this task. The key is to understand that your research questions have both *substance*—for example, What is my study about?—and *form*—for example, am I asking a "who," "what," "where," "why," or "how" question? Others have focused on some of the substantively important issues (see Campbell, Daft, & Hulin, 1982); the point of the preceding discussion is that the form of the question can provide an important clue regarding the appropriate research method to be used. Remember, too, that the methods can overlap. Thus, for some questions, a choice among methods might actually exist. Be aware, finally, that you (or your academic department) may be predisposed to favor a particular method regardless of the study question. If so, be sure to create the form of the study question best matching the method you were predisposed to favor in the first place.

Exercise 1.3   Identifying the Research Questions Covered When Other Research Methods Are Used

Locate a research study based solely on the use of a survey, history, or experiment (but not a case study). Identify the research question(s) addressed by the study. Does the type of question differ from those that might have appeared as part of a case study on the same topic, and if so, how?

(b) *Extent of control over behavioral events (see Figure 1.2, column 2) and* (c) *degree of focus on contemporary as opposed to entirely historical events (see Figure 1.2, column 3).* Assuming that "how" and "why" questions are to be the focus of study, these two remaining conditions help to distinguish further among a history, case study, and experiment.

A history is the preferred method when there is virtually no such control or access. The distinctive contribution of the historical method is in dealing with the "dead" past—that is, when direct observations of the event(s) being studied are not possible and when no relevant persons are alive to report, even retrospectively, what occurred. The historian must then rely on primary documents, secondary documents, and cultural and physical artifacts as the main sources of evidence. A history can, of course, be done about fairly recent events, as in conducting an oral history (e.g., Janesick, 2010); in this situation, the method begins to overlap with that of the case study.

The case study is preferred when examining contemporary events, but when the relevant behaviors cannot be manipulated. The case study relies on many of the same techniques as a history, but it adds two sources of evidence not usually available as part of the historian's repertoire: direct observation of the events being studied and interviews of the persons involved in the events. Again, although case studies and histories can overlap, the case study's unique strength is its ability to deal with a full variety of evidence—documents, artifacts, interviews, and observations—beyond what might be available in a conventional historical study. Moreover, in some situations, such as participant-observation (see Chapter 4), informal manipulation can occur.

Finally, experiments are done when an investigator can manipulate behavior directly, precisely, and systematically. This can occur in a laboratory setting, in which an experiment may focus on one or two isolated variables (and presumes that the laboratory environment can "control" for all the remaining variables beyond the scope of interest), or it can be done in a field setting, where the term *field (or social) experiment* has emerged to cover research where investigators "treat" whole groups of people in different ways, such as providing them with different kinds of vouchers to purchase services (Boruch & Foley, 2000).

The full range of experimental science also includes those situations in which the experimenter cannot manipulate behavior but in which the logic of experimental design still may be applied. These situations have been commonly regarded as *quasi-experimental* situations (e.g., Campbell & Stanley, 1966; Cook & Campbell, 1979) or *observational studies* (e.g., Rosenbaum, 2002). The quasi-experimental approach even can be used in a historical setting, where, for instance, an investigator may be interested in studying race riots or lynchings (see Spilerman, 1971) and use a quasi-experimental design because no control over the behavioral event was possible. In this case, the experimental method begins to overlap with histories.

A special situation in evaluation research. In the field of evaluation, Boruch and Foley (2000) have made a compelling argument for the desirability of one type of field experiment—*randomized field trials*—to be used in virtually all evaluations. For instance, the authors maintain that the field trials design, emulating the design of laboratory experiments, can be and has been used even when evaluating complex community initiatives. However, you should be cautioned about the possible limitations of this design.

In particular, the design may work well when, within a community, individual consumers or users of services are the units of analysis. Such a situation would exist if a community intervention consisted, say, of a health promotion campaign and the outcome of interest was the incidence of certain illnesses among the community's residents. The random assignment might designate a few communities to have the campaign, compared to a few that did not, and the outcomes would compare the condition of the residents in both sets of communities.

In many community studies, however, the actual outcomes of interest and therefore the appropriate unit of analysis may be at the community or collective level and not at the individual level. For instance, efforts to upgrade neighborhoods may be concerned with improving a neighborhood's economic base (e.g., the number of jobs per residential population). Now, although the candidate communities still can be randomly assigned, the degrees of freedom in any later statistical analysis are limited by the number of communities as well as the number of residents (the technical tool would be a two-level hierarchical linear model). Most field experiments will not be able to support the participation of a sufficiently large number of communities to overcome the severity of the subsequent statistical constraints.

The limitations when communities or collective entities are the units of analysis are extremely important because many public policy objectives focus on the collective rather than individual level. For instance, the thrust of federal education policy in the early 2000s focused on *school* performance. Schools were held accountable for year-to-year performance even though the composition of the students enrolled at the schools changed each year. Creating and implementing a field trial based on a large number of schools, as opposed to a large number of students, would present an imposing challenge and the need for extensive research resources. In fact, Boruch (2007) found that a good number of the randomized field trials inadvertently used the incorrect unit of analysis (individuals rather than collectives), thereby making the findings from the trials less usable.

Field experiments with a large number of collective entities (e.g., neighborhoods, schools, or organizations) also raise a number of practical challenges:

- any randomly selected "control" sites may adopt important components of the intervention of interest before the end of the field experiment and no longer qualify as "no-treatment" sites;
- the funded intervention may call for the experimental communities to reorganize their entire manner of providing certain services—that is, a "systems" change— thereby creating site-to-site variability in the unit of assignment (the experimental design assumes that the unit of assignment is the same at every site, both intervention and control);
- the same systems change aspect of the intervention also may mean that the organizations or entities administering the intervention may not necessarily remain stable over the course of time (the design requires such stability until the random field trials have been completed); and
- the experimental or control sites may be unable to continue using the same instruments and measures (the design, which will ultimately cluster the data to compare intervention sites as a group with comparison sites as a second group, requires common instruments and measures across sites).

The existence of any of these conditions will likely lead to the need to find alternatives to randomized field trials.

Summary. You should be able to identify some situations in which all research methods might be relevant (such as exploratory research) and other situations in which two methods might be considered equally attractive. You also can use multiple methods in any given study (for example, a survey within a case study or a case study within a survey). To this extent, the various methods are not mutually exclusive. But you also should be able to identify some situations in which a specific method has a distinct advantage. For case study research, this niche is when

- A "how" or "why" question is being asked about
  - a contemporary set of events,
  - over which a researcher has little or no control.

To determine the questions that are the most pressing on a topic, as well as to gain some precision in formulating these questions, requires much preparation. One way is to review the literature on the topic (Cooper, 1984). Note that such a literature review is therefore a means to an end, and not—as many people have been taught to think—an end in itself. Novices may think that the purpose of a literature review is to determine the *answers* about what is known on a topic; in contrast, experienced investigators review previous research to develop sharper and more insightful *questions* about the topic.

VARIATIONS IN CASE STUDIES, BUT A COMMON DEFINITION   △

Our discussion has progressed without formally defining *case study*. Moreover, commonly asked questions about case study research still have been unanswered. For example, (1) Is it still a case study when more than one case is included in the same study? (2) Does a case study preclude the use of quantitative evidence? (3) Can a case study be used to do evaluations? Let us now attempt to define the case study as a research method and then answer these three questions.

Definition of the Case Study as a Research Method

Some definitions of case studies have merely repeated the types of topics to which case studies have been applied. For example, in the words of one observer,

> The essence of a case study, the central tendency among all types of case study, is that it tries to illuminate a *decision* or set of decisions: why they were taken, how they were implemented, and with what result. (Schramm, 1971, emphasis added)

This definition thus cites cases of "decisions" as the major focus of case studies. Other common cases include "individuals," "organizations," "processes," "programs," "neighborhoods," "institutions," and even "events." However, dwelling on the definition of a case study "by interest in an individual case, not by the methods of inquiry used" (e.g., Stake, 2005, p. 443) would seem insufficient to establish the complete basis for case studies as a research *method*.

Alternatively, many of the earlier social science textbooks failed to consider case study research as a formal method at all. As discussed previously, one common shortcoming was to consider case study research as the exploratory stage of some other type of research method.

Another definitional shortcoming was to confuse case study research with doing "fieldwork," as in ethnography or participant-observation. Thus, early textbooks limited their discussion of case studies to descriptions of participant-observation or of fieldwork as a data collection process, without elaborating further on a definition of case study research (e.g., Kidder & Judd, 1986; Nachmias & Nachmias, 1992).

In a historical overview of the case study in American methodological thought, Jennifer Platt (1992) explains the reasons for these treatments. She traces the practice of doing case studies back to the conduct of life histories, the work of the Chicago school of sociology, and casework in social work. She then shows how *participant-observation* emerged as a data collection technique, effectively eliminating any further recognition of case study research. Thus, she found ample references to case study research in methodological textbooks up to 1950 but hardly any references to case studies or to case study research in textbooks from 1950 to 1980 (Platt, 1992, p. 18). Finally, Platt explains how the first edition of this book (1984) definitively dissociated case study research from the limited perspective of only doing some kind of field-work. She then also found a renewed discussion of case study research in textbooks, largely occurring from 1980 to 1989 and continuing thereafter (also see this book's preface for a Google Ngram analysis of the trends from 1980 to 2008). Case study research, in her words, had now come to be appreciated as having its own "logic of design . . . a strategy to be preferred when circumstances and research problems are appropriate rather than an ideological commitment to be followed whatever the circumstances" (Platt, 1992, p. 46).

Twofold definition of case study. And just what is this research method? The critical features first appeared in earlier publications (Yin, 1981a, 1981b), predating the first edition of this book. The resulting definition as it has evolved over the four previous editions of this book reflects a twofold definition of case studies. The first part begins with the *scope of a case study:*

1. A case study is an empirical inquiry that
   - investigates a contemporary phenomenon (the "case") in depth and within its real-world context, especially when
   - the boundaries between phenomenon and context may not be clearly evident.

In other words, you would want to do case study research because you want to understand a real-world case and assume that such an understanding is likely to involve important contextual conditions pertinent to your case (e.g., Yin & Davis, 2007).

This first part of the definition therefore helps you to continue distinguishing case study research from the other methods that have been discussed. An experiment, for instance, deliberately separates a phenomenon from its context, attending only to the phenomenon of interest and only as represented by a few variables (typically, the context is entirely ignored because it is "controlled" by the laboratory environment). A history, by comparison, does deal with the entangled situation between phenomenon and context but usually in studying *non*contemporary events. Finally, surveys can try to deal with phenomenon and context, but a survey's ability to investigate the context is extremely limited. The survey designer, for instance, constantly struggles to limit the number of items in a questionnaire (and hence the number of questions that can be analyzed) to fall safely within the allotted degrees of freedom (usually constrained by the number of respondents who are to be surveyed).

The second part of the definition of case studies arises because phenomenon and context are not always sharply distinguishable in real-world situations. Therefore, other methodological characteristics become relevant as the *features of a case study:*

2. A case study inquiry
   - copes with the technically distinctive situation in which there will be many more variables of interest than data points,[1] and as one result
   - relies on multiple sources of evidence, with data needing to converge in a triangulating fashion, and as another result
   - benefits from the prior development of theoretical propositions to guide data collection and analysis.

In essence, the twofold definition—covering the scope and features of a case study—shows how case study research comprises an all-encompassing method—covering the logic of design, data collection techniques, and specific approaches to data analysis. (For a further elaboration on this definition, see Tutorial 1-1 at the end of this chapter.) In this sense, case study research is not limited to being a data collection tactic alone or even a design feature alone (Stoecker, 1991). How the method is practiced is the topic of this entire book.

Applicability of different epistemological orientations. This all-encompassing method also can embrace different epistemological orientations—for example, a *relativist* or *interpretivist* compared to a *realist* orientation.[2] Much of case study research as it is described in this book appears to be oriented toward a *realist* perspective, which assumes the existence of a single reality that is independent of any observer. However, case study research also can excel in accommodating a *relativist* perspective—acknowledging multiple realities having multiple meanings, with findings that are observer dependent. For instance, Chapter 2 will later discuss the importance of "theory" in designing case studies. If you want to assume a relativist perspective, your theory in designing a case study may very well concern the way that you will capture the perspectives of different participants, and how and why you believe their different meanings will illuminate your topic of study.

Exercise 1.4 Finding and Analyzing an Existing Case Study from the Literature

Retrieve an example of case study research from the research literature. The case study can be on any topic, but it must have some empirical method and present some empirical (qualitative or quantitative) data. Why is this a case study? What, if anything, is distinctive about the findings that could not be learned by using some other type of social science method focusing on the same topic?

Variations in Case Studies as a Research Method

Certain other characteristics of case study research are not critical for defining the method. They may be considered variations in case studies, which now also provide the opportunity to answer the three questions posed at the outset of this subsection.

Yes, case study research includes both single- and multiple-case studies. Although some fields, such as political science and public administration, have tried to distinguish between these two approaches (and have used such terms as the *comparative case method* as a distinctive form of multiple-case studies; see Agranoff & Radin, 1991; Dion, 1998; Lijphart, 1975), single- and multiple-case studies are in reality but two variants of case study designs (see Chapter 2 for more). BOX 3 contains two examples of multiple-case studies.

BOX 3
Multiple-Case Studies: Case Studies
Containing Multiple "Cases"

Case studies can cover multiple cases and then draw a single set of "cross-case" conclusions. The two examples below both focused on a topic of continuing public interest: identifying successful programs to improve U.S. social conditions.

3A. A Cross-Case Analysis following the Presentation of Separate, Single Cases

Jonathan Crane (1998) edited a book that has nine social programs as separate cases. Each case has a different author and is presented in its own chapter. The programs had in common strong evidence of their effectiveness, but they varied widely in their focus—from education to nutrition to drug prevention to preschool programs to drug treatment for delinquent youths. The editor then presents a cross-program analysis in a final chapter, attempting to draw generalizable conclusions that could apply to many other programs.

3B. A Book Whose Entire Text Is Devoted to the Multiple-Case ("Cross-Case") Analysis

Lisbeth Schorr's (1997) book is about major strategies for improving social conditions, illustrated by four policy topics: welfare reform, strengthening the child protection system, education reform, and transforming neighborhoods. The book continually refers to specific cases of successful programs, but these programs do not appear as separate, individual chapters. Also citing data from the literature, the author develops numerous generalizations based on the case studies, including the need for successful programs to be "results oriented." Similarly, she identifies six other attributes of highly effective programs (also see BOX 41A and 41B, Chapter 6, p. 183).

And yes, case study research can include, and even be limited to, quantitative evidence. In fact, any contrast between quantitative and qualitative evidence does not set apart the various research methods. Note that, as analogous examples, some experiments (such as studies of perceptions) and some survey questions (such as those seeking categorical rather than numerical responses) rely on qualitative and not quantitative evidence. Likewise, historical research can include enormous amounts of quantitative evidence.

As a related but important note, case study research is not just a form of qualitative research, even though some have recognized the case study as being among the array of qualitative research choices (e.g., Creswell, 2012). The use of a mix of quantitative and qualitative evidence, along with the necessity for defining a "case," are but two of the ways that case study research goes beyond being a type of qualitative research. As a further example, case study research need not always engage in the *thick description* (Geertz, 1973) or detailed observational evidence that marks most forms of qualitative research.

And yes (and as discussed in greater detail in Appendix B of this book), case study research has its own place in doing evaluations (see Cronbach & Associates, 1980; Patton, 2002; U.S. Government Accountability Office, 1990; Stufflebeam & Shinkfield, 2007, pp. 309–324). There are at least four different applications (U.S. Government Accountability Office, 1990). The most important is to *explain* the presumed causal links in real-world interventions that are too complex for survey or experimental methods. A second application is to *describe* an intervention and the real-world context in which it occurred. Third, a case study can *illustrate* certain topics within an evaluation, again in a descriptive mode. Fourth, case study research may be used to *enlighten* those situations in which the intervention being evaluated has no clear, single set of outcomes. Whatever the application, one constant theme is that program sponsors—rather than researchers alone—may have a prominent role in defining the evaluation questions and relevant data categories.

ADDRESSING TRADITIONAL CONCERNS ABOUT ⬚ CASE STUDY RESEARCH

Although the case study is a distinctive form of empirical inquiry, many researchers nevertheless disdain the method. In other words, as a research endeavor, the case study has been viewed as a less desirable form of inquiry than either an experiment or a survey. Why is this?

Rigorous enough? Perhaps the greatest concern has arisen over a presumed need for greater rigor in doing case study research. Too many times, a case study researcher has been sloppy, has not followed systematic procedures, or has allowed equivocal evidence to influence the direction of the findings and conclusions. In doing case study research, you need to avoid such practices. Interestingly, a lack of rigor is presumed to be less likely when using the other methods—possibly because of the existence of numerous methodological texts providing researchers with specific procedures to be followed. In contrast, only a small (though increasing) number of texts besides the present one cover case study research in similar fashion.

Confusion with teaching cases? The possibility also exists that people have confused case study research with the case studies used in teaching. In teaching, case study materials may be deliberately altered to demonstrate a particular point more effectively (e.g., Ellet, 2007; Garvin, 2003). In research, any such step would be strictly forbidden. Thus, if a person's main prior exposure to case studies has been to one or more teaching cases, the exposure may taint the person's view of the case study as a research method.

In doing case study research, you must work hard to report all evidence fairly, and this book will help you to do so. What is often forgotten is that bias also can enter into the conduct of experiments (see Rosenthal, 1966) and the use of other research methods, such as designing questionnaires for surveys (Sudman & Bradburn, 1982) or in conducting historical research (Gottschalk, 1968). The problems are not different, but in case study research, they may occur more frequently and demand greater attention.

Exercise 1.5   Examining Case Studies Used for Teaching Purposes

Obtain a copy of a case study designed for teaching purposes (e.g., a case in a textbook used in a business school course). Identify the specific ways in which this type of "teaching" case is different from research case studies. Does the teaching case cite primary documents, contain evidence, or display data? Does the teaching case discuss how this evidence was fairly collected? What appears to be the main objective of the teaching case?

Generalizing from case studies? A third common concern about case study research is an apparent inability to generalize from case study findings. "How can you generalize from a single case?" is a frequently heard question. The answer is not simple (Kennedy, 1976). However, consider for the moment that the same question had been asked about an experiment: "How can you generalize from a single experiment?" In fact, generalizations in science are rarely based on single experiments; they are usually based on a multiple set of experiments that have replicated the same phenomenon under different conditions.

The same approach can be used with case studies but requires a different concept of the appropriate research designs, discussed in detail in Chapter 2. The short answer is that case studies, like experiments, are generalizable to theoretical propositions and not to populations or universes. In this sense, the case study, like the experiment, does not represent a "sample," and in doing case study research, your goal will be to expand and generalize theories (analytic generalizations) and not to extrapolate probabilities (statistical generalizations). Or, as three notable social scientists describe in their *single* case study done years ago, the goal is to do a "generalizing" and not a "particularizing" analysis (Lipset, Trow, & Coleman, 1956, pp. 419–420).[3]

Unmanageable level of effort? A fourth frequent concern about case study research is that case studies can potentially take too long and that they can result in massive, unreadable documents. This concern may be appropriate, given the way case studies have been done in the past (e.g., Feagin, Orum, & Sjoberg, 1991), but this is not necessarily the way case studies must be done in the future. Chapter 6 discusses alternative ways of composing a case study (whether presenting the case study in writing or orally)—including an option in which the traditional, flowing (and potentially lengthy) narrative can be avoided.

Nor need case studies take a long time. This incorrectly confuses case study research with a specific method of data collection, such as ethnography (e.g., O'Reilly, 2005) or participant-observation (e.g., DeWalt & DeWalt, 2011). Ethnographies usually require long periods in the field and emphasize detailed observational and interview evidence. Participant-observation may similarly assume a hefty investment of field effort. In contrast, a case study is a form of inquiry that does *not* depend solely on ethnographic or participant-observer data. You could even do a valid and high-quality case study without leaving the telephone or Internet, depending on the topic being studied.

Comparative advantage? A fifth possible concern with case study research has to do with its unclear comparative advantage, in contrast to other research methods. This issue especially emerged during the first decade of the 21st century, which favored randomized controlled trials (RCTs) or "true experiments," especially in education and related topics. These kinds of experiments were esteemed because they aimed to establish the effectiveness of various treatments or interventions (e.g., Jadad, 1998). In the eyes of many, the emphasis led to a downgrading of case study research because case studies (and other types of nonexperimental methods) cannot directly address this issue.

Overlooked has been the possibility that case studies can offer important insights not provided by RCTs. Noted quantitative scholars suggest, for instance, that RCTs, though addressing the effectiveness question, are limited in their ability to explain "how" or "why" a given treatment or intervention necessarily worked (or not), and that case studies are needed to investigate such issues (e.g., Shavelson & Towne, 2002, pp. 99–106)—or, as succinctly captured by the subtitle of an excellent article on evaluating public programs, "not whether programs work, but how they work" (Rogers, 2000).[4] In this sense, case study research does indeed offer its own advantage. At a minimum, case studies may be valued "as adjuncts to experiments rather than as alternatives to them" (Cook & Payne, 2002). In clinical psychology, a "large series of single case studies," confirming predicted behavioral changes after the initiation of treatment, may augment the evidence of efficaciousness from a field trial (e.g., Veerman & van Yperen, 2007). Finally, in a similar manner, case study research can readily complement the use of other quantitative and statistical methods (see BOX 4).

BOX 4
Complementarity of Case Study
and Statistical Research

In the field of international politics, a major proposition has been that "democracies seldom if ever make war upon one another" (George & Bennett, 2004, p. 37). The proposition has been the subject of an extensive body of research, involving statistical studies as well as case studies. An excellent chapter by George and Bennett (2004, pp. 37–58) shows how the statistical studies may have tested the correlation between regime types and war, but how case studies have been needed to examine the underlying processes that might explain such a correlation. For instance, one of the more prominent explanations has been that democracies are able to make formal commitments with each other that make the use of military force unnecessary for resolving disputes (p. 57). The review shows how the relevant research has taken place over many decades, involving many different scholars. The entire body of research, based on both the statistical and case studies, illustrates the complementarity of these methods.

Summary. Despite the fact that these five common concerns can be allayed, as above, one major lesson is that a good case study is still difficult to do. The inability to screen for a researcher's ability to do a good case study further compounds the problem. People know when they cannot play music; they also know when they cannot do mathematics beyond a certain level, and they can be tested for other skills, such as the bar examination in law. Somehow, the skills for doing good case study research have not yet been formally defined. As a result, "most people feel that they can prepare a case study, and nearly all of us believe we can understand one. Because neither view is well founded, the case study receives a good deal of approbation it does not deserve" (Hoaglin, Light, McPeek, Mosteller, & Stoto, 1982, p. 134). This quotation is from a book by five prominent *statisticians*. Surprisingly, from another field, even they recognize the challenge of doing a good case study.

SUMMARY △

This chapter has introduced the importance of case study research. Like other methods, it is a way of investigating an empirical topic by following a set of desired procedures. Articulating these procedures will dominate the remainder of this book.

The chapter has provided an operational definition of the case study and has identified some of the variations in case studies. The chapter also has attempted to distinguish case study research from alternative methods in social science, indicating the situations in which doing a case study may be preferred, for instance, to doing a survey. Some situations may have no clearly preferred method, as the strengths and weaknesses of the various methods may overlap. The basic goal, however, is to consider all the methods in an inclusive and pluralistic fashion—before settling on your method of choice in conducting a new social science study.

Finally, the chapter has addressed some of the major concerns about case study research, suggesting possible responses to these concerns. However, we must all work hard to overcome the problems of doing case study research, including the recognition that some of us were not meant, by skill or disposition, to do such research in the first place. Case study research is remarkably hard, even though case studies have traditionally been considered to be "soft" research, possibly because researchers have not followed systematic procedures. By offering an array of such procedures, this book tries to make case study research easier to follow and your own case study better.

NOTES TO CHAPTER 1 △

1. Appendix A has a full discussion of the reasons for the large number of variables in a case study.

2. These terms were deliberately chosen even though they oversimplify two contrasting perspectives. Ignored are the many more subtle orientations that investigators may bring to their research. For brief definitions, see Schwandt's (2007) dictionary of qualitative inquiry, which characterizes *realism* as "the doctrine that there are real objects that exist independently of our knowledge of their existence" (p. 256), *relativism* as "the doctrine that denies that there are universal truths" (p. 261), and *interpretivism* as a term that has "occasionally been used as a synonym for all qualitative inquiry" (p. 160).

3. There nevertheless may be exceptional circumstances when a single case is so unique or important that a case study investigator has no desire to generalize to any other cases. See Stake's (2005) "intrinsic" case studies and Lawrence-Lightfoot and Davis's (1997) "portraits."

4. Scholars also point out that the classic experiments only can test simple causal relationships—that is, when a single treatment such as a new drug is hypothesized to produce an effect. However, for many social and behavioral topics, the relevant causes may be complex and involve multiple interactions, and investigating these may well be beyond the capability of any single experiment (George & Bennett, 2004, p. 12).

Tutorial 1.1:
More on Defining "Case Study"

In this book, a "case study" means a particular kind of research inquiry. The term parallels those used to refer to other kinds of inquiries, such as an "experiment," a "survey," and a "history." "Case study research" is then a more formal label (again parallel to "experimental research," "survey research," and "historical research"), and the method of doing case study research is the topic of this entire book.

The definition of case study in Chapter 1 of this fifth edition retains the essence stated in this book's first edition (1984). The definition has two parts: (a) the scope of a case study inquiry and (b) its features. Concepts implicit in the original definition now appear explicit, including notions such as an "in-depth" inquiry, the phenomenon being studied as the "case," the "triangulation of evidence," and having "more variables of interest than data points."

Communicating a clear definition is difficult. Some reference works (e.g., Abercrombie, Hill, & Turner, 2006; Schwandt, 2007) give short but incomplete definitions. Other works may use several pages and still not attain clarity (e.g., David, 2006b; Mills et al., 2010b). This book's definition also can be enhanced, to avoid misinterpretations that have arisen with the book's earlier editions. The enhancements are as follows:

1. The lack of sharpness between *phenomenon* and *context* does not minimize the need to identify a "case" and its singularity as the essential feature of a case study; on the contrary, Chapter 2 (see pp. 35–40) discusses the challenge of defining the "case" in great detail.

2. The term *in-depth,* especially when studying a *contemporary phenomenon,* implies the likely need for some kind of fieldwork, to get you up close to the case being studied.

3. The term *contemporary phenomenon* embraces a broad notion of studying the present but that does not exclude the recent past—just not those events extending back to the "dead" past, where no direct observations can be made and no people are alive to be interviewed (doing a history would be the relevant method under those conditions).

4. Having *more variables of interest than data points* arises from the complexity of the case and its context (hence, many variables), with the case being the only "data point." The use of this language does not mean that case studies are variable-based; on the contrary, the multiplicity of variables raises doubts about the usefulness of conventional variable-based methods in analyzing case study data, hence favoring holistic approaches.

As a final note, the book's discussion of when to use case study research (pp. 4–6) focuses on its "niche," compared to other methods, and the discussion was not intended to be used as the definition of "case study."

Briefly Annotated References for Tutorial 1.1

Abercrombie, N., Hill, S., & Turner, B. S. (2006). *The Penguin dictionary of sociology* (5th ed.). London: Penguin. Presents a pocket dictionary, with references, of terms used in sociology.

David, M. (2006b). Editor's introduction. In M. David (Ed.), *Case study research* (pp. xxiii–xlii). London: Sage. Contains nearly 100 reprints of source materials for case study research.

Mills, A. J., Durepos, G., & Wiebe, E. (2010b). Introduction. In A. J. Mills, G. Durepos, & E. Wiebe (Eds.), *Encyclopedia of case study research* (pp. xxxi–xxxvi). Thousand Oaks, CA: Sage. Introduces a two-volume encyclopedia devoted to case study research.

Schwandt, T. A. (2007). *The Sage dictionary of qualitative inquiry* (3rd ed.). Los Angeles: Sage. Defines terms, with references, used in qualitative research.

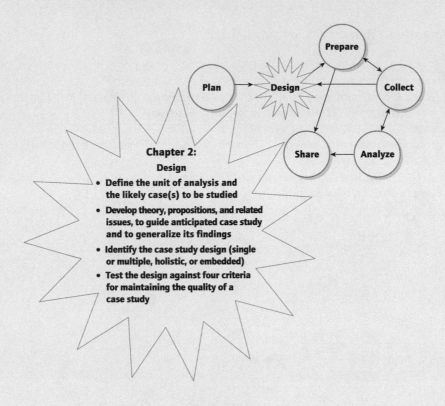

Chapter 2:

Design

- Define the unit of analysis and the likely case(s) to be studied
- Develop theory, propositions, and related issues, to guide anticipated case study and to generalize its findings
- Identify the case study design (single or multiple, holistic, or embedded)
- Test the design against four criteria for maintaining the quality of a case study

ABSTRACT

A research design is the logic that links the data to be collected (and the conclusions to be drawn) to the initial questions of study. Every empirical study has an implicit, if not explicit, research design. Articulating a "theory" about what is being studied and what is to be learned helps to strengthen a research design when doing case study research. Good theoretical propositions also lay the groundwork for generalizing the findings from the case study to other situations, by making *analytic* rather than *statistical generalizations*.

Critical to the design will be to define the "case" or unit of analysis to be studied, as well as to set some limits or bounds to the case. You can then examine the quality of your emerging design in relation to four tests commonly used in social science research: (a) construct validity, (b) internal validity, (c) external validity, and (d) reliability.

Among the specific case study designs, four major types follow a 2 × 2 matrix. The first pair consists of single-case and multiple-case designs. The second pair, which can occur in combination with either of the first pair, distinguishes between holistic and embedded designs. Whether holistic or embedded, in a multiple-case study, the selection of the cases should follow a replication rather than sampling logic. Although single-case studies can yield invaluable insights, most multiple-case study designs are likely to be stronger than single-case study designs. Trying to use even a "two-case" design is therefore a worthy objective, compared to doing a single-case study. Case study research also can be used in combination with other methods, as part of a larger mixed methods study.

2

DESIGNING CASE STUDIES

Identifying Your Case(s) and Establishing the Logic of Your Case Study

GENERAL APPROACH TO DESIGNING CASE STUDIES △

Chapter 1 has shown when you might choose to do case study research, as opposed to other types of research, to carry out a new study. The next step is to design your case study. For this purpose, as in designing any other type of research investigation, you need a plan or *research design*.

The development of this research design calls for careful craftwork. Unlike other research methods, a comprehensive and standard catalog of research designs for case study research has yet to emerge. There are no textbooks, like those in the biological and psychological sciences, covering such design considerations as the assignment of subjects to different groups, the selection of different stimuli or experimental conditions, or the identification of various response measures (see Cochran & Cox, 1957; Fisher, 1935, cited in Cochran & Cox, 1957; Sidowski, 1966). In a laboratory experiment, each of these choices reflects an important logical connection to the issues being studied. Nor have any common case study designs emerged—such as the *panel studies,* for example—used in survey research (see Kidder & Judd, 1986, chap. 6).

One pitfall to be avoided, however, is to consider case study designs to be a subset or variant of the research designs used for other methods, such as quasi-experiments (e.g., Campbell & Stanley, 1966; Cook & Campbell, 1979). For a long time, scholars incorrectly thought that the case study was but one type of quasi-experimental design (the "one-shot post-test-only" design—Campbell & Stanley, 1966, pp. 6–7). Although the misperception lingers to this very day, it was later corrected when one of the original authors made the following statement in the revision to the original work on quasi-experimental designs:

> Certainly the case study as normally practiced should not be demeaned by identification with the one-group post-test-only design. (Cook & Campbell, 1979, p. 96)

In other words, the one-shot, post-test-only design as a quasi-experimental design still may be considered flawed, but the case study has now been recognized as something different. In fact, case study research is a separate method that has its own research designs.

Tip: *How should I select the case(s) for my case study?*

You need sufficient access to the data for your potential case—whether to interview people, review documents or records, or make field observations. Given such access to more than a single candidate case, you should choose the case(s) that will most likely illuminate your research questions. Absent such access, you should consider changing your research questions, hopefully leading to new candidates to which you do have access.

Do you think access should be so important?

Unfortunately, case study research designs have not been codified. The following chapter therefore expands on the methodological ground broken by earlier editions of this book and describes a basic set of research designs for doing single- and multiple-case studies. Although these designs will need to be continually modified and improved in the future, in their present form they will nevertheless help you to design more rigorous and methodologically sound case studies.

Definition of Research Designs

Every type of empirical research study has an implicit, if not explicit, research design. In the most elementary sense, the design is the logical sequence that connects the empirical data to a study's initial research questions and, ultimately, to its conclusions. Colloquially, a research design is *a logical plan for getting from here to there,* where *here* may be defined as the initial set of questions to be answered, and *there* is some set of conclusions (answers) about these questions. Between *here* and *there* may be found a number of major steps, including the collection and analysis of relevant data. As a summary definition, another textbook has described a research design as a plan that

> guides the investigator in the process of collecting, analyzing, and interpreting observations. It is a *logical model of proof* that allows the researcher to draw inferences concerning causal relations among the variables under investigation. (Nachmias & Nachmias, 1992, pp. 77–78, emphasis added)

Another way of thinking about a research design is as a "blueprint" for your research, dealing with at least four problems: what questions to study, what data are relevant, what data to collect, and how to analyze the results (Philliber, Schwab, & Samsloss, 1980).

Note that a research design is much more than a work plan. The main purpose of the design is to help to avoid the situation in which the evidence does not address the initial research questions. In this sense, a research design deals with a *logical* problem and not a *logistical* problem. As a simple example, suppose you want to study a single organization. Your research questions, however, have to do with the organization's relationships with other organizations—their competitive or collaborative nature, for example. Such questions can be properly answered only if you collect information directly from the other organizations and not merely from the one you started with. If you complete your study by examining an organization's relationships from the vantage point of only one organization, you cannot draw unbiased conclusions about the relationships. This is a flaw in your research design, not in your work plan. The outcome could have been avoided if you had developed an appropriate research design in the first place.

Components of Research Designs

In case study research, five components of a research design are especially important:

1. a case study's questions;

2. its propositions, if any;

3. its unit(s) of analysis;

4. the logic linking the data to the propositions; and

5. the criteria for interpreting the findings.

Study questions. This first component has already been described in Chapter 1, which suggested that the *form* of the question—in terms of "who," "what," "where," "how," and "why"—provides an important clue regarding the most relevant research method to be used. Case study research is most likely to be appropriate for "how" and "why" questions, so your initial task is to clarify precisely the nature of your study questions in this regard.

More troublesome may be your having to come up with the substance of the questions. Many students take an initial stab, only to be discouraged when they find the same question(s) already well covered by previous research. Other less desirable questions focus on too trivial or minor parts of an issue. A helpful hint is to move in three stages. In the first, try to use the literature to narrow your interest to a key topic or two, not worrying about any specific research questions. In the second, examine closely—even dissect—a few key studies on your topic of interest. Identify the questions in those few studies and whether they conclude with new questions or loose ends for future research.

These may then stimulate your own thinking and imagination, and you may find yourself articulating some potential questions of your own. In the third stage, examine another set of studies on the same topic. They may reinforce the relevance and importance of your potential questions or even suggest ways of sharpening them.

Study propositions. As for the second component, each proposition directs attention to something that should be examined within the scope of study. For instance, assume that your research, on the topic of interorganizational partnerships, began with the following question: How and why do organizations collaborate with one another to provide joint services (for example, a manufacturer and a retail outlet collaborating to sell certain computer products)? These "how" and "why" questions, capturing what you are really interested in addressing, led you to case study research as the appropriate method in the first place. Nevertheless, these "how" and "why" questions do not sufficiently point to what you should study.

Only if you are forced to state some propositions will you move in the right direction. For instance, you might think that organizations collaborate because they derive mutual benefits. This proposition, besides reflecting an important theoretical issue (that other incentives for collaboration do not exist or are unimportant), also begins to tell you where to look for relevant evidence (that is, to define and ascertain the extent of specific benefits to each organization).

At the same time, some studies may have a legitimate reason for not having any propositions. This is the condition—which exists in experiments, surveys, and the other research methods alike—in which a topic is the subject of "exploration." Every exploration, however, should still have some purpose. Instead of propositions, the design for an exploratory study should state this purpose, as well as the criteria by which an exploration will be judged successful (or not). Consider the analogy in BOX 5 for exploratory case studies. Can you imagine how you would ask for support from Queen Isabella to do your exploratory study?

BOX 5
"Exploration" as an Analogy
for an Exploratory Case Study

When Christopher Columbus went to Queen Isabella to ask for support for his "exploration" of the New World, he had to have some reasons for asking for three ships (Why not one? Why not five?), and he had some rationale for going westward (Why not south? Why not south and then east?). He also had some (mistaken) criteria for recognizing the Indies when he actually encountered it. In short, his exploration began with some rationale and direction, even if his initial assumptions might later have been proved wrong (Wilford, 1992). This same degree of rationale and direction should underlie even an exploratory case study.

Unit of analysis—the "case." This third component is related to the fundamental problem of defining the "case" to be studied—a problem that rightfully confronts many researchers at the outset of their case studies (e.g., Ragin & Becker, 1992). You will need to consider at least two different steps: defining the case and bounding the case.

In *defining the case,* for instance, the classic case studies usually focus on an individual person as the case (e.g., Bromley, 1986, p. 1). Jennifer Platt (1992) has noted how the early case studies by scholars in the Chicago school of sociology were life histories of such persons as juvenile delinquents or derelict men. You also can imagine case studies of clinical patients, of exemplary students, or of certain types of leaders. In each situation, an individual person is the case being studied, and the individual is the primary unit of analysis. Information about the relevant individual would be collected, and several such individuals or "cases" might be included in a multiple-case study.

You would still need study questions and study propositions to help identify the relevant information to be collected about this individual or individuals. Without such questions and propositions, you might be tempted to cover "everything" about the individual(s), which is impossible to do. For example, the propositions in studying these individuals might be limited to the influence of early childhood or the role of peer relationships. Such seemingly general topics nevertheless represent a vast narrowing of the relevant data. The more a case study contains specific questions and propositions, the more it will stay within feasible limits.

Of course, the "case" also can be some event or entity other than a single individual. Case studies have been done about a broad variety of topics, including small groups, communities, decisions, programs, organizational change, and specific events. Feagin et al. (1991) contains some classic examples of these single cases in sociology and political science.

Beware of these types of cases—none is easily defined in terms of the beginning or end points of the "case." For example, a case study of a specific program may reveal (a) variations in program definition, depending upon the perspective of different actors, and (b) program components that preexisted the formal designation of the program. Any case study of such a program would therefore have to confront these conditions in delineating the unit of analysis. Similarly, you might at first identify a specific locale, such as a "city," as your case. However, your research questions and data collection might in fact be limited to tourism in the city, city policies, or city government. These choices would differ from defining the geographic city and its population as your case.

As a general guide, the tentative definition of your case (or of the unit of analysis) is related to the way you define your initial research question(s). Suppose, for example, you want to study the role of the United States in the global economy. Years ago, Peter Drucker (1986) wrote a provocative essay (but not a case study) about fundamental changes in the world economy, including the importance of "capital movements" independent of the flow of goods and services. If you were interested in doing a case study on this topic, Drucker's work would only serve as a starting point. You would still need to define the research question(s) of interest to you, and each question might point to a different unit of analysis (or "case"). Depending upon your question(s), the appropriate case might be a country's economy, an industry in the world marketplace, an economic policy, or the trade or capital flow between countries. Each unit of analysis and its related questions and propositions would call for a different case study, each having its own research design and data collection strategy.

If your research questions do not lead to the favoring of one unit of analysis over another, your questions may be too vague or too numerous—and you may have trouble doing a case study. However, when you do eventually arrive at a definition of the unit of analysis, do not consider closure permanent. Your choice of the unit of analysis, as with other facets of your research design, can be revisited as a result of discoveries during your data collection (see discussion and cautions about maintaining an adaptive posture, throughout this book and at the end of this chapter).

Sometimes, the unit of analysis may have been defined one way, even though the phenomenon being studied actually follows a different definition. Most frequently, investigators have confused case studies of neighborhoods with case studies of small groups (as another example, confusing a new technology with the workings of an engineering team in an organization; see BOX 6A). How a geographic *area* such as a neighborhood copes with racial transition, upgrading, and other phenomena can be quite different from how a small *group* copes with these same phenomena. For instance, *Street Corner Society* (Whyte, 1943/1993; see BOX 2A in Chapter 1 of this book) and *Tally's Corner* (Liebow, 1967; see BOX 9, this chapter) often have been mistaken for being case studies of neighborhoods when in fact they are case studies of small groups (note that in neither book is the neighborhood geography described, even though the small groups lived in a small area with clear neighborhood definitions if not boundaries). In contrast, BOX 6B presents a good example of how units of analyses can be defined in a more discriminating manner—in the field of world trade.

BOX 6
Defining the Unit of Analysis

6A. What Is the Unit of Analysis?

The Soul of a New Machine (1981) was a Pulitzer Prize–winning book by Tracy Kidder. The book, also a best seller, is about the development of a new minicomputer, produced by Data General Corporation, intended to compete with one produced by a direct competitor, Digital Equipment Corporation (also see BOX 29, Chapter 5, p. 144).

This easy-to-read book describes how Data General's engineering team invented and developed the new computer. The book begins with the initial conceptualization of the

(Continued)

(Continued)

computer and ends when the engineering team relinquishes control of the machine to Data General's marketing staff.

The book is an excellent example of a case study. However, the book also illustrates a fundamental problem in doing case studies—that of defining the unit of analysis. Is the "case" being studied the minicomputer, or is it about the dynamics of a small group—the engineering team? The answer is critical for understanding how the case study might relate to any broader body of knowledge—that is, whether to generalize to a technology topic or to a group dynamics topic. Because the book is not an academic study, it does not need to, nor does it, provide an answer.

6B. A Clearer Choice among Units of Analysis

Ira Magaziner and Mark Patinkin's (1989) book, *The Silent War: Inside the Global Business Battles Shaping America's Future,* presents nine individual case studies (also see BOX 36, Chapter 5, p. 165). Each case helps the reader to understand a real-life situation of international economic competition.

Two of the cases appear similar but in fact have different main units of analysis. One case covers a firm—the Korean firm Samsung—and the critical policies that make it competitive. Understanding Korean economic development is part of the context, and the case study also contains an embedded unit—Samsung's development of the microwave oven as an illustrative product. The other case covers a country—Singapore—and the policies that make it competitive. Within the country case study is an embedded unit of analysis—the development of an Apple computer factory in Singapore, serving as an illustrative example of how the national policies affect foreign investments.

To reduce the confusion and ambiguity in defining the unit of analysis or "case," one recommended practice is to discuss your potential case selection with a colleague. Try to explain to that person what questions you are trying to address and why you have chosen a specific case or group of cases as a way of addressing those questions. This may help you to avoid incorrectly identifying the unit of analysis.

Once the general definition of the case has been established, other clarifications—sometimes called *bounding the case*—become important. If the unit of analysis is a small group, for instance, the persons to be included within the group (the immediate topic of the case study) must be distinguished from those who are outside of it (the context for the case study). Similarly, if the case is about the local services in a specific geographic area, you need to decide which services to cover. Also desirable, for almost any topic that might be chosen, are the specific time boundaries to define the estimated beginning and ending of the case, for the purposes of your study (e.g., whether to include the entire or only some part of the life cycle of the entity that is to be the case).

Bounding the case in these ways will help to determine the scope of your data collection and, in particular, how you will distinguish data about the subject of your case study (the "phenomenon") from data external to the case (the "context").

Exercise 2.1   Defining the Boundaries of a Case

Select a topic for a case study you would like to do. Identify some research questions to be answered or propositions to be examined by your case study. Does the naming of these questions or propositions clarify the boundaries of your case with regard to the time period covered by the case study; the relevant social group, organization, or geographic area; the type of evidence to be collected; and the priorities for data collection and analysis? If not, should you sharpen the original questions?

These latter cautions regarding the need for spatial, temporal, and other concrete boundaries underlie a key but subtle aspect in defining your case. The desired case should be some real-life phenomenon that has some concrete manifestation. The case cannot simply be an abstraction, such as a claim, an argument, or even a hypothesis. These abstractions could rightfully serve as the starting points for research studies using other kinds of methods and not just case study research. To justify doing case study research, you need to go one step further: You need to define a specific, real-life "case" to be a concrete manifestation of the abstraction. (For examples of more concrete and less concrete case study topics, see Figure 2.1.)

Take the concept of "neighboring." Alone, it could be the subject of research studies using methods other than the case study method. The other methods might include a survey of the relationships among neighbors, a history of the evolution of the sense of neighboring and the creation of neighborhood boundaries, or an experiment in which young children do tasks next to each other to determine the distracting effects, if any, of their "neighbors" in a classroom. These examples show how the abstract concept of "neighboring" does not alone produce the grounds for a case study. However, the concept could readily become a case study topic if it were accompanied by your selecting a specific neighborhood ("case") to be studied and posing study questions and propositions about the neighborhood in relation to the concept of "neighboring."

One final point pertains to the role of the available research literature and needs to be made about defining the case and the unit of analysis. Most researchers will want to compare their findings with previous research. For this reason, the key definitions used in your study should not be idiosyncratic. Rather, each case study and unit of analysis either should be similar to those previously studied by others or should innovate in clear, operationally defined ways. In this manner, the previous literature also can become a guide for defining the case and unit of analysis.

Figure 2.1 Illustrative Cases for Case Studies

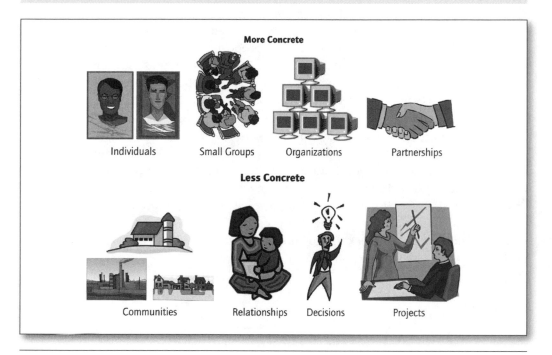

SOURCE: Clip Art © Jupiter Images.

Linking data to propositions. The fourth component has been increasingly better developed in doing case study research. The component foreshadows the data analysis steps in your case study. Chapter 5 covers these steps and the various analytic techniques and choices in detail. However, during the design stage, you need to be aware of the choices and how they might suit your case study. In this way, your research design can create a more solid foundation for the later analysis.

Exercise 2.2 Defining the Unit of Analysis (and the "Case") for a Case Study

Examine Figure 2.1. Discuss each subject, which illustrates a different unit of analysis. Find a published case study on at least one of these subjects, indicating the actual "case" that was being studied. Understanding that each subject illustrates a different unit of analysis and involves the selection of different cases to be studied, do you think that the more concrete units might be easier to define than the less concrete ones? Why?

All of the analytic techniques in Chapter 5 represent ways of *linking data to propositions:* pattern matching, explanation building, time-series analysis, logic models, and cross-case synthesis. The actual analyses will require that you combine or assemble your case study data as a direct reflection of your initial study propositions. For instance, knowing that some or all of your propositions cover a temporal sequence would mean that you might eventually use some type of time-series analysis. If you noted this strong likelihood during the design phase, you might make sure that your planned data collection included the collection of appropriate time markers as part of the case being studied.

As a caution, if you have had limited experience in conducting empirical studies, you may not easily identify the likely analytic technique(s) or anticipate the needed data to use the techniques to their full advantage. Even more experienced researchers often note how they have either (a) collected too much data that were not later used in any analysis or (b) collected too little data that prevented the proper use of a desired analytic technique. Sometimes, the latter situation even may force researchers to return to their data collection phase (if they can), to supplement the original data. The more you can avoid either of these situations, the better off you will be.

Criteria for interpreting a case study's findings. For many studies, a common illustration of this fifth component arises when statistical analyses are relevant. For instance, by convention, quantitative studies consider a *p* level of less than .05 to demonstrate that observed differences are "statistically significant" and therefore associated with more robust findings. In other words, the statistical estimates serve as the criteria for interpreting the findings. However, much case study analysis will not rely on the use of statistics, leading to the need to find other ways of thinking about such criteria.

When doing case studies, a major and important alternative strategy is to identify and address rival explanations for your findings. Addressing such rivals becomes a criterion for interpreting your findings: The more rivals that have been addressed and rejected, the stronger will be your findings. Again, Chapter 5 discusses this strategy and how it works. At the design stage of your work, the challenge is to anticipate and enumerate the important rivals, so you will include data about them as part of your data collection. If you only think of rival explanations after data collection has been completed, you will be starting to justify and design a *future* study, but you will not be helping to complete your *current* case study. For this reason, specifying important rival explanations is a part of a case study's research design work.

Summary. A research design should include five components. The first three components—that is, defining your study's questions, propositions, and unit of analysis—will lead your research design into identifying the data that are to be collected. The last two components—that is, defining the logic linking the data to the propositions and the criteria for interpreting the findings—will lead the design into anticipating your case study analysis, suggesting what is to be done after the data have been collected.

THE ROLE OF THEORY OR THEORETICAL PROPOSITIONS IN △ RESEARCH DESIGNS

Covering the preceding five components of research designs will effectively force you to begin constructing some preliminary theory or theoretical propositions related to your topic of study. This role of theory development, prior to the conduct of any data collection, is one point of difference between case study research and related qualitative methods such as ethnography (Lincoln & Guba, 1985; Van Maanen, 1988) and *grounded theory* (Corbin & Strauss, 2007). Typically, these related methods may deliberately avoid specifying any theoretical propositions at the outset of an inquiry (nor do these methods have to cope with the challenge of defining a "case"). As a result, students who may consider these methods to be interchangeable with case study research wrongly think that, by having selected the case study method, they can proceed quickly into their fieldwork (e.g., by rushing to establish their field contacts as quickly as possible). No presumption could be more misleading. Among other considerations, the relevant field contacts depend upon an understanding—or theory—of what is being studied.

Theory Development

For case studies, some theory development as part of the design phase is highly desired. The needed theory can be plain and simple. For example, a case study on the implementation of a new management information system (MIS) started with the following straightforward theoretical statement:

> The case study will show why implementation only succeeded when the organization was able to re-structure itself, and not just overlay the new MIS on the old organizational structure. (Markus, 1983)

The statement presents the nutshell of a theory of MIS implementation—that is, that organizational restructuring is needed to make MIS implementation work.

The same MIS case study then added the following theoretical statement:

> The case study will also show why the simple replacement of key persons was not sufficient for successful implementation. (Markus, 1983)

This second statement presents the nutshell of a *rival* theory—that is, that MIS implementation fails because of the resistance to change on the part of individual people and that the replacement of such people is the main requirement for implementation to succeed.

You can see that as these two initial statements are elaborated, the stated ideas will increasingly cover the questions, propositions, units of analysis, logic connecting data to propositions, and criteria for interpreting the findings—that is, the five components of the needed research design. In this sense, the complete research design embodies a "theory" of what is being studied.

This theory should by no means be considered with the formality of grand theory in social science, nor are you being asked to be a masterful theoretician. Rather, the simple goal is to have a sufficient blueprint for your study, and this requires theoretical propositions, usefully noted by Sutton and Staw (1995) as "a [hypothetical] story about why acts, events, structure, and thoughts occur" (p. 378). The theoretical propositions can represent key issues from the research literature or practical matters such as differing types of instructional leadership styles or partnering arrangements in a study of organizations. Such propositions will enable the complete research design to provide surprisingly strong guidance in determining the data to collect and the strategies for analyzing the data. For this reason, some theory development prior to the collection of any case study data is desirable. Paul Rosenbaum notes that, for nonexperimental studies more generally, the preferred theoretical statements should elaborate a complex pattern of expected results—the more complex the better (Rosenbaum, 2002, pp. 5–6 and 277–279). The benefit is a stronger design and a heightened ability to interpret your eventual data.

However, theory development takes time and can be difficult (Eisenhardt, 1989). For some topics, existing works may provide a rich theoretical framework for designing a specific case study. If you are interested in international economic development, for instance, Peter Drucker's (1986) "The Changed World Economy" cited earlier is an exceptional source of theories and hypotheses. Drucker claims that the world economy has changed significantly from the past. He points to the "uncoupling" between the primary products (raw materials) economy and the industrial economy, a similar uncoupling between low labor costs and manufacturing production, and the uncoupling between financial markets and the real economy of goods and services. To test these propositions might require different studies, some focusing on the different uncouplings, others focusing on specific industries, and yet others explaining the plight of specific countries. Each different study would likely call for a different unit of analysis. Drucker's theoretical framework would provide guidance for designing these studies and even for collecting relevant data.

In other situations, the appropriate theory may be a descriptive theory (see BOX 2A in Chapter 1 for another example), and your concern should focus on such issues as (a) the purpose of the descriptive effort, (b) the full but realistic range of topics that might be considered a "complete" description of what is to be studied, and (c) the likely topic(s) that will be the essence of the description. Good answers to these questions, including the rationales underlying the answers, will help you go a long way toward developing the needed theoretical base—and research design—for your study.

For yet other topics, the existing knowledge base may be poor, and the available literature will provide no conceptual framework or hypotheses of note. Such a knowledge base does not lend itself to the development of good theoretical statements, and any new empirical study is likely to assume the characteristic of an "exploratory" study. Nevertheless, as noted earlier with the illustrative case in BOX 5, even an exploratory case study should be preceded by statements about what is to be explored, the purpose of the exploration, and the criteria by which the exploration will be judged successful.

Overall, you may want to gain a richer understanding of how theory is used in case studies by reviewing specific case studies that have been successfully completed. For instance, Yin (2012, chap. 3) shows how theory was used in exploratory, descriptive, and explanatory situations by discussing five actual case studies.

Illustrative Topics for Theories

In general, to overcome the barriers to theory development, you should try to prepare for your case study by doing such things as reviewing the literature related to what you would like to study (e.g., see H. M. Cooper, 1984), discussing your topic and ideas with colleagues or teachers, and asking yourself challenging questions about what you are studying, why you are proposing to do the study, and what you hope to learn as a result of the study.

As a further reminder, you should be aware of the full range of theories that might be relevant to your study. For instance, note that the earlier MIS example illustrated MIS "implementation" theory and that this is but one type of theory that can be the subject of study. Other types of theories for you to consider include:

- individual theories—for example, theories of individual development, cognitive behavior, personality, learning and disability, individual perception, and interpersonal interactions;
- group theories—for example, theories of family functioning, informal groups, work teams, supervisory-employee relations, and interpersonal networks;
- organizational theories—for example, theories of bureaucracies, organizational structure and functions, excellence in organizational performance, and interorganizational partnerships; and
- societal theories—for example, theories of urban development, international conflicts, cultural institutions, technological development, and marketplace functions.

Other examples cut across these illustrative types. Decision-making theory (Carroll & Johnson, 1992), for instance, can involve individuals, organizations, or social groups. As another example, a common topic of case study research is the evaluation of publicly supported programs, such as federal, state, or local programs. In this situation, the development of a theory of how a program is supposed to work is essential to the design of the evaluation. In this situation, Bickman (1987) reminds us that the theory needs to distinguish between the substance of the program (e.g., how to make education more effective) and the process of program implementation (e.g., how to install an effective program). The distinction would avoid situations where policy makers might want to know the desired substantive remedies (e.g., findings about a newly effective curriculum) but where an evaluation unfortunately focused on managerial issues (e.g., the need to hire a good project director). Such a mismatch can be avoided by giving closer attention to the substantive theory.

Use of Theory to Generalize From Case Studies

Besides making it easier to design your case study, having some theory or theoretical propositions will later play a critical role in helping you to generalize the lessons learned from your case study. This role of theory has been characterized throughout this book as *analytic generalization* and has been contrasted with another way of generalizing the results from empirical studies, known as *statistical generalization*. Understanding the distinction between these two types of generalization may be your most notable accomplishment in doing case study research.

Let us first take the more commonly recognized way of generalizing—*statistical* generalization—although it is the less relevant one for doing case study research. In statistical generalization, an inference is made about a population (or universe) on the basis of empirical data collected from a sample of that universe. This is shown graphically as a Level One inference in Figure 2.2.[1] This method of generalizing is commonly followed when doing surveys (e.g., Fowler, 1988; Lavrakas, 1987) or analyzing archival data such as in studying housing or employment trends. As another example, political polls need to generalize their findings beyond their sample of respondents and to apply to the larger population, and research investigators readily follow quantitative procedures to determine the confidence with which such extrapolations can be made.

A fatal flaw in doing case studies is to consider statistical generalization to be the way of generalizing the findings from your case study. This is because your case or cases are not "sampling units" and also will be too small in number to serve as an adequately sized sample to represent any larger population.

Rather than thinking about your case as a sample, you should think of it as the opportunity to shed empirical light about some theoretical concepts or principles, not unlike the motive of a laboratory investigator in conceiving of and then conducting a new experiment.[2] In this sense, both a case study and an experiment may have an interest in going beyond the specific case or experiment. Both kinds of studies are likely to strive for generalizable findings or lessons learned—that is, analytic generalizations—that go beyond the setting for the specific case or specific experiment that had been studied (see Tutorial 2-1). For example, the lessons learned could assume the form of a *working hypothesis*

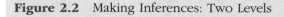

Figure 2.2 Making Inferences: Two Levels

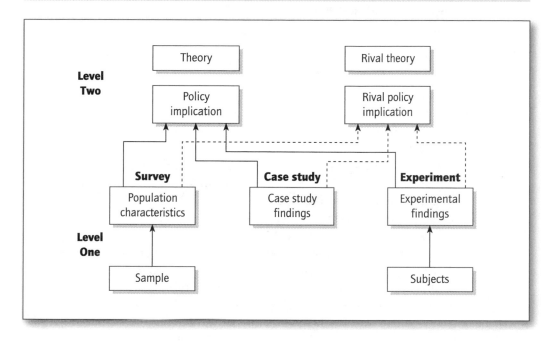

(Cronbach, 1975), either to be applied in reinterpreting the results of existing studies of other concrete situations (that is, other cases or experiments) or to define new research focusing on yet additional concrete situations (that is, new cases or experiments). Note that the aim of an analytic generalization is still to generalize to these other concrete situations and not just to contribute to abstract theory building. Also note that the generalizations, principles, or lessons learned from a case study may potentially apply to a variety of situations, far beyond any strict definition of the hypothetical population of "like-cases" represented by the original case.

The theory or theoretical propositions that went into the initial design of your case study, as empirically enhanced by your case study's findings, will have formed the groundwork for an analytic generalization. Alternatively, a new generalization may emerge from the case study's findings alone. In other words, the *analytic generalization* may be based on either (a) corroborating, modifying, rejecting, or otherwise advancing theoretical concepts that you referenced in designing your case study or (b) new concepts that arose upon the completion of your case study. The important point is that, regardless of whether the generalization was derived from the conditions you specified at the outset or uncovered at the conclusion of your case study, the generalization will be at a conceptual level higher than that of the specific case (or experiment)—shown graphically as a Level Two inference in Figure 2.2.

Several prominent case studies illustrate how analytic generalizations can use a case study's findings to implicate new situations. First, consider how the three initial case studies of this book (cited in BOXES 1, 2A, and 2B of Chapter 1) treated the generalizing function:

- **BOX 1:** Allison's case (1971) is about the Cuban missile crisis, and he relates the three theoretical models from his case study to many other situations, first to other international confrontations, such as between the United States and North Vietnam in the 1960s (p. 258). The later edition of the case study (Allison & Zelikow, 1999) then discusses the models' relevance to the "rethinking of nuclear threats to Americans today" (p. 397) as well as to the broader challenge of inferring the motives underlying actions taken by a foreign power.
- **BOX 2A:** Whyte's study (1943/1993) is well known for uncovering the relationship between individual performance and group structure, highlighted by a bowling tournament where he directly experienced the impact on his own performance ("as if something larger than myself was controlling the ball"—p. 319) and observed how the gang members' bowling scores, with one notable exception, emulated their standing in the gang. Whyte generalizes his findings by later commenting that "I believed then (and still believe now) that this sort of relationship may be observed in other group activities everywhere" (p. 319).
- **BOX 2B:** Neustadt and Fineberg (1983) show yet another variation, claiming no generalization but concluding with an extensive discussion of the usefulness of their case study in teaching public policy courses (pp. 231–250).

Second, BOX 7 contains four additional illustrations. All show how findings from a single-case study nevertheless can be generalized to a broad variety of other situations. The fourth of these case studies has one other notable feature: It demonstrates how an entire case study can be published as a journal article (the first three examples appeared in the form of rather lengthy books).

Analytic generalization can be used whether your case study involves one or several cases, which shall be later referenced as single-case or multiple-case studies. Also to come, this chapter's later discussion under the topic of *external validity* adds a further insight about making analytic generalizations. The main point at this juncture is that you should try to aim toward analytic generalizations in doing case studies, and you should avoid thinking in such confusing terms as "the sample of cases" or the "small sample size of cases," as if a single-or multiple-case study were equivalent to respondents in a survey. In other words, again as graphically depicted in Figure 2.2, you should aim for Level Two inferences when doing case studies.

In a like manner, even referring to your case or cases as a "purposive sample" may raise similar conceptual and terminological problems. You may have intended to convey that the "purposive" portion of the term reflects your selection of a case that will illuminate the theoretical propositions of your case study. However, your use of the

BOX 7
Generalizing from Single-Case Studies:
Four More Examples

7A. A Sociology of "Mistake"

The tragic loss of the space shuttle *Challenger* in 1986, vividly shown in repeated TV replays of the spaceship's final seconds, certainly qualifies as a unique case. The causes of this loss became the subject of a Presidential Commission and of a case study by Diane Vaughan (1996). Vaughan's detailed study shows how the social structure of an organization (the NASA space agency) had, over time, transformed deviance into acceptable and routine behavior.

Vaughan's ultimate explanation differs markedly from that of the Presidential Commission, which pointed to individual errors by middle managers as the main reasons for failure. In Vaughan's words, her study "explicates the sociology of mistake" (p. xiv)—that "mistakes are systemic and socially organized, built into the nature of professions, organizations, cultures, and structures" (p. 415). She shows how deviance is transformed into acceptable behavior through the institutionalization of production pressures (originating in the organizational environment), leading to "nuanced, unacknowledged, pervasive effects on decisionmaking" (p. xiv). Her final discussion applies this generalization to a diverse array of other situations. As examples, she cites studies showing the research distortions created by the worldview of scientists, the uncoupling of intimate relationships, and the inevitability of accidents in certain technological systems.

7B. The Origins of Social Class

The second example is about the uncovering and labeling of a social class structure based on a case study of a small American city, Yankee City (Warner & Lunt, 1941). This classic case study in sociology made a critical contribution to social stratification theory and an understanding of the social differences among "upper," "upper-middle," "middle-middle," "upper-lower," and "lower" classes. Over the years, the insights from these differences have applied to a broad range of situations (by no means limited to other small cities).

7C. Contribution to Urban Planning

The third example is Jane Jacobs and her famous book, *The Death and Life of Great American Cities* (1961). The book is based mostly on experiences from a single case, New York City. The book's chapters then show how these New York experiences can be used to develop broader theoretical principles in urban planning, such as the role of sidewalks, the role of neighborhood parks, the need for primary mixed uses, the need for small blocks, and the processes of slumming and unslumming.

(Continued)

(Continued)

Jacobs's book created heated controversy in the planning profession. New empirical inquiries were made about one or another of her rich and provocative ideas. These inquiries helped to test the broader applicability of her principles to other concrete settings, and in this way Jacobs's work still stands as a significant contribution in the field of urban planning.

7D. Government Management of "Spoiled" National Identity

The fourth example creatively extended Erving Goffman's well-known sociological theory, regarding the management of stigma by individual people, to an institutional level (Rivera, 2008). A field-based case study of Croatia showed how the stigma created by the wars of Yugoslav secession had demolished the country's image as a desirable tourist destination, but then how the country successfully used an impression management strategy to revive the tourism. Croatia thus presented "an exciting case of reputation management in action" (p. 618). The author suggests that her adapted theoretical model can be used as "a launching point for understanding the public representation dilemmas faced by other states and organizational actors that have undergone reputation-damaging events" (p. 615). In so doing, the case study has provided another illustration of analytic generalization.

"sample" portion of the term still risks misleading others into thinking that the case comes from some larger universe or population of like-cases, undesirably reigniting the specter of statistical generalization. The most desirable posture may be to avoid referring to any kind of sample (purposive or otherwise). (The preferred criteria and terminology for selecting cases, as part of either a single- or a multiple-case study, are discussed later in this chapter under the topic of "case study designs.") In this sense, case study research directly parallels experimental research: Few if any people would consider that a new experiment should be designed as a sample (of any kind) from a larger population of like-experiments—and few would consider that the main way of generalizing the findings from a single experiment would be in reference to a population of like-experiments.

Summary

This section has suggested that a complete research design, while including the five components previously described, will benefit from the development of theoretical propositions. A good case study researcher should pursue such propositions and take advantage of this benefit, whether the case study is to be exploratory, descriptive, or explanatory. The use of theory and theoretical propositions in doing case studies is an immense aid in defining the appropriate research design and data to be collected. The same theoretical orientation also will become the main vehicle for generalizing the findings from the case study.

CRITERIA FOR JUDGING THE QUALITY OF RESEARCH DESIGNS △

Because a research design is supposed to represent a logical set of statements, you also can judge the quality of any given design according to certain logical tests. Concepts that have been offered for these tests include trustworthiness, credibility, confirmability, and data dependability (U.S. Government Accountability Office, 1990).

Four tests, however, have been commonly used to establish the quality of any empirical social research. Because case study research is part of this larger body, the four tests also are relevant to case study research. An important innovation of this book is the identification of several tactics for dealing with these four tests when doing case study research. Figure 2.3 lists the four widely used tests and the recommended case study tactics, as well as a cross-reference to the phase of research when the tactic is to be used. (Each tactic is described in detail in the referenced chapter of this book.)

Because the four tests are common to all social science methods, the tests have been summarized in numerous textbooks (e.g., see Kidder & Judd, 1986, pp. 26–29). The tests also have served as a framework for assessing a large group of case studies in the field of strategic management (Gibbert, Ruigrok, & Wicki, 2008). The four tests are:

Figure 2.3 Case Study Tactics for Four Design Tests

TESTS	Case Study Tactic	Phase of Research in which Tactic Occurs
Construct validity	• use multiple sources of evidence • establish chain of evidence • have key informants review draft case study report	data collection (see Chap. 4) data collection (see Chap. 4) composition (see Chap. 6)
Internal validity	• do pattern matching • do explanation building • address rival explanations • use logic models	data analysis (see Chap. 5) data analysis (see Chap. 5) data analysis (see Chap. 5) data analysis (see Chap. 5)
External validity	• use theory in single-case studies • use replication logic in multiple-case studies	research design (see Chap. 2) research design (see Chap. 2)
Reliability	• use case study protocol • develop case study database	data collection (see Chap. 3) data collection (see Chap. 4)

- *Construct validity:* identifying correct operational measures for the concepts being studied
- *Internal validity* (for explanatory or causal studies only and not for descriptive or exploratory studies): seeking to establish a causal relationship, whereby certain conditions are believed to lead to other conditions, as distinguished from spurious relationships
- *External validity:* defining the domain to which a study's findings can be generalized
- *Reliability:* demonstrating that the operations of a study—suchas the data collection procedures—can be repeated, with the same results

Each item on this list deserves explicit attention. For case study research, an important revelation is that the several tactics to be used in dealing with these tests should be applied throughout the subsequent conduct of a case study, not just at its beginning. Thus, the "design work" for doing case studies may actually continue beyond the initial design plans.

Construct Validity

This first test is especially challenging in case study research. People who have been critical of case studies often point to the fact that a case study researcher fails to develop a sufficiently operational set of measures and that "subjective" judgments—ones tending to confirm a researcher's preconceived notions (Flyvberg, 2006; Ruddin, 2006)—are used to collect the data.[3] Take an example such as studying "neighborhood change"—a common case study topic (e.g., Bradshaw, 1999; Keating & Krumholz, 1999): Over the years, concerns have arisen over how certain urban neighborhoods have changed their character. Any number of case studies has examined the types of changes and their consequences. However, without any prior specification of the significant, operational events that constitute "change," a reader cannot tell whether the claimed changes in a case study genuinely reflect the events in a neighborhood or whether they happen to be based on a researcher's impressions only.

Neighborhood change can cover a wide variety of phenomena: racial turnover, housing deterioration and abandonment, changes in the pattern of urban services, shifts in a neighborhood's economic institutions, or the turnover from low- to middle-income residents in revitalizing neighborhoods. The choice of whether to aggregate blocks, census tracts, or larger areas also can produce different results (Hipp, 2007).

To meet the test of construct validity, an investigator must be sure to cover two steps:

1. define neighborhood change in terms of specific concepts (and relate them to the original objectives of the study) and

2. identify operational measures that match the concepts (preferably citing published studies that make the same matches).

For example, suppose you satisfy the first step by stating that you plan to study neighborhood change by focusing on trends in neighborhood crime. The second step now demands that you select a specific measure, such as police-reported crime (which happens to be the standard measure used in the FBI Uniform Crime Reports) as your measure of crime. The literature will indicate certain known shortcomings in this measure, mainly that unknown proportions of crimes are not reported to the police. You will then need to discuss how the shortcomings nevertheless will not bias your study of neighborhood crime and hence neighborhood change.

As previously shown in Figure 2.3, three tactics are available to increase construct validity when doing case studies. The first is the use of *multiple sources of evidence,* in a manner encouraging convergent lines of inquiry, and this tactic is relevant during data collection (see Chapter 4). A second tactic is to establish a *chain of evidence,* also relevant during data collection (also Chapter 4). The third tactic is to have the draft case study report reviewed by key informants (a procedure described further in Chapter 6).

Internal Validity

This second test has been given the greatest attention in experimental and quasi-experimental research (see Campbell & Stanley, 1966; Cook & Campbell, 1979). Numerous "threats" to internal validity have been identified, mainly dealing with spurious effects. However, because so many textbooks already cover this topic, only two points need to be made here.

First, internal validity is mainly a concern for explanatory case studies, when an investigator is trying to explain how and why event x led to event y. If the investigator incorrectly concludes that there is a causal relationship between x and y without knowing that some third factor—z—may actually have caused y, the research design has failed to deal with some threat to internal validity. Note that this logic is inapplicable to descriptive or exploratory studies (whether the studies are case studies, surveys, or experiments), which are not concerned with this kind of causal situation.

Second, the concern over internal validity, for case study research, extends to the broader problem of making inferences. Basically, a case study involves an inference every time an event cannot be directly observed. An investigator will "infer" that a particular event resulted from some earlier occurrence, based on interview and documentary evidence collected as part of the case study. Is the inference correct? Have all the rival explanations and possibilities been considered? Is the evidence convergent? Does it appear to be airtight? A research design that has anticipated these questions has begun to deal with the overall problem of making inferences and therefore the specific problem of internal validity.

However, the specific tactics for achieving this result are difficult to identify when doing case study research. Figure 2.3 (previously shown) suggests four analytic tactics.

All are described further in Chapter 5 because they take place during the analytic phase of doing case studies: *pattern matching, explanation building, addressing rival explanations,* and *using logic models.*

External Validity

The third test deals with the problem of knowing whether a study's findings are generalizable beyond the immediate study, regardless of the research method used (e.g., experiments, surveys, or case studies). For case studies, the issue relates directly to the earlier discussion of *analytic generalization* and the reference to Level Two in Figure 2.2. To repeat the earlier discussion further, referring to *statistical generalization* and any analogy to samples and populations would be misguided.

Another insight on this issue derives from observing the form of the original research question(s) posed in doing your case study. The form of the question(s) can help or hinder the preference for seeking generalizations—that is, striving for external validity.

Recall that the decision to favor case study research should have started with the posing of some "how" and "why" question(s). For instance, many descriptive case studies deal with the "how" of a situation, whereas many explanatory case studies deal with the "why" of situations. However, if a case study has no pressing "how" or "why" questions—such as a study merely wanting to document the social trends in a neighborhood, city, or country or the employment trends in an organization (and essentially posing a "what" question)—arriving at an analytic generalization may be more difficult. To avoid this situation, augmenting the study design with "how" and "why" questions (and collecting the additional data) can be extremely helpful. (Alternatively, if in the illustrative examples a study's research interest is entirely limited to documenting social trends, using some other method might serve the study's objectives better than using the case study method.)

In this manner, the form of the initial research question(s) can directly influence the strategies used in striving for external validity. These research question(s) should have been settled during the research design phase of your case study, if not earlier. For this reason, Figure 2.3 as previously shown points to the research design phase, with the identification of appropriate theory or theoretical propositions, as being the most appropriate time for establishing the groundwork for starting to address the external validity of your case study.

Reliability

Most people are probably already familiar with this final test. The objective is to be sure that, if a later researcher follows the same procedures as described by an earlier researcher and conducts the same case study over again, the later investigator should arrive at the same findings and conclusions. (Note that the emphasis is on doing the *same* case over again, not on "replicating" the results of one case by doing another case study.) The goal of reliability is to minimize the errors and biases in a study.

One prerequisite for allowing this other investigator to repeat an earlier case study is the need to document the procedures followed in the earlier case. Without such documentation, you could not even repeat your own work (which is another way of dealing with reliability). In the past, case study research procedures have been poorly documented, making external reviewers suspicious of the reliability of the case study method.[4] As previously shown, Figure 2.3 suggests two specific tactics for overcoming these shortcomings—the use of a *case study protocol* to deal with the documentation problem in detail (discussed in Chapter 3) and the development of a *case study database* (discussed in Chapter 4).

The general way of approaching the reliability problem is to make as many steps as operational as possible and to conduct research as if someone were looking over your shoulder. Accountants and bookkeepers always are aware that any calculations must be capable of being audited. In this sense, an auditor also is performing a reliability check and must be able to produce the same results if the same procedures are followed. A good guideline for doing case studies is therefore to conduct the research so that an auditor could in principle repeat the procedures and hopefully arrive at the same results.

Summary

Four tests may be considered relevant in judging the quality of a research design. In designing and doing case studies, various tactics are available to deal with these tests, though not all of the tactics occur at the same phase in doing a case study. Some of the tactics occur during the data collection, data analysis, or compositional phases of the research and are therefore described in greater detail in subsequent chapters of this book.

Exercise 2.3 Defining the Criteria for Judging the Quality of Research Designs

Define the four criteria for judging the quality of research designs: (a) construct validity, (b) internal validity, (c) external validity, and (d) reliability. Give an example of each type of criterion in a case study you might want to do.

CASE STUDY RESEARCH DESIGNS △

Traditional case study research has not usually included the idea of having formal designs, as might be found when doing survey or experimental research. You still may successfully conduct a new case study without any formal design. However, attending to the potential case study research designs can make your case studies stronger and, possibly, easier to do. You might therefore find the remainder of this section to be useful. It covers four types of designs, based on the 2 × 2 matrix in Figure 2.4.

Figure 2.4 Basic Types of Designs for Case Studies

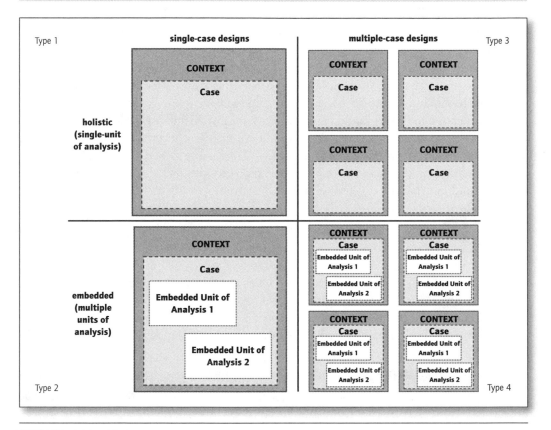

SOURCE: COSMOS Corporation.

The matrix first shows that every type of design will include the desire to analyze contextual conditions in relation to the "case," with the dotted lines between the two signaling that the boundaries between the case and the context are not likely to be sharp. The matrix then shows that single- and multiple-case studies reflect different design situations and that, within these two variants, there also can be unitary or multiple units of analysis. The resulting four types of designs for case studies are (Type 1) single-case (holistic) designs, (Type 2) single-case (embedded) designs, (Type 3) multiple-case (holistic) designs, and (Type 4) multiple-case (embedded) designs. The rationale for these four types of designs is as follows.

What Are the Potential Single-Case Designs (Types 1 and 2)?

Five rationales for single-case designs. A primary distinction in designing case studies is between *single-* and *multiple-*case study designs. This means the need for a decision, prior to any data collection, on whether you are going to use a single case or multiple cases in your case study.

The single-case study is an appropriate design under several circumstances, and five single-case rationales—that is, having a *critical, unusual, common, revelatory,* or *longitudinal* case—are given below. Recall that a single-case study is analogous to a single experiment, and many of the same conditions that justify a single experiment also can justify a single-case study.

Recall, too, that the selection of your case should be related to your theory or theoretical propositions of interest. These form the substantive context for each of the five rationales. Thus, the first rationale for a single case—selecting a *critical case*—would be critical to your theory or theoretical propositions (again, note the analogy to the critical *experiment*). The theory should have specified a clear set of circumstances within which its propositions are believed to be true. The single case then can be used to determine whether the propositions are correct or whether some alternative set of explanations might be more relevant. In this manner, like Graham Allison's comparison of three theories and the Cuban missile crisis (described in Chapter 1, BOX 2), the single case can represent a significant contribution to knowledge and theory building by confirming, challenging, or extending the theory. Such a study even can help to refocus future investigations in an entire field. (See BOX 8 for another example, in the field of organizational innovation.)

BOX 8
The Critical Case as a Single-Case Study

One rationale for selecting a single-case rather than a multiple-case design is that the single case can represent the critical test of a significant theory. Gross, Bernstein, and Giacquinta (1971) used such a design by focusing on a single school in their book, *Implementing Organizational Innovations* (also see BOX 20B, p. 114).

The school was selected because it had a prior history of innovation and could not be claimed to suffer from "barriers to innovation." In the prevailing theories, such barriers had been prominently cited as the major reason that innovations failed. Gross et al. (1971) showed that, in this school, an innovation also failed but that the failure could not be attributed to any barriers. Implementation processes, rather than barriers, appeared to account for the failure.

In this manner, the book, though limited to a single case, represented a watershed in organizational innovation theory. Prior to the study, analysts had focused on the identification of barriers to innovation; since the study, the literature has been much more dominated by studies of the implementation process, not only in schools but also in many other types of organizations.

A second rationale for a single case is where the case represents an *extreme* case or an *unusual* case, deviating from theoretical norms or even everyday occurrences. For instance, such cases can occur in clinical psychology, where a specific injury or disorder may offer a distinct opportunity worth documenting and analyzing. In clinical research, a common research strategy calls for studying these unusual cases because the findings may reveal insights about normal processes. In this manner, the value of a case study can be connected to a large number of people, well beyond those suffering from the original clinical syndrome.

Conversely, a third rationale for a single case is the *common* case. Here, the objective is to capture the circumstances and conditions of an everyday situation—again because of the lessons it might provide about the social processes related to some theoretical interest. In this manner, a street scene and its sidewalk vendors can become the setting for learning about the potential social benefits created by informal entrepreneurial activity (e.g., Duneier, 1999), a study of a small business can yield insights into innovations and innovative processes (e.g., see Yin, 2012, chap. 9), and the social and institutional structure within a single, low-income urban neighborhood can provide insights into the relationship between poverty and social capital (e.g., Small, 2004).

A fourth rationale for a single-case study is the *revelatory* case. This situation exists when a researcher has an opportunity to observe and analyze a phenomenon previously inaccessible to social science inquiry, such as Whyte's (1943/1993) *Street Corner Society,* previously described in Chapter 1, BOX 2A. Another example is Phillippe Bourgois's (2003) study of crack and the drug-dealing marketplace in Spanish Harlem—a neighborhood in New York City. The author gained the trust and long-term friendship of two dozen street dealers and their families, revealing a lifestyle that few had been able to study up to that time. For another example, see Elliot Liebow's (1967) famous case study of unemployed men, *Tally's Corner* (BOX 9). When researchers have similar types of opportunities and can uncover some prevalent phenomenon previously inaccessible to social scientists, such conditions justify the use of a single-case study on the grounds of its revelatory nature.

BOX 9
The Revelatory Case as a Single-Case Study

Another rationale for selecting a single case is that the researcher has access to a situation previously inaccessible to empirical study. The case study is therefore worth conducting because the descriptive information alone will be revelatory.

Such was the situation in Elliot Liebow's (1967) sociological classic, *Tally's Corner.* The book is about a single group of African American men living in a poor, inner-city neighborhood. By befriending these men, the author was able to learn about their lifestyles, their

(Continued)

(Continued)

coping behavior, and in particular their sensitivity to unemployment and failure. The book provided insights into socioeconomic conditions that have prevailed in many U.S. cities for a long time, but that only had been obscurely understood. The single case showed how investigations of such topics could be done, thus stimulating much further research and eventually the development of needed public policy actions.

A fifth rationale for a single-case study is the *longitudinal* case: studying the same single case at two or more different points in time. The theory of interest would likely specify how certain conditions and their underlying processes change over time. The desired time intervals would presumably reflect the anticipated stages at which the changes should reveal themselves. They may be pre-specified time intervals, such as prior to and then after some critical event, following a "before" and "after" logic. Alternatively, they might not deal with specific time intervals but cover trends over an elongated period of time, following a developmental course of interest. Under exceptional circumstances, the same case might be the subject of two consecutive case studies, such as occurred with *Middletown* (Lynd & Lynd, 1929) and *Middletown in Transition* (Lynd & Lynd, 1937). Whatever the time intervals or periods of interest, the processes being studied should nevertheless reflect the theoretical propositions posed by the case study. The desired time intervals would presumably reflect the anticipated stages at which the changes should reveal themselves, and the processes being observed should again reflect the theoretical propositions posed by the case study.

These five serve as major rationales for selecting a single-case study. There are other situations in which the single-case study may be used as a pilot case that might be the beginning of a multiple-case study. However, in this latter situation, the single-case portion of the study would not be regarded as a complete study on its own.

Whatever the rationale for doing single-case studies (and there may be more than the five mentioned here), a potential vulnerability of the single-case design is that a case may later turn out not to be the case it was thought to be at the outset. Single-case designs therefore require careful investigation of the potential case, to minimize the chances of misrepresentation and to maximize the access needed to collect the case study evidence. A fair warning is not to commit yourself to any single-case study until these major concerns have been covered.

Holistic versus embedded case studies. The same single-case study may involve units of analysis at more than one level. This occurs when, within a single case, attention is also given to a subunit or subunits (see BOX 10). For instance, even though a case

BOX 10
An Embedded, Single-Case Design

Union Democracy (1956) is a highly regarded case study by three eminent academicians—Seymour Martin Lipset, Martin Trow, and James Coleman. The case study is about the inside politics of the International Typographical Union and involves several units of analysis (see "Kinds of Data" table, below). The main unit was the organization as a whole, the smallest unit was the individual member, and several intermediary units also were important. At each level of analysis, different data collection techniques were used, ranging from historical to survey analysis.

Kinds of Data					
Unit Being Characterized	Total System	Intermediate Units		Individuals	
	Issues, Data on Occupation; Union Laws; Policies; Historical Data; Convention Reports	*Locals' Histories and Voting Records; Issues on Local Level; Size of Locals*	*Shops' Voting Records; Shop Size*	*Interviews with Leaders*	*Interviews of the Sample of Men*
International Typographical Union as a whole	Structural, environmental, behavioral properties	By inference, communication network (structural)			
Locals	Behavioral properties (militancy, etc.)	Behavioral properties, size	By inference, communication network (structural)	Structural, environmental, behavioral properties	
Shops	Shops		Behavioral properties, size		Distributions of individual properties
Other immediate social environment of men	The social climate, by inference from dominant issues and election outcome	The social climate, by inference from dominant issues and election outcome			Chapel chairman's attributes; friends' attributes
Men	By inference, dominant values and interests	By inference: values, interests, and loyalties (e.g., local over international)	By inference: values, interests, loyalties (e.g., to shop over local)	By inference: values	Behavior, background, values, attitudes

SOURCE: Lipset, Trow, and Coleman (1956, p. 422). Reprinted by permission.

study might be about a single organization, such as a hospital, the analysis might include outcomes about the clinical services and staff employed by the hospital (and possibly even some quantitative analyses based on the employee records of the staff). In an evaluation study, the single case might be a public program that involves large numbers of funded projects—which would then be the embedded units (see Appendix B for more details). In either situation, these embedded units can be selected through sampling or cluster techniques (McClintock, 1985). No matter how the units are selected, the resulting design would be called an *embedded case study design* (see Figure 2.4, Type 2). In contrast, if the case study examined only the global nature of an organization or of a program, a *holistic design* would have been used (see Figure 2.4, Type 1).

These two variants of single-case studies both have their strengths and weaknesses. The holistic design is advantageous when no logical subunits can be identified or when the relevant theory underlying the case study is itself of a holistic nature. Potential problems arise, however, when a global approach allows a researcher to avoid examining any specific phenomenon in operational detail. Thus, a typical problem with the holistic design is that the entire case study may be conducted at an unduly abstract level, lacking sufficiently clear measures or data.

A further problem with the holistic design is that the entire nature of the case study may shift, unbeknownst to the researcher, during the course of study. The initial study questions may have reflected one orientation, but as the case study proceeds, a different orientation may emerge, and the evidence begins to address different research questions. Although some people have claimed such flexibility to be a strength of case study research, in fact the largest criticism of case studies is based on this type of shift—in which the implemented research design is no longer appropriate for the research questions being asked (see COSMOS Corporation, 1983). Because of this problem, you need to avoid such unsuspected slippage; if the relevant research questions really do change, you should simply start over again, with a new research design. One way to increase the sensitivity to such slippage is to have a set of subunits. Thus, an embedded design can serve as an important device for focusing a case study inquiry.

An embedded design, however, also has its pitfalls. A major one occurs when the case study focuses only on the subunit level and fails to return to the larger unit of analysis. For instance, an evaluation of a program consisting of multiple projects may include project characteristics as a subunit of analysis. The project-level data may even be highly quantitative if there are many projects. However, the original evaluation becomes a project study (i.e., a multiple-case study of different projects) if no investigating is done at the level of the original case—that is, the program. Similarly, a study of organizational climate may involve individual employees as a subunit of study. However, if the data focus only on individual employees, the study will in fact become an employee and not an organizational study. In both examples, what has happened is that the original phenomenon of interest (a program or organizational climate) has become the context and not the target of study.

Summary. Single-case studies are a common design for doing case study research, and two variants have been described: those using holistic designs and those using embedded units of analysis. Overall, the single-case design is eminently justifiable under certain conditions—where the case represents (a) a critical test of existing theory, (b) an extreme or unusual circumstance, or (c) a common case, or where the case serves a (d) revelatory or (e) longitudinal purpose.

A major step in designing and conducting a single case is defining the unit of analysis (or the case itself). An operational definition is needed, and some caution must be exercised—before a total commitment to the whole case study is made—to ensure that the case in fact is relevant to the issues and questions of interest.

Within the single-case study may still be incorporated subunits of analyses, so that a more complex (or embedded) design is developed. The subunits can often add significant opportunities for extensive analysis, enhancing the insights into the single case. However, if too much attention is given to these subunits, and if the larger, holistic aspects of the case begin to be ignored, the case study itself will have shifted its orientation and changed its nature. If the shift is justifiable, you need to address it explicitly and indicate its relationship to the original inquiry.

What Are the Potential Multiple-Case Designs (Types 3 and 4)?

The same study may contain more than a single case. When this occurs, the study has used a multiple-case design, and such designs have increased in frequency in recent years. A common example is a study of school innovations (such as the use of new curricula, rearranged school schedules, or a new educational technology), in which individual schools adopt some innovation. Each school might be the subject of an individual case study, but the study as a whole covers several schools and in this way uses a multiple-case design.

Multiple- versus single-case designs. In some fields, multiple-case studies have been considered a different "methodology" from single-case studies. For example, both anthropology and political science have developed one set of rationales for doing single-case studies and a second set for doing what have been considered "comparative" (or multiple-case) studies (see Eckstein, 1975; Lijphart, 1975). This book, however, considers single- and multiple-case designs to be variants within the same methodological framework—and no broad distinction is made between the so-called classic (that is, single) case study and multiple-case studies. The choice is considered one of research design, with both being included under case study research.

Multiple-case designs have distinct advantages and disadvantages in comparison to single-case designs. The evidence from multiple cases is often considered more compelling, and the overall study is therefore regarded as being more robust (Herriott & Firestone, 1983). At the same time, the rationale for single-case designs cannot usually be satisfied by multiple cases. By definition, the unusual or extreme case, the critical case, and the revelatory case all are likely to involve only single cases. Moreover, the conduct of a multiple-case study can require extensive resources and time beyond the means of a single student or independent research investigator. Therefore, the decision to undertake multiple-case studies cannot be taken lightly.

Selecting the multiple cases also raises a new set of questions. Here, *a major insight is to consider multiple cases as one would consider multiple experiments*—that is, to follow a "replication" design. This is far different from a misleading analogy that incorrectly considers multiple cases to be similar to the multiple respondents in a survey (or to the multiple subjects within an experiment)—that is, to follow a "sampling" design. The methodological differences between these two views are revealed by the different rationales underlying the replication as opposed to sampling designs.

Replication, not sampling logic, for multiple-case studies. The replication logic is analogous to that used in multiple experiments (see Hersen & Barlow, 1976). For example, upon uncovering a significant finding from a single experiment, an ensuing and pressing priority would be to replicate this finding by conducting a second, third, and even more experiments. Some of the replications might attempt to duplicate the exact conditions of the original experiment. Other replications might alter one or two experimental conditions considered unimportant to the original finding, to see whether the finding could still be duplicated. Only with such replications would the original finding be considered robust.

The logic underlying the use of multiple-case studies is the same. Each case must be carefully selected so that it either (a) predicts similar results (a *literal replication*) or (b) predicts contrasting results but for anticipatable reasons (a *theoretical replication*). The ability to conduct 6 or 10 case studies, arranged effectively within a multiple-case design, is analogous to the ability to conduct 6 to 10 experiments on related topics; a few cases (2 or 3) would be literal replications, whereas a few other cases (4 to 6) might be designed to pursue two different patterns of theoretical replications. If all the cases turn out as predicted, these 6 to 10 cases, in the aggregate, would have provided compelling support for the initial set of propositions. If the cases are in some way contradictory, the initial propositions must be revised and retested with another set of cases. Again, this logic is similar to the way researchers deal with conflicting experimental findings.

The logic underlying these replication procedures also should reflect some theoretical interest, not just a prediction that two cases should simply be similar or different. For example, one might consider the initial proposition that an increase in using a new computer system in small business environments will occur when the system is used for both administrative (e.g., accounting and personnel) and business (e.g., sales and production) applications, but not either alone. To pursue this proposition in a multiple-case study design, 3 or 4 small businesses (or cases) might be selected in which both types of applications are present, to determine whether, in fact, use of the system did increase over a period of time (the investigation would be predicting a literal replication in these 3 or 4 cases). Three or 4 additional cases might be selected in which only administrative applications are present, with the prediction being little increase in use (predicting a theoretical replication). Finally, 3 or 4 other cases would be selected in which only business applications are present, with the same prediction of little increase in use, but for different reasons than the administrative-only cases (another theoretical replication). If this entire pattern of results across these multiple cases is indeed found, the 9 to 12 cases, in the aggregate, would provide substantial support for the initial proposition.

Another example of a multiple-case replication design comes from the field of urban studies (see BOX 11). You also can find examples of three entire case studies, all following a replication design but covering university administration, the transformation of business firms, and HIV/AIDS prevention, in the companion text (Yin, 2012, chaps. 11, 12, and 15).

BOX 11
A Multiple-Case, Replication Design

A common problem in the 1960s and 1970s was how to get good advice to city governments. Peter Szanton's (1981) book, *Not Well Advised,* reviewed the experiences of numerous attempts by university and research groups to collaborate with city officials.

The book is an excellent example of a multiple-case replication design. Szanton starts with eight case studies, showing how different university groups all failed to help city governments. The eight cases are sufficient "replications" to convince the reader of a general phenomenon. Szanton then provides five more case studies, in which nonuniversity groups also failed, concluding that failure was therefore not necessarily inherent in the academic enterprise. Yet a third group of cases shows how university groups have successfully helped business, engineering firms, and sectors other than city government. A final set of three cases shows that those few groups able to help city government were concerned with implementation and not just with the production of new ideas, leading to the major conclusion that city governments may have peculiar needs in receiving but also then putting advice into practice.

Within each of the four groups of case studies, Szanton has illustrated the principle of literal replication. Across the four groups, he has illustrated theoretical replication. This potent case study design can and should be applied to many other topics.

This replication logic, whether applied to experiments or to case studies, must be distinguished from the sampling logic commonly used in surveys. The sampling logic requires an operational enumeration of the entire universe or pool of potential respondents and then a statistical procedure for selecting a specific subset of respondents to be surveyed. The resulting data from the sample that is actually surveyed are assumed to reflect the entire universe or pool, with inferential statistics used to establish the confidence intervals for which this representation is presumed accurate. The entire procedure is commonly used when a researcher wishes to determine the prevalence or frequency of a particular phenomenon.

Any application of this sampling logic to case study research would be misplaced. First, case studies are not the best method for assessing the prevalence of phenomena. Second, a case study would have to cover both the phenomenon of interest and its context, yielding a large number of potentially relevant variables. In turn, this would require an impossibly large sample of cases—too large to allow more than a superficial examination of any given case.

Third, if a sampling logic had to be applied to all types of research, many important topics could not be empirically investigated, such as the following problem: Your investigation deals with the role of the presidency of the United States, and you are interested in doing a multiple-case study of (a few) presidents to test your theory about presidential leadership. However, the complexity of your topic means that your choice of a small number of cases could not adequately represent all the 44 presidents since the beginning of the Republic. Critics using a sampling logic might therefore deny the acceptability of your study. In contrast, if you use a replication logic, the study is eminently feasible.

The replication approach to multiple-case studies is illustrated in Figure 2.5. The figure indicates that the initial step in designing the study must consist of theory development, and then shows that case selection and the definition of specific measures are important steps in the design and data collection process. Each individual case study consists of a "whole" study, in which convergent evidence is sought regarding the facts and conclusions for the case; each case's conclusions are then considered to be the information needing replication by other individual cases. Both the individual cases and the multiple-case results can and should be the focus of a summary report. For each individual case, the report should indicate how and why a particular proposition was demonstrated (or not demonstrated). Across cases, the report should indicate the extent of the replication logic and why certain cases were predicted to have certain results, whereas other cases, if any, were predicted to have contrasting results.

An important part of Figure 2.5 is the dashed-line feedback loop. The loop represents the situation where important discovery occurs during the conduct of one of the individual case studies (e.g., one of the cases did not in fact suit the original design). Such a discovery may require you to reconsider one or more of the study's original theoretical propositions. At this point, "redesign" should take place before proceeding

Figure 2.5 Multiple-Case Study Procedure

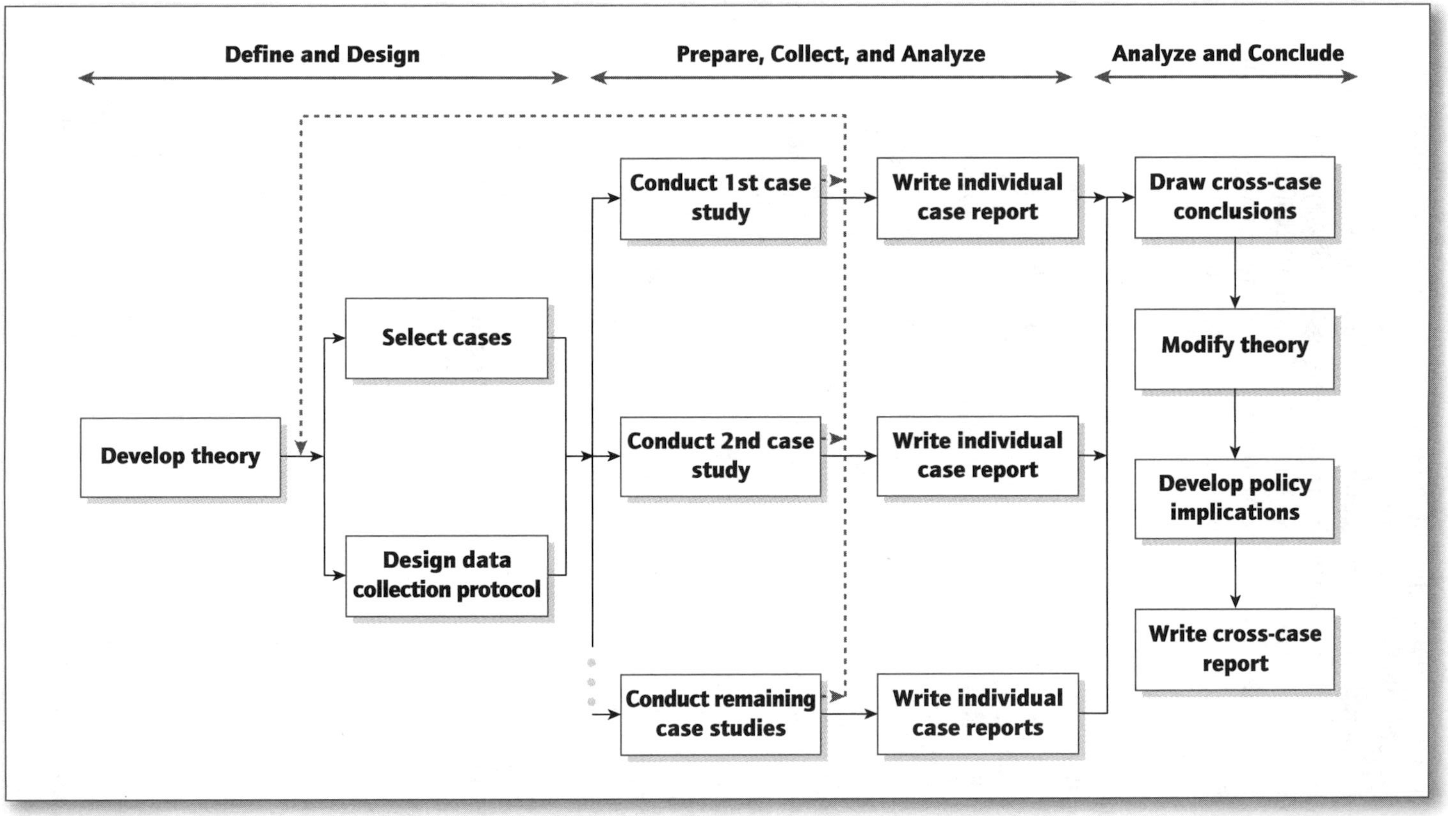

SOURCE: COSMOS Corporation.

further. Such redesign might involve the selection of alternative cases or changes in the case study protocol (see Chapter 3). Without such redesign, you risk being accused of distorting or ignoring the discovery, just to accommodate the original design. This condition leads quickly to a further accusation—that you have been selective in reporting your data, to suit your preconceived ideas (that is, the original theoretical propositions).

Overall, Figure 2.5 depicts a different logic from that of a sampling design. The logic as well as its contrast with a sampling design may be difficult to follow and is worth extensive discussion with colleagues before proceeding with any multiple-case study.

When using a multiple-case design, a further question you will encounter has to do with the *number* of cases deemed necessary or sufficient for your study. However, because a sampling logic should not be used, the typical criteria regarding the use of a power analysis to determine the desired sample size (e.g., Lipsey, 1990) also are irrelevant. Instead, you should think of the number of case replications—both literal and theoretical—that you need or would like to have in your study.

Your judgment will be a discretionary, not formulaic, one. Such discretionary judgments occur in non–case study research, such as in setting the criterion for defining a "significant effect" in experimental science. Thus, designating a "$p < .05$" or "$p < .01$" likelihood of detection, to set the confidence level for accepting or rejecting the null hypothesis, is not based on any formula but is a matter of discretionary, judgmental choice. Note that when patient safety and well-being are at stake, as in a clinical trial, investigators will usually not even settle for a "$p < .01$" significance level but may choose to attain a "$p < .0001$" or even more stringent level. Analogously, designating the number of replications depends upon the certainty you want to have about your multiple-case results. For example, you may want to settle for two or three literal replications when your theory is straightforward and the issue at hand does not demand an excessive degree of certainty. However, if your theory is subtle or if you want a higher degree of certainty, you may press for five, six, or more replications.

In deciding upon the number of replications, an important consideration is related to your sense of the strength and importance of rival explanations. The stronger the rivals, the more additional cases you might want, each case showing a different result when some rival explanation had been taken into account. For example, your original hypothesis might be that summer reading programs improve students' reading scores, and you already might have shown this result through several cases that served as literal replications. A rival explanation might be that parents also work more closely with their children during the summer and that this circumstance can account for the improved reading scores. You would then find another case, with parent participation but no summer reading program, and in this theoretical replication you would predict that the scores would not improve. Having two such theoretical replications would provide even greater support for your findings.

Rationale for multiple-case designs. In short, the rationale for multiple-case designs derives directly from your understanding of literal and theoretical replications. The simplest multiple-case design would be the selection of two or more cases that are believed to be literal replications, such as a set of cases with exemplary outcomes in relation to some evaluation question, such as "how and why a particular intervention has been implemented smoothly." Selecting such cases requires prior knowledge of the outcomes, with the multiple-case inquiry focusing on how and why the exemplary outcomes might have occurred and hoping for literal (or direct) replications of these conditions from case to case.[5]

More complicated multiple-case designs would likely result from the number and types of theoretical replications you might want to cover. For example, investigators have used a "two-tail" design in which cases from both extremes (of some important theoretical condition, such as extremely good and extremely bad outcomes) have been deliberately chosen. Multiple-case rationales also can derive from the prior hypothesizing of different types of conditions and the desire to have subgroups of cases covering each type. These and other similar designs are more complicated because the study should still have at least two individual cases within each of the subgroups, so that the theoretical replications across subgroups are complemented by literal replications within each subgroup.

Multiple-case studies: Holistic or embedded. The fact that a design calls for multiple-case studies does not eliminate the variation identified earlier with single-case studies: Each individual case may still be holistic or embedded. In other words, a multiple-case study may consist of multiple holistic cases (see Figure 2.4, Type 3) or of multiple embedded cases (see Figure 2.4, Type 4).

The difference between these two variants depends upon the type of phenomenon being studied and your research questions. In an embedded design, a study even may call for the conduct of a survey at each case study site. For instance, suppose a study is concerned with the impact of the same type of curriculum adopted by different nursing schools. Each nursing school may be the topic of a case study, with the theoretical framework dictating that nine such schools be included as case studies, three to replicate a direct result (literal replication) and six others to deal with contrasting conditions (theoretical replications).

For all nine schools, an embedded design is used because surveys of the students (or, alternatively, examination of students' archival records) are needed to address research questions about the performance of the schools. However, the results of each survey will *not* be pooled across schools. Rather, the survey data will be part of the findings for each individual nursing school, or case. These data may be highly quantitative and even involve statistical tests, focusing on the attitudes and behavior of individual students, and the data will be used along with information about the school to interpret the success and operations with the curriculum at that particular school. If, in contrast, the survey data are pooled across schools, a replication design is no longer being used. In fact, the study has now become an embedded, single-case study, in which all nine schools and their students have now become part of some larger, main unit of analysis that might not have been specified at the outset. Such a turn of events would create a pressing need to discard the original multiple-case design. The newly designed single-case study would require a complete redefinition of the main unit of analysis and entail extensive revisions to the original theories and propositions of interest.

Summary. This section has dealt with situations in which the same investigation may call for multiple-case studies. These types of designs are becoming more prevalent, but they are more expensive and time-consuming to conduct.

Any use of multiple-case designs should follow a replication, not a sampling, logic, and a researcher must choose each case carefully. The cases should serve in a manner similar to multiple experiments, with similar results (a literal replication) or contrasting results (a theoretical replication) predicted explicitly at the outset of the investigation.

The individual cases within a multiple-case study design may be either holistic or embedded. When an embedded design is used, each individual case study may in fact include the collection and analysis of quantitative data, including the use of surveys within each case study.

Exercise 2.4   Defining a Case Study Research Design

Select one of the case studies described in the BOXES of this book, reviewing the entire case study (not just the material in the BOX). Describe the research design of this case study. How did it justify the relevant evidence to be sought, given the main research questions to be answered? What methods were used to identify the findings, based on the evidence? Is the design a single- or multiple-case design? Is it holistic or does it have embedded units of analysis?

MODEST ADVICE IN SELECTING CASE STUDY DESIGNS △

Now that you know how to define case study designs and are prepared to carry out design work, you might want to consider three pieces of advice.

Single- or Multiple-Case Designs?

The first word of advice is that, although all designs can lead to successful case studies, when you have the choice (and resources), multiple-case designs may be preferred over single-case designs. If you can do even a "two-case" case study, your chances of doing a good case study will be better than using a single-case design. Single-case designs are vulnerable if only because you will have put "all your eggs in one basket." More important, the analytic benefits from having two (or more) cases may be substantial.

To begin with, even with two cases, you have the possibility of direct replication. Analytic conclusions independently arising from two cases, as with two experiments, will be more powerful than those coming from a single case (or single experiment) alone. Alternatively, you may have deliberately selected your two cases because they offered contrasting situations, and you were not seeking a direct replication. In this design, if the subsequent findings support the hypothesized contrast, the results represent a strong start toward theoretical replication—again strengthening your findings compared to those from a single-case study alone (e.g., Eilbert & Lafronza, 2005; Hanna, 2005; also see BOX 12).

BOX 12
Two, "Two-Case" Case Studies

12A. Contrasting Cases for Community Building

Chaskin (2001) used two case studies to illustrate contrasting strategies for capacity building at the neighborhood level. The author's overall conceptual framework, which was the main topic of inquiry, claimed that there could be two approaches to building community capacity—using a collaborative organization to (a) reinforce existing networks of community organizations or (b) initiate a new organization in the neighborhood. After thoroughly airing the framework on theoretical grounds, the author presents the two case studies, showing the viability of each approach.

12B. Contrasting Strategies for Educational Accountability

In a directly complementary manner, Elmore, Abelmann, and Fuhrman (1997) chose two case studies to illustrate contrasting strategies for designing and implementing educational accountability (i.e., holding schools accountable for the academic performance of their students). One case represented a lower cost, basic version of an accountability system. The other represented a higher cost, more complex version.

In general, criticisms about single-case studies usually reflect fears about the uniqueness or artifactual conditions surrounding the case (e.g., special access to a key informant). As a result, the criticisms may turn into skepticism about your ability to do empirical work beyond having done a single-case study. Having two cases can begin to blunt such criticism and skepticism. Having more than two cases will produce an even stronger effect. In the face of these benefits, having at least two cases should be your goal. If you do use a single-case design, you should be prepared to make an extremely strong argument in justifying your choice for the case.

Exercise 2.5 Establishing the Rationale for a Multiple-Case Study

Develop some preliminary ideas about a "case" for your case study. Alternatively, focus on one of the single-case studies presented in the BOXES in this book. In either situation, now think of a companion "case" that might augment the single case. In what ways might the companion case's findings supplement those of the first case? Could the data from the second case fill a gap left by the first case or respond better to some obvious shortcoming or criticism of the first case? Would the two cases together comprise a stronger case study? Could yet a third case make the findings even more compelling?

Closed or Adaptive Designs?

Another word of advice is that, despite this chapter's details about design choices, you should not think that a case study's design cannot be modified by new information or discovery during data collection. Such revelations can be enormously important, leading to your altering or modifying your original research design.

As examples, in a single-case study, what was thought to be a critical or unusual case might have turned out not to be so, after initial data collection had started; ditto a multiple-case study, where what was thought to be parallel cases for literal replication turn out not to be so. With these revelations, you have every right to conclude that your initial design needs to be modified. However, you should undertake any alterations only given a serious caution. The caution is to understand precisely the nature of the alteration: Are you merely selecting different cases, or are you also changing your original theoretical concerns and objectives? The point is that the needed adaptiveness should not lessen the rigor with which case study procedures are followed.

Mixed Methods Designs: Mixing Case Studies with Other Methods?

Researchers have given increasing attention to *mixed methods research*—a "class of research where the researcher mixes or combines quantitative and qualitative research techniques, methods, approaches, concepts or language into a *single* study" (Johnson & Onwuegbuzie, 2004, p. 17, emphasis added). Confinement to a single study forces the methods being mixed into an integrated mode. The mode differs from the conventional situation whereby different methods are used in *separate* studies that may later be synthesized.

Mixed methods research forces the methods to share the same research questions, to collect complementary data, and to conduct counterpart analyses (e.g., Yin, 2006b)— in short, to follow a mixed methods design. As such, mixed methods research can permit researchers to address more complicated research questions and collect a richer and stronger array of evidence than can be accomplished by any single method alone. Depending upon the nature of your research questions and your ability to use different methods, mixed methods research opens a class of research designs that deserve your attention.

The earlier discussion of embedded case study designs in fact points to the fact that certain kinds of case studies already represent a form of mixed methods research: Embedded case studies may rely on holistic data collection strategies for studying the main case and then call upon surveys or other quantitative techniques to collect data about the embedded unit(s) of analysis. In this situation, other research methods are embedded within case study research.

The opposite relationship also can occur. Your case study may be part of a larger, mixed methods study. The main investigation may rely on a survey or other quantitative techniques, and your case study may help to investigate the conditions within one of the entities being surveyed. The contrasting relationships (survey within case or case within survey) are illustrated in Figure 2.6 (also see Appendix B for further discussion of these mixtures in relation to evaluation studies).

Figure 2.6   Mixed Methods: Two Nested Arrangements

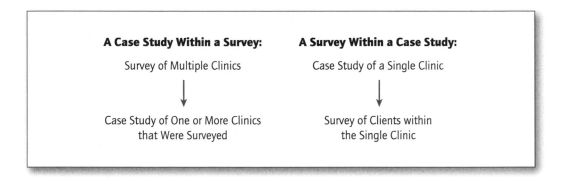

At the same time, mixed methods research need not include the use of case study research at all. For instance, a clinical study could be combined with historical work that embraces the quantitative analysis of archival records, such as newspapers and other file material. Going even further, mixed methods research need not be limited to combinations of quantitative and qualitative methods. For instance, a study could employ a mix of two quantitative methods: a survey to describe certain conditions, complemented by an experiment that tries to manipulate some of those conditions (e.g., Berends & Garet, 2002).

By definition, studies using mixed methods research are more difficult to execute than studies limited to single methods. However, mixed methods research can enable you to address broader or more complicated research questions than case studies alone. As a result, mixing case study research with other methods should be among the possibilities meriting your consideration.

NOTES TO CHAPTER 2 △

1. Figure 2.2 focuses only on the formal research design process, not on data collection activities. For all three types of research (survey, case study, and experiment), data collection techniques might be depicted as the level below Level One in the figure. For example, for case study research, this might include using multiple sources of evidence, as described further in Chapter 4. Similar data collection techniques can be described for surveys or experiments—for example, questionnaire design for surveys or stimulus presentation strategies for experiments.

2. Whether experiments also need to address statistical generalizations has been the topic of sharp debate in psychology. According to the statistical argument, the human subjects in an experiment should be considered a population sample, with the experimental results therefore limited to the universe of the same population. The debate began over the excessive use of college sophomores in behavioral research (e.g., Cooper, McCord, & Socha, 2011; Gordon, Slade, & Schmitt, 1986; McNemar, 1946; Peterson, 2001; Sears, 1986) and has since extended to an awareness that the subjects in most behavioral research have been white males from industrialized countries (Henrich, Heine, & Norenzayan, 2010), even though the experimental findings are intended to apply as "the norm for all human beings" (Prescott, 2002, p. 38).

3. One of the anonymous reviewers of the third edition of this book pointed out that construct validity also has to do with whether interviewees understand what is being asked of them.

4. For other suggested guidelines for reviewers of case study proposals or manuscripts, see Yin (1999).

5. Strictly quantitative studies that select cases with known outcomes follow the same design and have alternatively been called "case-control," "retrospective," or "case referent" studies (see Rosenbaum, 2002, p. 7).

Tutorial 2.1:
More on Defining "Analytic Generalization"

An analytic generalization consists of a carefully posed theoretical statement, theory, or theoretical proposition. The generalization can take the form of a lesson learned, working hypothesis, or other principle that is believed to be applicable to other situations (not just other "like cases"). Thus, the preferred analytic generalization is posed at a conceptual level higher than that of the specific case (presumably, this higher level was needed to justify the importance of studying the chosen case in the first place).

Though not using the same terminology, other prominent works have devoted attention to analytic generalization, also distinguishing it from statistical generalization: (1) Mitchell's (1983) discussion of *logical inference* and *statistical inference;* (2) Bromley's (1986) discussion of *case inference* compared with *statistical inference* (pp. 290–291); and Donmoyer's (1990) *schema.* A fourth work, by Burawoy (1991), covers the *extended case method*—his way of describing how a generalization "extends" a narrow case to some broader significance (pp. 271–280).

The more difficult and contrary position—that the studied case should be construed as an instance, example, or sample of some larger group of cases—undesirably returns to statistical generalization (the relationship between a sample and its population—e.g., Gomm, Hammersley, & Foster, 2000, pp. 99–103). That position dwells on the fact that a "case" seems to be an instance or example of other "like cases." However, such a claim is inappropriate when thinking about analytic generalization, where the findings from a case study can have implications going well beyond the same kind of case and extend to a whole host of other unlike situations (see BOX 7, p. 43, in the main text for three examples). Moreover, unless a case study has included a large number of cases—typically dozens or scores if not hundreds of cases (see Tutorial 5-3)—the study will face an uphill battle by invoking the sample to population analogy and its concomitant need to employ statistical analyses to assess the strength of any relationship.

Small (2009) provides two excellent examples and an insightful discussion of analytic generalization, also citing the same key works as referenced above. To him, the preferred logic represents "a different perspective and language of inquiry" (p. 18). He further notes the importance of starting with a substantive proposition (e.g., a causal relationship) rather than a numeric one (e.g., the representativeness of a case) to make analytic generalizations work.

Briefly Annotated References for Tutorial 2.1

Bromley, D. B. (1986). *The case-study method in psychology and related disciplines.* Chichester, England: Wiley.
    Provides comprehensive guidance on case study research in psychology.
Burawoy, M. (1991). The extended case method. In M. Burawoy, A. Burton, A. A. Ferguson, K. J. Fox, J. Gamson, N. Gartrell, et al. (Eds.), *Ethnography unbound: Power and resistance in the modern metropolis*

(pp. 271–287). Berkeley: University of California Press. Presents the extended case method for analyzing participant-observation data.

Donmoyer, R. (1990). Generalizability and the single-case study. In E. W. Eisner & A. Peshkin (Eds.), *Qualitative inquiry in education: The continuing debate* (pp. 175–200). New York: Teachers College Press. Offers a way of generalizing from single studies, not based on sampling and statistical significance.

Gomm, R., Hammersley, M., & Foster, P. (2000). Case study and generalization. In R. Gomm, M. Hammersley, & P. Foster (Eds.), *Case study method* (pp. 98–115). London: Sage. Highlights use of the case study method for generalizing, rather than merely studying a case for its own sake.

Mitchell, J. C. (1983). Case and situation analysis. *Sociological Review, 31,* 187–211. Emphasizes case study research as a method for preserving the unitary character of the social object being studied and discusses the challenge of generalizing from the case(s).

Small, M. L. (2009). "How many cases do I need?" On science and the logic of case selection in field-based research. *Ethnography, 10,* 5–38. Poses a thoughtful article on key issues in designing field-based research, including the challenge of generalizing from field situations.

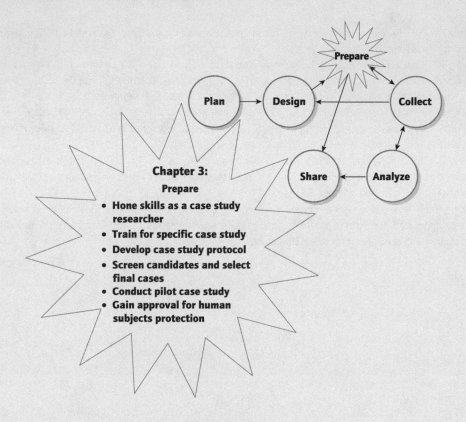

Chapter 3:

Prepare

- **Hone skills as a case study researcher**
- **Train for specific case study**
- **Develop case study protocol**
- **Screen candidates and select final cases**
- **Conduct pilot case study**
- **Gain approval for human subjects protection**

ABSTRACT

Preparing to do a case study starts with a researcher's prior skills and values and covers the preparation and training for the specific case study (including procedures for protecting human subjects).

With regard to skills, many people incorrectly believe they are sufficiently skilled to do case study research because they think the method is easy to do. In fact, case study research is among the hardest types of research because of the absence of well-documented procedures. Case study researchers therefore need to feel comfortable in addressing procedural uncertainties that may arise during the course of a study. Other desirable traits include the ability to ask good questions, "listen," be adaptive, have a firm grasp of the issues being studied, and know how to avoid bias and bring high ethical standards to the research.

A researcher can prepare to do a high-quality case study through intensive training. The most important part of the training will cover the development of a case study protocol, to guide the actual data collection. The protocol is especially critical if the case study uses a multiple-case design or involves multiple researchers, or both. Two final preparatory steps include the screening of candidate cases to be part of the case study, and the conduct of a pilot case study.

3

PREPARING TO COLLECT CASE STUDY EVIDENCE

What You Need to Do before Starting to Collect Case Study Data

Even though doing a case study begins with the research questions to be addressed and the development of a case study design, most people associate the doing of a case study with the collection of the case study data, and this and the following chapter focus on the data collection activity. This chapter deals with the needed preparation. The next covers the actual data collection techniques.

The preparation for data collection can be complex. If not done well, the entire case study can be jeopardized, and all of the earlier work—in defining the research questions and designing the case study—will have been for naught. Moreover, gaining approval for your case study, showing how human subjects will be protected, can pose another challenge.

Good preparation begins with (1) the *desired skills and values* on the part of the case study investigator. These have seldom been the topic of explicit attention in the past. Yet, some are critical and can be learned or practiced. Four additional topics also should be a formal part of any case study preparation: (2) *training* for a specific case study, (3) developing a *protocol* for the study, (4) *screening* candidate cases, and (5) conducting a *pilot case study*. The protocol is an especially effective way of dealing with the overall problem of increasing the reliability of case studies. However, success with all five topics is needed to ensure that case study data collection will proceed smoothly. The following chapter therefore covers each topic.

△ THE CASE STUDY RESEARCHER: DESIRED SKILLS AND VALUES

Too many people are drawn to case study research because they believe it is "easy." Many social scientists—especially budding ones—think case study research can be mastered without much difficulty. They believe that they only will have to learn a minimal set of technical procedures; that any of their own shortcomings in formal, analytic skills will be unimportant; and that a case study will allow them simply to "tell it like it is." No beliefs could be farther from the truth.

In actuality, the demands of a case study on your intellect, ego, and emotions are far greater than those of any other research method. This is because the data collection procedures are *not* routinized. In laboratory experiments or in surveys, for instance, the data collection phase of a research project can be largely, if not wholly, conducted by one (or more) research assistant(s). The assistant(s) will carry out the data collection activities with a minimum of discretionary behavior, and in this sense, the activity is routinized—and analytically boring.

Conducting case studies offers no such parallel. Rather, a well-trained and experienced researcher is needed to conduct a high-quality case study because of the continuous interaction between the theoretical issues being studied and the data being collected. Mediating this interaction will require delicate judgment calls. They can involve technical aspects of the data collection but also ethical dilemmas, such as dealing with the sharing of private information or coping with other possible field conflicts. Only an alert researcher will be able to take advantage of unexpected opportunities rather than being trapped by them—while still exercising sufficient care to avoid potentially biased procedures.

Unfortunately, there are no tests for distinguishing those persons likely to become good case study researchers from those who are not. Compare this situation to that in mathematics or even a profession such as law. In math, people are able to score themselves for their abilities and to screen themselves from further advancement because they simply cannot

---

Tip: *When am I ready to start collecting the case study data?*

You have just designed your case study, following the suggestions in Chapter 2, and you are anxious to start collecting data because time is short, and available data collection opportunities are present. Your readiness, however, should not be defined by external time constraints or conditions. Instead, your "readiness" depends upon your own skill levels for doing case studies, as well as your having completed formal and preparatory procedures prior to collecting actual data, such as having properly selected the case to be studied.

Have you practiced these skills, and do you think case study research needs to follow formal procedures in preparing for data collection?

carry out higher levels of math problems. To practice law, a person must pass the bar examination in a particular state. Again, many people screen themselves out of the field by failing to pass this test.

No such gatekeepers exist for assessing the skills and values needed to do good case studies. However, a basic list of desired attributes might be the ability to:

- *Ask good questions*—and interpret the answers fairly.
- *Be a good "listener"* not trapped by existing ideologies or preconceptions.
- *Stay adaptive,* so that newly encountered situations can be seen as opportunities, not threats.
- *Have a firm grasp of the issues being studied,* even when in an exploratory mode.
- *Avoid biases* by being sensitive to contrary evidence, also knowing how to *conduct research ethically.*

Any absence of these attributes is remediable, as anyone missing one or more of them can work on developing them. But everyone must be honest in assessing her or his capabilities in the first place. You might therefore check yourself against the following profiles.

Asking Good Questions

More than with the other research methods discussed in Chapter 1, case study research requires an inquiring mind *during* data collection, not just before or after the activity. The ability to pose and ask good questions is therefore a prerequisite for case study researchers. The desired result is for the researcher to create a rich dialogue with the evidence, an activity that encompasses

> pondering the possibilities gained from deep familiarity with some aspect of the world, systematizing those ideas in relation to kinds of information one might gather, checking the ideas in the light of that information, dealing with the inevitable discrepancies between what was expected and what was found by rethinking the possibilities of getting more data, and so on. (Becker, 1998, p. 66)

Case study data collection does follow a formal protocol, but the specific information that may become relevant to a case study is not readily predictable. As you collect case study evidence, you must quickly review the evidence and continually ask yourself why events or perceptions appear as they do. Your judgments may lead to the immediate need to search for additional evidence.

If you are able to ask good questions throughout the data collection process, a good prediction is that you also will be mentally and emotionally exhausted at the end of each day when doing fieldwork. This depletion of analytic energy is far different from the experience in collecting experimental or survey data—that is, testing "subjects" or administering questionnaires. In these situations, data collection is highly routinized, and the data collector must complete a certain volume of work but exercise minimal discretionary behavior. Furthermore, any substantive review of the evidence does not come until some later time. The result is that such a data collector may become physically exhausted but will have been mentally untested after a day of data collection.

One insight into asking good questions is to understand that research is about questions and not necessarily about answers. If you are the type of person for whom one tentative answer immediately leads to a whole host of new questions, and if these questions eventually aggregate to some significant inquiry about how or why the world works as it does, you are likely to be a good asker of questions.

Being a Good "Listener"

For case studies, "listening" means receiving information through multiple modalities—for example, making keen observations or sensing what might be going on—not just using the aural modality. Being a good listener means being able to assimilate large amounts of new information without bias. As an interviewee recounts an incident, a good listener hears the exact words used by the interviewee (sometimes, the terminology reflects an important perspective), captures the mood and affective components, understands the context from which the interviewee is perceiving the world, and infers the meaning intended by the interviewee (not by the researcher).

The listening skill also needs to be applied to the inspection of documentary evidence, as well as to observations of real-life situations. In reviewing documents, listening takes the form of worrying whether the originator of the document intended any important messages *between* the lines; any inferences, of course, would need to be corroborated with other sources of information, but important insights might be gained in this way. Poor "listeners" may not even realize that there can be information between the lines. Other listening deficiencies include having a closed mind, being selective in what is retained, or simply having a poor memory.

Staying Adaptive

Few case studies will end exactly as planned. Inevitably, you will have to make minor if not major changes, ranging from the need to pursue an unexpected lead (potentially minor) to the need to identify a new "case" for study (potentially major). The skilled researcher must remember the original purpose of the case study but then must be willing to adapt procedures or plans if unanticipated events occur (see BOX 13).

BOX 13
Adaptiveness in Designing a Case Study

Peter Blau's study of behavior in large government agencies (*The Dynamics of Bureaucracy*, 1955) is still valued for its insights into the relationship between the formal and informal organization of work groups, even more than 50 years later.

Although his study focused on two government agencies, that was not Blau's initial design. As the author notes, he first intended to study a single organization and later switched to a plan to compare two organizations—a public one and a private one (Blau, 1955, pp. 272–273). However, his initial attempts to gain access to a private firm were unsuccessful, and in the meanwhile, he had developed a stronger rationale for comparing two different kinds of government agencies.

These shifts in the initial plans are examples of the kinds of changes that can occur in the design of a case study. Blau's experience shows how a skilled researcher can take advantage of changing opportunities, as well as shifts in theoretical concerns, to produce a classic case study.

When a shift is made, you must maintain an unbiased perspective and acknowledge those situations in which, in fact, you may have inadvertently begun to pursue a totally new study. When this occurs, many completed steps—including the initial design of the case study—must be repeated and redocumented. One of the worst complaints about the conduct of case study research is that researchers change directions without knowing that their original research design was inappropriate for the eventual case study, thereby leaving unknown gaps and biases. Thus, the need for you to balance adaptability with *rigor*—but not rigidity—cannot be overemphasized.

The desired adaptability also should not result in any exploitative tendencies on your part. For instance, if an interviewee wants to take more time to respond to your questions, being adaptive should not then mean that you can now extend the interview time far beyond what appears to have been the interviewee's original commitment to the interview. Similarly, if an organization pleasantly surprises you by permitting you to retrieve and read some key documents previously withheld from you, you should not think immediately of copying them, unless your host voluntarily signals that this would be an acceptable procedure.

Having a Firm Grasp of the Issues Being Studied

The main way of staying on target is to recall and understand the purpose of the case study in the first place. Every case study researcher must understand the theoretical or policy issues because analytic judgments have to be made throughout the data collection phase. Without a firm grasp of the issues, you could miss important clues and would not know when a deviation was acceptable or even desirable. The point is that case study data collection is not merely a matter of *recording* data in a mechanical fashion, as it is in some other types of research. You must be able to *interpret* the information as it is being collected and to know immediately, for instance, if several sources of information contradict one another and lead to the need for additional evidence—much like a good detective.

In fact, the detective role offers some keen insights into case study fieldwork. Note that the detective arrives on a scene *after* a crime has occurred and is basically being called upon to make *inferences* about what actually transpired. The inferences, in turn, must be based on convergent evidence from witnesses and physical evidence, as well as some unspecifiable element of common sense. Finally, the detective may have to make inferences about multiple crimes, to determine whether the same perpetrator committed them. This last step is similar to the replication logic underlying multiple-case studies.

Avoiding Bias and Conducting Research Ethically

All of the preceding conditions will be negated if a researcher only seeks to use a case study to substantiate a preconceived position. Case study researchers are especially prone to this problem because they must understand the issues beforehand (see Becker, 1958, 1967), and this understanding may undesirably sway them toward supportive evidence and away from contrary evidence. You also may have elected to do a case study to enable you (wrongly) to pursue or (worse yet) advocate a particular orientation to the issues.[1]

One test of this possible bias is the degree to which you are open to contrary evidence. For example, researchers studying "nonprofit" organizations may be surprised to find that many of these organizations have entrepreneurial and capitalistic motives (even though the organizations don't formally make profits). If such findings are based on compelling evidence, the conclusions of the case study would have to reflect these contrary findings. To test your own tolerance for contrary findings, report your preliminary findings—possibly while still in the data collection phase—to two or three critical colleagues. The colleagues should offer alternative explanations and suggestions for data collection. If the quest for contrary findings can produce documentable rebuttals, the likelihood of bias will have been reduced.

Avoiding bias is but one facet of a broader set of values that falls under the rubric of "research ethics." A good case study researcher, like any other social scientist, will strive for the highest ethical standards while doing research. These include having a responsibility to scholarship, such as neither plagiarizing nor falsifying information, as well as being honest, avoiding deception, and accepting responsibility for one's own work. These also include maintaining a strong professional competence that includes keeping up with related research, ensuring accuracy, striving for credibility, and understanding and divulging the needed methodological qualifiers and limitations to one's work.

You can learn more about the particular ethical standards that have been promoted by different academic disciplines by familiarizing yourself with any one of several documents: American Anthropological Association (1998); American Association of University Professors (2006); American Educational Research Association (2000); American Evaluation Association (2004); American Political Science Association Committee on Professional Ethics, Rights, and Freedom (2008); American Psychological Association (2010); and American Sociological Association (1999).

Exercise 3.1 Identifying the Skills for Doing Case Study Research

Name the various skills that are important for a case study researcher to have. Do you know any people that have been successful in doing case study research? What strengths and weaknesses do they have as research investigators? Are these similar to the ones you have just named?

Exercise 3.2 Analyzing Your Own Skills for Doing Case Study Research

What distinctive skills do you believe equip you to do a case study? Have you done previous studies requiring the collection and analysis of original data? Have you done any fieldwork, and if so, in what ways are you a good "listener" or an observant person? If you identify some case study skills that you still might need to strengthen, how would you go about the task?

PREPARATION AND TRAINING FOR A SPECIFIC CASE STUDY △

Protecting Human Subjects

Specific ethical considerations arise for all research involving human "subjects"—those people who will participate in your study or about whom you might collect previously recorded data, such as personnel or client records or students' grades. As a result, sometime between the completion of your design and the start of your data collection, you will need to show how you plan to protect the human subjects in your case study. You will need to obtain formal approval for your plan, and you should not view such approval merely as a nominal oversight process.

The need for protecting human subjects comes from the fact that nearly all case studies, like those covered by this book, are about human affairs. In this manner, you and other social scientists differ from scientists who study physical, chemical, or other nonhuman systems or from historians who may be studying the "dead past." The study of "a contemporary phenomenon in its real-world context" obligates you to important ethical practices akin to those followed in medical research.

As part of the protection, you are responsible for conducting your case study with special care and sensitivity—going beyond the research design and other technical considerations covered throughout this book. The care usually involves (National Research Council, 2003, pp. 23–28):

- gaining *informed consent* from all persons who may be part of your case study, by alerting them to the nature of your case study and formally soliciting their volunteerism in participating in the study;
- protecting those who participate in your study from any *harm,* including avoiding the use of any *deception* in your study;
- protecting the *privacy and confidentiality* of those who participate so that, as a result of their participation, they will not be unwittingly put in any undesirable position, even such as being on a roster to receive requests to participate in some future study, whether conducted by you or anyone else;
- taking special precautions that might be needed to protect *especially vulnerable groups* (for instance, research involving children); and
- selecting participants *equitably,* so that no groups of people are unfairly included or excluded from the research.

Formal approval of your plan will come from an institutional review board (IRB). The board is charged with reviewing and approving all human subjects research before such research can proceed. As a result, the most imperative step before proceeding with your case study is to seek out the IRB at your institution, follow its guidance, and obtain its approval.

The board's review will cover the objectives and design of your study and how you plan to protect the human subjects in it. Note that your interactions with the specific human subjects in your study take place through both direct contact (as in interviews) and the potential use of archival records (such as employee or school records). Compared to its review of studies using other methods, an IRB may devote extra attention to a proposed case study because of a lack of familiarity with case study research. For instance, case study interviews may be more challenging because the interactions are not as structured as in survey interviews and their close-ended questionnaires. The board will want to know such information as how you plan to interact with those being studied, the protocols or data collection instruments you are planning to use, and how you will ensure such protections as informed consent, avoidance of harm, and privacy and confidentiality (see Tutorial 3-1 for more detail about preparing for and interacting with an IRB).

More general guidance comes from your own professional ethics and professional research associations that promulgate their own standards for doing human subjects research, not just case studies (e.g., Joint Committee on Standards for Educational Evaluation, 1981—and also see the seven professional association documents cited above, on pp. 87–88). Also important, your institutional setting will have its own expectations—whether you are part of a university or of an independent research organization—and you need to follow its guidance and procedures.

Training to Do the Case Study

Training also is a necessary step in doing case study research. The timing of the training, relative to the timing for seeking human subjects approval, will not always be linear. You need to have some data collection plans before seeking approval, but, as pointed out below, the finalization of the plans cannot occur until after the approval has been granted. The training activities described below may therefore take place over an extended period of time, starting before but ending after the approval process.

For case study research, the key to understanding the needed training is to understand that every case study researcher must be able to operate as a "senior" researcher. Once you have started collecting data, you should think of yourself as an independent researcher who cannot rely on a rigid formula to guide your inquiry. You must be able to make intelligent decisions throughout the data collection process.

In this sense, training to do a case study actually begins with the definition of the research questions being addressed and the development of the case study design. If these steps have been satisfactorily conducted, as described in Chapters 1 and 2, only minimal further effort may be needed, especially if there is only a single case study researcher.

However, it often happens that a case study needs to be conducted by a *case study team,*[2] for any of three reasons:

1. a single case calls for intensive data collection at the same site, requiring a "team" of researchers (see BOX 14);

2. a case study involves multiple cases, with different persons being needed to cover each site or to rotate among the sites (Stake, 2006, p. 21); or

3. a combination of the first two conditions.

BOX 14
The Logistics of Field Research, Circa 1924–1925

Arranging schedules and gaining access to relevant sources of evidence are important to the *management* of a case study. The modern researcher may feel that these activities have only emerged with the growth of "big" social science during the 1960s and 1970s.

In a famous field study done decades ago, however, many of the same management techniques already had been practiced. The two principal investigators and their staff secretary opened a local office in the city they were studying. This office was used by other project staff for extended periods of time. From this vantage point, the research team participated in local life, examined documentary materials, compiled local statistics, conducted interviews, and distributed and collected questionnaires. This extensive fieldwork resulted 5 years later in the publication of the now-classic study of small-town America, *Middletown* (1929), by Robert and Helen Lynd.

Under these circumstances, all team members should have contributed to the development of a draft case study protocol. This draft would then have been the version submitted for IRB approval, with the IRB-approved version subsequently being considered the final version of the protocol.

When multiple researchers or team members participate in the same case study, all need to learn to be "senior" researchers. Training takes the form of group collaboration rather than didactic instruction: Much time has to be allowed for reading, preparing for the training, and holding the training. (See Figure 3.1 for an agenda of an illustrative training session.)

Figure 3.1   Multisession Agenda for Case Study Training

Preparatory Readings: Should include the original case study proposal, if any; a field-oriented methodological text; several works on the substance of the case study; and sample case studies (reports or publications) from previous case study research.

Session 1: Discussion of the Purpose of the Case Study, the Main Research Questions, and the Selection of the Case(s)

Session 2: Review of the Case Study Protocol

    A. Discussion of relevant theoretical frameworks and literature

    B. Development or review of the hypothetical logic model, if relevant

(Continued)

(Continued)

   C. In-depth discussion of protocol topics (discuss importance of topic and possible types of evidence to be collected in relation to each topic)

   D. Anticipated topics to be covered in the eventual case study report (creates preliminary expectations about the study's end goals)

Session 3: Methodological Review

   A. Arrangements for contacting field informants (e.g., draft confirmation letter or email)

   B. Fieldwork procedures (discuss methodological principles)

   C. Use of evidence (review types of evidence and need for convergence)

   D. Note taking and other field practices

   E. Follow-up activities (e.g., draft thank-you note)

   F. Study schedule, including key deadlines

Typically, the training will cover all phases of the planned case study, including readings on the subject matter, the theoretical issues that led to the case study design, and the case study methods and tactics. You might review examples of the tools used in other case studies (see BOX 15) to add as illustrations to the methodological portion of the training.

BOX 15
Reviewing the Tools and Methods Used in Other Case Studies, Circa the 21st Century

Websites have provided new opportunities to access the tools and methods used in other case studies. For example, in online versions of articles, academic journals may reproduce supplementary materials that might not have appeared in the printed version of the article. For one case study, the supplementary materials included the formal case study protocol, the case study coding book, evidentiary tables linking claims to sections of the case study database, and a list of documents in the case study database (Randolph & Eronen, 2007).

The goal of the training is to have all team members understand the basic concepts, terminology, and methodological issues relevant to the study. Each team member needs to know

- why the case study is being done,
- what evidence is being sought,

- what procedural variations can be anticipated (and what should be done if such variations occur), and
- what would constitute supportive or contrary evidence for any given proposition.

Discussions, rather than lectures, are the key part of the training effort, to test whether the desired level of understanding has been achieved.

This approach to case study training can be contrasted to the training for other types of data collection—for example, group training for survey interviewers. The survey training does involve discussions, but it mainly emphasizes a didactic approach that covers the questionnaire items or terminology to be used. The survey training may or may not cover the global or conceptual concerns of the study, as interviewers may not need to have any broader understanding beyond the mechanics of the survey instrument. Survey training rarely involves any outside reading about the substantive issues, and the survey interviewer generally does not know how the survey data are to be analyzed or what issues are to be investigated. Such an approach may feed the strengths of doing surveys but would be insufficient for case study training.

Protocol development and review. The next subsection will say more about the *content* of the case study protocol. However, a legitimate and desirable training task is the understanding of the protocol by the entire case study team.

To reinforce such an understanding, each team member may be assigned one portion of the substantive topics covered by the protocol. Each member might then be responsible for reviewing the appropriate reading materials related to the assigned portion, adding any other information that may be relevant, and leading a discussion that clarifies that portion of the protocol's questions. In this manner, such an arrangement should ensure that the team members have mastered the content of the protocol and done so as part of a group collaboration. The aim is for each individual member, as well as the team as a whole, to emerge with a deep and shared understanding of the protocol.

Problems to be addressed during training. The training also provides an important opportunity for uncovering problems within the case study plan or with the research team's capabilities. If such problems do emerge, one consolation is that they will be more troublesome if they are only recognized later, after the data collection begins. Good case study researchers should therefore press to be certain, during the training period, that potential problems are brought into the open.

The most obvious problem is that the training may reveal flaws in the case study design or even the initial definition of the study questions. If this occurs, you must be willing to make the necessary revisions, even if more time and effort are necessary. Sometimes, the revisions will challenge the basic purpose of the case study, as in a situation in which the original objective may have been to investigate a technological phenomenon, such as the use of personal computers, but in which the case study really turns out to be about an organizational phenomenon, such as poor supervision. Any revisions, of course, also may lead to the need to review a slightly different literature and to recast the entire case study and its audience. You also should check your IRB's procedures to see whether it will need to conduct a new human subjects review. Despite these unexpected developments, changing the basic premise of your case study is fully warranted if the training has demonstrated the unrealistic (or uninteresting) nature of the original plan.

A second problem is that the training may reveal incompatibilities among the team members—and in particular, the fact that some team members may not share the perspective of the study or its sponsors. In one multiple-case study of community organizations, for instance, team members varied in their beliefs regarding the efficacy of such organizations (U.S. National Commission on Neighborhoods, 1979). When such biases are discovered, one way of dealing with the differing orientations is to suggest to the team that contrary evidence will be respected if it is collected and verifiable. A team member still has the choice, of course, of continuing to participate in the study or deciding to drop out.

A third problem is that the training may reveal some impractical time deadlines or expectations regarding available resources. For instance, a case study may have assumed that 20 persons were to be contacted for open-ended interviews during fieldwork, as part of the data collection. The training may have revealed, however, that the time needed for meeting with these persons is likely to be much longer than anticipated. Under such circumstances, any expectation for interviewing 20 persons would have to depend on revising the original fieldwork schedule.

Finally, the training may uncover some positive features, such as the fact that two or more team members have complementary skills and are able to work productively together. Such rapport and productivity during the training session may readily extend to the actual data collection period and may therefore suggest certain pairings for the fieldwork teams. In general, the training should have the effect of creating group norms for the ensuing data collection activity. This norm-building process is more than an amenity; it will help ensure supportive reactions, should unexpected problems arise during the data collection.

Exercise 3.3 Conducting Training for Doing a Case Study

Describe the major ways in which the preparation and training to do a case study are *different* from those for doing studies using other types of research strategies (e.g., surveys, experiments, histories, and archival analysis). Develop a training agenda to prepare for a case study you might be considering, in which two or three persons are to collaborate.

△　THE CASE STUDY PROTOCOL

A case study protocol has only one thing in common with a survey questionnaire: Both are directed at a single data point—either a single case (even if the case is part of a larger, multiple-case study) or a single respondent.

Beyond this similarity are major differences. The protocol is more than a questionnaire or instrument. First, the protocol contains the instrument but also contains the procedures and general rules to be followed in using the protocol. Second, the protocol is directed at an entirely different party than that of a survey questionnaire, explained below. Third, having a case study protocol is desirable under all circumstances, but it is essential if you are doing a multiple-case study.

The protocol is a major way of increasing the *reliability* of case study research and is intended to guide the researcher in carrying out the data collection from a single case (again, even if the single case is one of several in a multiple-case study). Figure 3.2 gives a *table of contents* from an illustrative protocol, which was used in a study of innovative law enforcement practices supported by federal funds. The practices had been defined earlier through a careful screening process (see later discussion in this chapter for more detail on "screening case study nominations"). Furthermore, because data were to be collected from 18 such cases as part of a multiple-case study, the information about any given case could not be collected in great depth, and thus the number of data collection questions—10 in all (see Section C, Figure 3.2)–was to be modest.

Figure 3.2　Table of Contents of Protocol for Conducting Case Studies of Innovative Law Enforcement Practices

A. **Overview of the Case Study**

　1. Mission and goals reflecting the interests of the case study's sponsor (if any) and audience

　2. Case study questions, hypotheses, and propositions

　3. Theoretical framework for the case study (*reproduces the logic model*); key readings

　4. Role of protocol in guiding the case study researcher (*notes that the protocol is a standardized agenda for the researcher's line of inquiry*)

B. **Data Collection Procedures**

　1. Names of contact persons for doing fieldwork

　2. Data collection plan (*covers the type of evidence to be expected, including the roles of people to be interviewed, the events to be observed, and any other documents to be reviewed when on site*)

　3. Expected preparation prior to fieldwork (*identifies specific information to be reviewed and issues to be covered, prior to fieldwork*)

(Continued)

(Continued)

C. Data Collection Questions (see Figure 3.4 for a detailed question)

1. The practice in operation and its innovativeness:

   a. Describe the practice in detail, including the deployment of personnel and technologies, if any.

   b. What is the nature, if any, of collaborative efforts across communities or jurisdictions that have been needed to put the practice into place?

   c. How did the idea for the practice start?

   d. Was there a planning process, and how did it work? What were the original goals and target populations or areas for the practice?

   e. In what ways is the practice innovative, compared to other practices of the same kind or in the same jurisdiction?

   f. Describe whether the practice has been supported from the jurisdiction's regular budget or as a result of funding from an external source.

2. Evaluation of the innovative practice

   a. What is the design for evaluating the practice, and who is doing the evaluation?

   b. What part of the evaluation has been implemented?

   c. What are the outcome measures being used, and what outcomes have been identified to date?

   d. What rival explanations have been identified and explored, for attributing the outcomes to the investment of the federal funds?

D. Guide for the Case Study Report

1. Audience(s) for the report and stylistic preferences for communicating with the audience(s)

2. The law enforcement practice in operation

3. Innovativeness of the practice

4. Outcomes from the practice, to date

5. Law enforcement agency context and history pertaining to the practice

6. Exhibits to be developed: chronology of events covering the implementation and outcomes of the practice at this site; logic model for the practice; arrays or presenting outcome or other data; references to relevant documents; list of persons interviewed

As a general matter, and as suggested by the illustrative example in Figure 3.2, a case study protocol should have four sections:

- Section A: an overview of the case study (objectives and auspices, case study issues, and relevant readings about the topic being investigated),
- Section B: data collection procedures (procedures for protecting human subjects, identification of likely sources of data, presentation of credentials to field contacts, and other logistical reminders),

- Section C: data collection questions (the specific questions thatthe case study researcher must keep in mind in collecting data and the potential sources of evidence for addressing each question—see Figure 3.4 for an example), and
- Section D: a guide for the case study report (outline, format for the data, use and presentation of other documentation, and bibliographical information).

A quick glance at these topics will indicate why the protocol is so important. First, it keeps you targeted on the topic of the case study. Second, preparing the protocol forces you to anticipate several problems, including the way that the case study reports are to be completed. This means, for instance, that you will have to identify the *audience(s)* for your case study report even before you have conducted your case study. Such forethought will help to avoid mismatches in the long run.

The table of contents of the illustrative protocol in Figure 3.2 reveals another important feature of the case study report: In this instance, the desired report outline starts by calling for a description of the innovative practice being studied (see Item D2 in Figure 3.2)—and only later covers the agency context and history pertaining to the practice (see Item D5). This choice reflects the fact that most researchers write too extensively about history and background conditions. While these are important, the description of the subject of the study—the innovative practice—needs more attention.

The four sections of the protocol are elaborated further, as follows.

Overview of the Case Study (Section A of the Protocol)

The overview should cover the background information about the case study, its substantive issues, and the relevant readings about the issues.

The background information can start by articulating the mission and goals of the case study's sponsor (if any) and audience (e.g., a thesis committee). Such perspectives need to be remembered in conducting the research. For instance, a sponsor or audience may desire the case study to show its relationship to certain other previous studies, use certain general formats for writing the case study report, or fit within a certain time schedule. The explicit recognition of these features belongs in the overview section.

A procedural portion of this background section is a statement about the case study that you can share with anyone who may want to know about the case study, its purpose and sponsor, and the people involved in conducting the case study. This statement can even be accompanied by a letter of introduction, to be sent to all major interviewees and organizations that may be the subject of study. (See Figure 3.3 for an illustrative letter.)

The bulk of the overview, however, should be devoted to the case study's substantive issues. The material may include the rationale for selecting the case(s), the propositions or hypotheses being examined, and the broader theoretical or policy relevance of

Figure 3.3 Illustrative Letter of Introduction

NATIONAL COMMISSION ON NEIGHBORHOODS
2000 K Street, N.W., Suite 350
Washington, D.C. 20006
202-632-5200

May 30, 1978

To Whom It May Concern:

This is to introduce
a highly qualified individual with wide experience
in the field of neighborhood revitalization and community organization.   has been engaged
by the National Commission on Neighborhoods to join
a team of experts now undertaking a series of 40-50
case studies commissioned by our Task Force on Gover-
nance.

Ultimately, by means of this case study
approach, the Commission hopes to identify and document answers to such questions as: What enables some
neighborhoods to survive, given the forces, attitudes
and investment policies (both public and private)
working against them? What preconditions are necessary in order to expand the number of neighborhoods
where successful revitalization, benefiting existing
residents, is possible? What can be done to promote
these preconditions?

This letter is directed to community leaders,
administrative staff and city officials. We must ask
you to give your time, experience and patience to our
interviewers. Your cooperation is most essential if
the case studies are to successfully guide and support
the final policy recommendations which the Commission
must forward to the President and to Congress.

On behalf of all twenty members of the Commission,
I wish to express our gratitude for your assistance.
Should you wish to be entered on our mailing list for
the Commission newsletter and final report, our interviewer will be glad to make the proper arrangements.

Again, thank you very much.

Sincerely,

/signed/
Senator Joseph F. Timilty
Chairman

the inquiry. For all topics, relevant readings should be cited, and the essential reading materials should be made available to everyone on the case study team.

A good overview will communicate to the informed reader (that is, someone familiar with the general topic of inquiry) the case study's purpose and setting. Some of the materials (such as a summary describing the case study effort) may be needed for other purposes anyway, so that writing the overview should be seen as a doubly worthwhile activity. In the same vein, a well-conceived overview even may later form the basis for the background and introductory sections in the final case study report.

Data Collection Procedures (Section B of the Protocol)

Chapter 1 has previously defined case studies as being about phenomena within their *real-world* contexts. This has important implications for defining and designing a case study, which have been discussed in Chapters 1 and 2.

For data collection, however, this characteristic of case studies also raises an important issue, for which properly designed field procedures are essential. You will be collecting data from people and institutions in *their* everyday situations, not within the controlled confines of a laboratory, the sanctity of a library, or the structured limitations of a survey questionnaire. In a case study, you must therefore learn to integrate real-world events with the needs of the data collection plan. In this sense, you do not have the control over the data collection environment as others might have in using the other research methods discussed in Chapter 1.

Note that in a laboratory experiment, human subjects are solicited to enter into a laboratory—an environment controlled nearly entirely by the research investigator. The subject, within ethical and physical constraints, must follow the researcher's instructions, which carefully prescribe the desired behavior. Similarly, the human respondent to a survey questionnaire cannot deviate (far) from the agenda set by the questions. Therefore, the respondent's behavior also is constrained by the ground rules of the researcher. Naturally, the subject or respondent who does not wish to follow the prescribed behaviors may freely drop out of the experiment or survey. Finally, in the historical archive, pertinent documents may not always be available, but except in rare instances, a researcher can inspect what exists at her or his own pace and at a time convenient to her or his schedule. In all three situations, the research investigator closely controls the formal data collection activity.

Collecting data for case studies involves an entirely different situation. To interview key persons, you must cater to the interviewees' schedules and availability, not your own. The nature of the interview is much more open-ended, and an interviewee may not necessarily cooperate in sticking to your line of questions. Similarly, in making observations of real-world activities, you are intruding into the world of the case and of the participants being studied rather than the reverse; under these conditions, you are the one who may have to make special arrangements to become an observer (or even as a participant-observer). As a result, your behavior—and not that of the field participants—is the one likely to be constrained.

This contrasting process of doing data collection leads to the need to have explicit and well-planned field procedures encompassing guidelines for "coping" behaviors. Imagine, for instance, sending a youngster to camp; because you do not know what to expect, the best preparation is to have the resources to be prepared. Case study field procedures should be the same way.

With the preceding orientation in mind, the data collection portion of the protocol needs to emphasize the major tasks in collecting data, including

- gaining access to key organizations or interviewees;
- having sufficient resources while doing fieldwork—including a personal computer, writing instruments, paper, paper clips, and a preestablished, quiet place to write notes privately;
- developing a procedure for calling for assistance and guidance, if needed, from other team members or colleagues;
- making a clear schedule of the data collection activities that are expected to be completed within specified periods of time; and
- providing for unanticipated events, including changes in the availability of interviewees as well as changes in your own energy, mood, and motivation while doing fieldwork.

These are the kinds of topics that can be included in the field procedures section of the protocol. Depending upon the actual case study being done, the specific procedures will vary.

The more operational these procedures are, the better. To take but one minor issue as an example, case study data collection frequently results in the accumulation of numerous documents at the field site. The burden of carrying such bulky documents can be reduced by two procedures. First, the case study team may have had the foresight to bring large, prelabeled envelopes, to send the documents back to its office rather than carry them. Second, field time may have been set aside for perusing the documents and then going to a local copier facility and copying only the few relevant pages of each document—and then returning the original documents to the informants at the field site. These and other operational details can enhance the overall quality and efficiency of case study data collection.

A final part of this portion of the protocol should carefully describe the procedures for protecting human subjects. First, the protocol should repeat the rationale for the IRB-approved field procedures. Then, the protocol should include the scripted words or instructions for the team to use in obtaining informed consent or otherwise informing case study interviewees and other participants of the risks and conditions associated with the research.

Data Collection Questions (Section C of the Protocol)

The heart of the protocol is a set of substantive questions reflecting your actual line of inquiry. Some people may consider this part of the protocol to be the case study "instrument." However, two characteristics distinguish case study questions from those in a survey instrument.

General orientation of the questions. First and foremost, the questions are posed *to you, the researcher,* not to an interviewee. In this sense, the protocol is directed at an entirely different party than a survey instrument. The protocol's questions, in essence, are queries to you, helping to remind you of the information that needs to be collected, and why. In some instances, the specific questions also may serve as prompts in asking questions during a case study interview. However, the main purpose of the protocol's questions is to keep you on track as data collection proceeds. (See Figure 3.4 for an illustrative question from a study of a school program; the complete protocol included dozens of such questions.)

Figure 3.4   Illustrative Protocol Question (from a Study of School Practices)

Define a practice put into place at the school two or more years ago, aimed directly at improving school instruction; does the practice have a name?

- Operationalize the practice by placing the actions and chronological events into a logic model framework, postulating how the practice was presumed to have improved school instruction.
- Collect data related to the nature and extent of any improvements for the relevant period of time—for example,
  - Raised expectations or strengthened consensus over goals
  - Improved educational standards or tightened academic requirements
  - Increased quality of the teaching staff
  - Increased participation by parents in their child's learning
  - Student performance (e.g., enrollment in specific courses, attendance, or results from achievement tests)
- Cite evidence supporting (or not) the initial logic model in explaining how and why the practice led to the improvements.

Each question should be accompanied by a list of likely sources of evidence. Such sources may include the names of individual interviewees, documents, or observations. This crosswalk between the questions of interest and the likely sources of evidence is extremely helpful in collecting case study data. Just before starting a field interview, for instance, a case study researcher can quickly review the major protocol questions that might pertain to the anticipated interview. (Again, the protocol questions form the structure of the inquiry and are not intended as the literal questions to be asked of any given interviewee.)

Five levels of questions. Second, the content of the case study protocol should distinguish clearly among different types or levels of questions. The potentially relevant questions can, remarkably, occur at any of five levels:

Level 1: questions asked of specific interviewees;

Level 2: questions asked of the individual case (these are the questions in the case study protocol to be answered by the researcher during a single case, even when the single case is part of a larger, multiple-case study);

Level 3: questions asked of the pattern of findings across multiple cases;

Level 4: questions asked of an entire study—for example, calling on information beyond the case study evidence and including other literature or published data that may have been reviewed; and

Level 5: normative questions about policy recommendations and conclusions, going beyond the narrow scope of the study.

Of these five levels, you should concentrate heavily on Level 2 for the case study protocol.

The difference between Level 1 and Level 2 questions is highly significant. The two types of questions are most commonly confused because researchers think that their questions of inquiry (Level 2) are synonymous with the specific questions they will ask of interviewees in the field (Level 1). To disentangle these two levels in your own mind, think about a clinician. The clinician has in mind what the course of events in an illness might be (Level 2), but the actual questions posed to any patient or client (Level 1) do not necessarily betray the clinician's thinking. The *verbal* line of inquiry is different from the *mental* line of inquiry, and this is the difference between Level 1 and Level 2 questions. For the case study protocol, explicitly articulating the Level 2 questions is therefore of much greater importance than any attempt to identify the Level 1 questions.

In the field, keeping in mind the Level 2 questions, while simultaneously articulating Level 1 questions in conversing with an interviewee, is not easy. In a like manner, you can lose sight of your Level 2 questions when examining a detailed document that will become part of the case study evidence (the common revelation occurs when you ask yourself, "Why am I reading this document?"). To overcome these problems, successful participation in the earlier training helps. Remember that being a "senior" investigator means maintaining a working knowledge of the entire case study inquiry. The (Level 2) questions in the case study protocol embody this inquiry.

The other levels also should be understood clearly. A cross-case question for a multiple-case study of organizational units, for instance (Level 3), may be whether the larger organizational units among your multiple cases are more responsive than the smaller ones, or whether complex bureaucratic structures make the larger ones more cumbersome and less responsive. However, this Level 3 question should not be part of the protocol for collecting data from the single case, because the single case only can address the responsiveness of a single organizational unit. The Level 3 question can only be addressed after the data from all the single cases (in a multiple-case study) have been examined. Thus, only the multiple-case analysis can cover Level 3 questions. Similarly, the questions at Levels 4 and 5 go well beyond the empirical data from the full case study, and you should note this limitation if you include such questions in the case study protocol. Remember: *The protocol is for the data collection from a single case (even when part of a multiple-case study) and is not intended to serve the entire project.*

Undesired confusion between unit of data collection and unit of analysis. Related to the distinction between Level 1 and Level 2 questions, a more subtle and serious problem can arise in articulating the questions in the case study protocol. The questions should cater to the unit of analysis of the case study, which may be at a different level from the unit of data collection of the case study. Confusion will occur if, under these circumstances, the data collection process leads to an (undesirable) distortion of the unit of analysis.

The common confusion begins because the data collection sources may be individual people (e.g., interviews with individuals), whereas the unit of analysis of your case study may be a collective (e.g., the organization to which the individual belongs)—a frequent design when the case study is about an organization, community, or social group. Even though your data collection may have to rely heavily on information from individual interviewees, your conclusions cannot be based entirely on the interviews as a source of information (your case study would have transformed into an open-ended survey, not a case study). In this example, the protocol questions need to be about the organization, not the individuals. The second row in Figure 3.5 covers such an organizational case study, indicating the kind of evidence that might be obtained from either individual interviewees (cell 1) or the organization's policy records and documentable outcomes (cell 2).

Figure 3.5 Design versus Data Collection: Different Units of Analysis

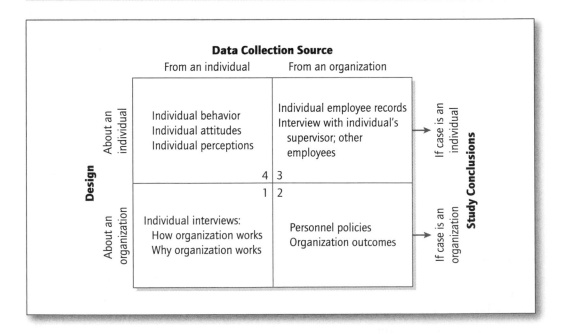

However, the reverse situation also can be true. Your case study may be about an individual, and the sources of information can include archival records (e.g., personnel files or student records) from an organization (cell 3). In this situation, you also would want to avoid basing your conclusions about the individual from the organizational sources of information only. In this example, the protocol questions therefore need to be about the individual, not the organization. The first row in Figure 3.5 covers such an individual case study.

Other data collection devices. The protocol questions can include *empty table shells* (for more detail, see Miles & Huberman, 1994). An empty table shell defines the axes of a table, by precisely labeling its rows and columns—prior to having any data in the table's cells. In this way, an empty table shell indicates the data to be collected, and your job is to collect the data called forth by the axes. The relevant data may be quantitative (numeric) or qualitative (categorical or narrative). If the latter, you would refer to the empty and completed table shell as a *word table.*

Empty table shells can help in several ways. First, the table shells force you to identify exactly what data are being sought. Second, the table shells ensure that parallel information will be collected from the different cases, when a multiple-case design is being used. Finally, the table shells aid in understanding what might be done with the data once they have been collected, as the completed table shell can actually become the basis for analysis.

Guide for the Case Study Report (Section D of the Protocol)

This topic is generally missing from most case study plans. Researchers neglect to think about the outline, format, or audience for the case study report until after the data have been collected. Yet, some planning at this preparatory stage—admittedly out of sequence in the typical conduct of most research—means that a tentative outline can (and should) appear in the case study protocol. (Such planning accounts for the arrow between "prepare" and "share" in the figure at the outset of this chapter.)

Again, one reason for the conventional linear sequence—that is, to complete data collection and only then to think about a report—comes from the practices with other research methods. For instance, there is less need to worry about the report of an experiment because the report's format and likely audience already have been dictated by the formats of academic journals. Thus, most reports of experiments follow a similar outline: the posing of the research questions and hypotheses; a description of the research design, apparatus, and data collection procedures; the presentation of the data collected; the analysis of the data; and a discussion of findings and conclusions.

Unfortunately, case study reports do not have such a uniformly acceptable outline. For this reason, every researcher should give at least a few preliminary thoughts, prior to the conduct of a case study, to the design of the final case study report (Chapter 6 further discusses such report preparation). One possibility can derive from the expectation that the quality of the final case study will warrant its publication in an academic journal. Anticipating and identifying a possible journal or two would then be a useful step, because the case study report could emulate what is believed to be acceptable to the journals. Another possibility is that a case study has been commissioned by some sponsor who already has a knowable reporting format and preference.

For either of the preceding possibilities, the development of the protocol will benefit from your perusing earlier works—for example, previous case studies that have appeared in the candidate journals or existing reports that have appeared under the sponsor's auspice. The guidance in the protocol can then point to the likely audience, topics, and length of the final case study report. For example, some sponsors of case studies might have an interest in reports that are peppered with interesting vignettes if not anecdotes, and the guidance would emphasize the need to be alert for opportunities to collect such data.

In addition to guidance about the report, this part of the protocol can indicate the extent of documentation for the case study report. Properly done, the data collection may lead to large amounts of documentary evidence, in the form of published reports, publications, memoranda, and other documents collected about the case. What is to be done with this documentation, for later presentation? In most studies, the documents are filed away and seldom retrieved. Yet, this documentation is an important part of the "database" for a case study (see Chapter 4). One possibility is to have the final case study report include an *annotated* bibliography itemizing each of the available documents. The annotations would help an inquisitive reader to identify the documents that might be relevant for further inspection.

In summary, to the extent possible, an initial profile of the case study report should be part of the protocol. This will facilitate the collection of relevant data and will reduce the possibility that a return visit to a fieldwork site will be necessary. At the same time, the existence of such a profile should not imply rigid adherence to a predesigned protocol. In fact, case study plans can change as a result of the initial data collection, and you are encouraged to consider having an adaptive posture—if used properly and without bias—as an advantage of case study research.

Exercise 3.4   Developing a Case Study Protocol

Select some phenomenon in need of explanation from the everyday life of your university or organization (past or present). Illustrative topics might be, for example, why the university or organization changed some policy or how it makes decisions about its curriculum or training requirements. For these illustrative topics (or a topic of your own choosing), design a case study protocol to collect the information needed to produce an adequate explanation. What would be your main research questions or propositions? What specific sources of data would you seek (e.g., persons to be interviewed, documents to be sought, and field observations to be made)? Would your protocol be sufficient in guiding you through the entire process of collecting the data for your case study?

SCREENING THE CANDIDATE CASES FOR YOUR CASE STUDY △

Another preparatory step is the final selection of the case to be the centerpiece of your case study. Sometimes, the selection is straightforward because you have chosen to study an unusual case whose identity has been known from the outset of your inquiry. Or, you already may know the case you will study because of some special arrangement or access that you have. However, at other times, there may be many qualified case candidates, and you must choose your final single case or array of multiple cases from among them. The goal of the screening procedure is to be sure that you identify the final cases properly, prior to formal data collection. The worst scenario would occur when, after having started formal data collection, the case turns out not to be viable or to represent something other than what you had intended to study.

A one-phase approach. When you have only a dozen or so of possible candidates that can serve as your cases (whether these candidates are organizations, individuals, or some other entity depends on your unit of analysis), the screening may consist of querying people knowledgeable about each candidate. You even may collect limited documentation about each candidate. To be avoided, at all costs, is an extensive screening procedure that effectively becomes a "mini" case study of every candidate case. Prior to collecting the screening data, you should have defined a set of operational criteria whereby candidates will be deemed qualified to serve as cases. If doing a single-case study, choose the case that is likely, all other things being equal, to have the most available data sources; if doing a multiple-case study, select cases that best fit your (literal or theoretical) replication design.

A two-phase approach. A large number of eligible candidates (e.g., 12 or more) warrants a two-stage screening procedure. The first stage should consist of collecting relevant quantitative data about the entire pool, from some archival source (e.g., statistical databases about individual schools or firms). You may have to obtain the archival data from some central source (e.g., a federal, state, or local agency or a national association). Once obtained, you should define some relevant criteria for either stratifying or reducing the number of candidates. The goal is to reduce the number of candidates to 12 or fewer and then to conduct the one-phase procedure described in the previous paragraph. Such a two-stage procedure was followed in a case study of local economic development, and the experience is fully reported in the companion text (Yin, 2012, chap. 3, pp. 32–39). (Also see BOX 16 for another example.)

In completing the screening process, you may want to revisit your earlier decision about the total number of cases to be studied. Respecting your resource constraints, if multiple candidates are qualified to serve as cases, the larger the number you can study, the better.

> ## BOX 16
> ## A Methodic Procedure for Selecting Cases
>
> A study of revitalization in urban neighborhoods began with the proposition that community organizations play a significant role in this process (Marwell, 2007). The study took place in two neighborhoods, with intense fieldwork covering the work of four different types of community organizations in each neighborhood.
>
> A detailed appendix describes the procedure for selecting the neighborhoods, which first used demographic data to reduce an initial array of 59 neighborhoods to 14 candidates, then used four additional criteria to select the two finalists from the 14 (pp. 241–247). Subsequently, the author canvassed these two neighborhoods for their community organizations, with the appendix giving the specific criteria for choosing these finalists (pp. 247–248). The descriptions provide good examples of how case selection procedures can work, as well as the unexpected issues that can arise (e.g., see Footnote 6, p. 244).

△ THE PILOT CASE STUDY

A pilot case study will help you to refine your data collection plans with respect to both the content of the data and the procedures to be followed. In this regard, it is important to note that a *pilot test* is not a *pretest*. The pilot case is more formative, assisting you to develop relevant lines of questions—possibly even providing some conceptual clarification for the research design as well. In contrast, the pretest is the occasion for a formal "dress rehearsal," in which the data collection plan that is used is as faithful to the final plan as possible. As a result, the pilot test might preferably occur before seeking final approval from an IRB, as discussed earlier in this chapter.

You may identify a pilot case in a number of ways. For example, you may know that the informants at a fieldwork site are unusually congenial and accessible, or the site may be geographically convenient or may have an unusual amount of documentation and data. Another possibility is that a pilot case might represent a complicated case, compared to the likely real cases, so that nearly all relevant data collection issues will be encountered in the pilot case. Under some circumstances, the pilot case study can be so important that substantial resources may be devoted to this phase of the research. For this reason, several subtopics are worth further discussion: the selection of pilot cases, the nature of the inquiry for the pilot cases, and the nature of the reports from the pilot cases.

Selection of Pilot Cases

In general, convenience, access, and geographic proximity can be the main criteria for selecting a pilot case or cases. This will allow for a less structured and more prolonged relationship between yourself and the participants than might occur in the "real" cases. The pilot case can then assume the role of a "laboratory" in detailing your protocol, allowing you to observe different phenomena from many different angles or to try different approaches on a trial basis.

One study of technological innovations in local services (Yin, 2012, pp. 29–32) actually had seven pilot cases, each focusing on a different type of technology. Four of the cases were located in the same metropolitan area as the research team's and were visited first. Three of the cases, however, were located in different cities and were the basis for a second set of visits. The cases were not chosen because of their distinctive technologies or for any other substantive reason. The main criterion, besides proximity, was the fact that access to the cases was made easy by some prior personal contact on the part of the research team. Finally, the interviewees in the cases also were congenial to the notion that the research team was at an early stage of its research and would not have a fixed agenda.

In return for serving as a pilot case, the main informants usually expect to receive some feedback from you about their case. Your value to them is as an external observer, and you should be prepared to provide such feedback. To do so, even though you should already have developed a draft protocol representing the topics of interest to your case study, you should adapt parts of the protocol to suit the informants' needs. You should then conduct the pilot case by following (and pilot-testing) your formal field procedures.

Scope of the Pilot Inquiry

The scope of the inquiry for the pilot case can be much broader than the ultimate data collection plan. Moreover, the inquiry can cover both substantive and methodological issues.

In the above-mentioned example, the research team used the seven pilot cases to improve its conceptualization of different types of technologies and their related organizational effects. The pilot studies were done prior to the selection of specific technologies for the final data collection—and prior to the final articulation of the study's theoretical propositions. Thus, the pilot data provided considerable insight into the basic issues being studied. This information was used in parallel with an ongoing review of relevant literature, so that the final research design was informed both by prevailing theories and by a fresh set of empirical observations.[3] The dual sources of information helped to ensure that the actual study reflected significant theoretical or policy issues as well as questions relevant to real-world cases.

Methodologically, the work on the pilot cases can provide information about relevant field questions and about the logistics of the field inquiry. In the technology pilot cases, one important logistical question was whether to observe the technology in action first or to collect information about the prevailing organizational issues first. This choice interacted with a further question about the deployment of the field team: If the team consisted of two or more persons, what assignments required the team to work together and what assignments could be completed separately? Variations in these procedures were tried during the pilot case studies, the trade-offs were acknowledged, and eventually a satisfactory procedure was developed for the formal data collection plan.

Reports from the Pilot Cases

The pilot case reports are mainly of value to the research team itself and need to be written clearly, even if only in the form of memos. One difference between the pilot reports and the actual case study reports is that the pilot reports should be explicit about the lessons learned about both the research design and the field procedures. The pilot reports might even contain subsections on these topics.

If more than a single pilot case is planned, the report from one pilot case also can indicate the modifications to be attempted in the next pilot case. In other words, the report can contain the agenda for the ensuing pilot case. If enough pilot cases are done in this manner, the agenda for the final pilot case may actually become a good prototype for the final case study protocol.

> **Exercise 3.5** Selecting a Case for Doing a Pilot Study
>
> Define the desired features for a pilot case, as a prelude to a new case study. How would you go about contacting potential participants and using such a case? Describe why you might want only one pilot case, as opposed to two or more pilot cases.

△ SUMMARY

This chapter has reviewed the preparations for data collection. Depending upon the scope of a case study—whether single or multiple cases will be involved or whether single or multiple researchers will be involved—the preparatory tasks will be correspondingly straightforward or complex.

The major topics have been the desired skills and values of the case study researcher, the preparation and training of the case study team for a specific case study, the nature of the case study protocol, the screening of candidate cases, and the role and purpose of a pilot case study. Every case study should follow these different steps to varying degrees, depending upon the specific inquiry.

As with the management of other affairs, the expertise with which these activities are conducted will improve with practice. Thus, one desirable sequence is for you to complete a relatively straightforward case study before attempting to do a more complex one, from a managerial standpoint. With the successful completion of each case study, the preparatory tasks may even become second nature. Furthermore, if the same case study team has conducted several different studies together, the team will work with increasing efficiency and professional satisfaction with each ensuing case study.

NOTES TO CHAPTER 3 △

1. Thacher (2006) argues forcefully in support of what he calls "normative" case studies. In such studies, the researchers do use case studies to advocate specific issues, at the risk of being challenged about the fairness of their data collection. Such risks may be best left to very senior investigators but are not recommended for those with less experience—much less novices—in doing case studies.

2. The difference between having a single case study researcher and needing multiple researchers can create a significantly different orientation to the entire case study. The classic single researchers have frequently been brilliant and creative—quickly and intuitively adapting to new conditions during data collection or finding newly appealing patterns during data analysis. With multiple researchers, such talents may have to be curbed because of the need for consistency across researchers, but the good discipline is rewarded by minimizing the likelihood of introducing bias into the case study.

3. The final study, in its published form, received the William E. Mosher Award, presented by the American Society for Public Administration, for the best article published in the journal (the *Public Administration Review*) in 1981.

Tutorial 3.1:

More on Review by Institutional Review Boards (IRBs)

Gaining approval from an institutional review board (IRB) has become a standard part of doing any research involving human subjects. However, the approval process can be anything but standard. For instance, if an IRB raises important questions about your research, you may have to undertake multiple submissions before gaining approval, and the time consumed by these submissions may affect your schedule for doing the research.

As a general matter, you will want to prepare carefully for the IRB's review. Every university and research organization has its own IRB, usually consisting of five or more senior colleagues who volunteer to serve on a rotating basis. You can obtain a sound understanding of your local IRB's expectations by first checking to see whether your IRB has its own website. Most such websites will provide detailed guidance about your particular IRB's review procedures and experiences.

Adding to this information, you might want to review previous submissions to your IRB that have covered research projects like the one you are proposing. Similarly, your literature review might highlight previous studies with highly similar topics and methods. If your study has an innovative flavor much less methodology, prepare ahead of time for the inevitable questions that the IRB might raise.

More broadly, you can familiarize yourself with the principles underlying the need to protect human subjects by reviewing other works that cover the procedures in greater depth, especially relying on sources reflecting your own substantive subject area (e.g., for business research, see Eriksson & Kovalainen, 2008, pp. 62–76; for social work and sociology, see Grinnell & Unrau, 2008, pp. 30–59; and for public health, see Speiglman & Spear, 2009). Likewise, you can consult the formal guidances issued by the various social science professions, selecting the one that you most identify with (e.g., see the citations to the several professional associations' documents listed under the heading "Avoiding Bias and Conducting Research Ethically" in Chapter 3, p. 76).

Remember that an IRB's specific concerns may vary from institution to institution and from IRB to IRB as its membership turns over. Do not hesitate to speak with a member or two of your own IRB ahead of time, to gain direct insight into the review process and its expectations.

Briefly Annotated References for Tutorial 3.1

Eriksson, P., & Kovalainen, A. (2008). *Qualitative methods in business research.* London: Sage. Treats case study research as one of nine methods in qualitative business research.

Grinnell, R. M., & Unrau, Y. A. (Eds.). (2008). *Social work research and evaluation: Foundations of evidence-based practice*. New York: Oxford University Press. Serves as a comprehensive textbook on research and evaluation in social work.

Speiglman, R., & Spear, P. (2009). The role of institutional review boards: Ethics: Now you see them, now you don't. In D. M. Mertens & P. E. Ginsberg (Eds.), *The handbook of social research ethics* (pp. 121–134). Thousand Oaks, CA: Sage. Describes the role of institutional review boards.

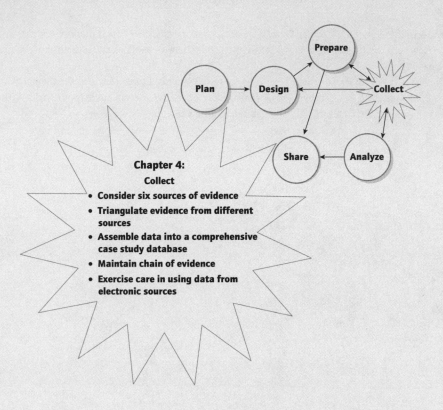

Chapter 4:
Collect
- Consider six sources of evidence
- Triangulate evidence from different sources
- Assemble data into a comprehensive case study database
- Maintain chain of evidence
- Exercise care in using data from electronic sources

ABSTRACT

Case study evidence may come from six sources: documents, archival records, interviews, direct observation, participant-observation, and physical artifacts. Using these six sources calls for mastering different data collection procedures. Throughout, your objective may be to collect data about actual human events and behavior or to capture the distinctive perspectives of the participants in your case study (or both). These extended inquiries mean that case study data collection can require much fieldwork time, including the conduct of prolonged interviews occurring over multiple sittings.

In addition to appreciating how to work with the six sources, four overriding principles are important to any data collection effort in doing case study research. One principle is to use multiple sources of evidence (evidence from two or more sources, converging on the same findings). Another is to create a case study database—a formal assembly of evidence, distinct from the final case study report, containing all your case study notes, the documents and tabular materials from the field, and your preliminary narratives or memos about the data. Other principles cover your sensitivity in maintaining a chain of evidence and exercising care when using electronic sources of evidence, such as social media communications. By incorporating all these principles into your case study, you will increase its quality substantially.

4

COLLECTING CASE STUDY EVIDENCE

The Principles You Should Follow in Working with Six Sources of Evidence

C ase study evidence can come from many sources. This chapter discusses six of them: documentation, archival records, interviews, direct observation, participant-observation, and physical artifacts. Each source is associated with an array of data or evidence. One purpose of this chapter is to review the six sources briefly. A second purpose is to convey four essential data collection principles, regardless of the sources used.

Supporting Textbooks

You may find the six sources of evidence all potentially relevant, even in doing the same case study. For this reason, having them briefly reviewed in this chapter, all in one place, may be helpful. For any given source of evidence, extensive further detail is available in numerous methodological textbooks and articles. Therefore, you also may want to check out some of these texts, especially if any single source of evidence is especially important to your case study. However, choosing among the texts and other works will require some searching and careful selection.

First, you can find guidance in (admittedly older) books devoted entirely to data collection (e.g., Bouchard, 1976; Fiedler, 1978; Murphy, 1980; Schatzman & Strauss, 1973;

Wax, 1971). These books usually have "fieldwork" or "field research" as part of their titles and are not oriented toward specific crafts, such as doing ethnography. Besides reviewing basic data collection procedures, the books also offer useful guidance on the logistics of planning and conducting fieldwork. Although the books do not focus directly on case study research, the similarity of the procedures makes the books valuable because they are easy to use. However, as you may have noticed by the publication dates of the cited works, these kinds of books appear to be diminishing.

Second, contemporary books are more readily available but make your choices more complicated. These books may only cover limited types of evidence or even specialize in one source of evidence only, such as field interviewing (e.g., Rubin & Rubin, 2011; Weiss, 1994), participant-observation (e.g., DeWalt & DeWalt, 2011; Jorgensen, 1989), or documentary evidence (e.g., Barzun & Graff, 1985), thereby losing the benefit of seeing how multiple sources might complement each other. Other works covering a broader range of evidence may nevertheless come with a dominant disciplinary orientation that may not match your needs, such as clinical research or research in primary care settings (e.g., Crabtree & Miller, 1999), program evaluations (e.g., Patton, 2002), social work research (e.g., Rubin & Babbie, 1993), or anthropology (e.g., Robben & Sluka, 2007).

Third, books that might at first appear to be comprehensive methodological texts also cover many topics in addition to data collection and, as a result, only devote a fraction of their entire text to data collection procedures (e.g., 1 of 11 chapters in Creswell, 2007, and 1 of 28 chapters in Silverman, 2010). Other books that do have a truly comprehensive range and that do discuss data collection techniques in greater detail are nevertheless designed to serve more as reference works than as textbooks to be used by individual researchers (e.g., Bickman & Rog, 2009).

Given these variations, you must overcome the complex if not fragmented nature of the methodological marketplace represented by these various texts. To do so will make your own data collection procedures even better.

Supporting Principles

In addition to your need to be familiar with the data collection procedures using the six different sources of evidence, you also need to continue addressing the design challenges enumerated in Chapter 2: construct validity, internal validity, external validity, and reliability.

Tip: *How much time and effort should I devote to collecting the case study data? How do I know whether I'm finished collecting the data?*

Unlike other methods, there is no clear cut-off point. You should try to collect enough data so that (a) you have confirmatory evidence (evidence from two or more different sources) for most of your main topics, and (b) your evidence includes attempts to investigate major rival hypotheses or explanations.

What do you think are some of the cut-off points for other methods, and why wouldn't they work in doing case study research?

For this reason, the latter part of this chapter gives much emphasis to its second purpose, the discussion of four principles of data collection.

These principles have been neglected in the past and are discussed at length: (a) using multiple, not just single, sources of evidence; (b) creating a case study database; (c) maintaining a chain of evidence; and (d) exercising care in using data from electronic sources of evidence, such as social media communications. The principles are extremely important for doing high-quality case studies, are relevant to all six types of sources of evidence, and should be followed whenever possible. In particular, these principles, as noted in Chapter 2 (see Figure 2.3), will help to deal with the problems of construct validity and reliability.

Exercise 4.1 Identifying Sources of Evidence in Other Case Studies

Select and retrieve one of the case studies cited in the BOXES of this book. Go through the case study and identify five findings important to the case study. For each finding, indicate the source or sources of evidence, if any, used to support the finding. In how many instances was there more than a single source of evidence?

Six Sources of Evidence △

The sources of evidence discussed here are the ones most commonly used in doing case study research: documentation, archival records, interviews, direct observations, participant-observation, and physical artifacts. However, you should be aware that a complete list of sources can be quite extensive—including films, photographs, and videotapes; projective techniques and psychological tests; proxemics; kinesics; "street" ethnography; and life histories (Marshall & Rossman, 2011).

A useful overview of the six major sources considers their comparative strengths and weaknesses (see Figure 4.1). You should immediately note that no single source has a complete advantage over all the others. In fact, the various sources are highly complementary, and a good case study will therefore want to rely on as many sources as possible (see the later discussion in this chapter on "multiple sources of evidence").

Documentation

Except for studies of preliterate societies, documentary information is likely to be relevant to every case study topic.[1] This type of information can take many forms and should be the object of explicit data collection plans. For instance, consider the following variety of documents:

Figure 4.1 Six Sources of Evidence: Strengths and Weaknesses

SOURCE OF EVIDENCE	Strengths	Weaknesses
Documentation	• Stable—can be reviewed repeatedly • Unobtrusive—not created as a result of the case study • Specific—can contain the exact names, references, and details of an event • Broad—can cover a long span of time, many events, and many settings	• Retrievability—can be difficult to find • Biased selectivity, if collection is incomplete • Reporting bias—reflects (unknown) bias of any given document's author • Access—may be deliberately withheld
Archival records	• *[Same as those for documentation]* • Precise and usually quantitative	• *[Same as those for documentation]* • Accessibility due to privacy reasons
Interviews	• Targeted—focuses directly on case study topics • Insightful—provides explanations as well as personal views (e.g., perceptions, attitudes, and meanings)	• Bias due to poorly articulated questions • Response bias • Inaccuracies due to poor recall • Reflexivity—interviewee gives what interviewer wants to hear
Direct observations	• Immediacy—covers actions in real time • Contextual—can cover the case's context	• Time-consuming • Selectivity—broad coverage difficult without a team of observers • Reflexivity—actions may proceed differently because they are being observed • Cost—hours needed by human observers
Participant-observation	• *[Same as above for direct observations]* • Insightful into interpersonal behavior and motives	• *[Same as above for direct observations]* • Bias due to participant-observer's manipulation of events
Physical artifacts	• Insightful into cultural features • Insightful into technical operations	• Selectivity • Availability

- letters, memoranda, e-mails, and other personal documents, such as diaries, calendars, and notes;
- agendas, announcements and minutes of meetings, and other written reports of events;
- administrative documents, such as proposals, progress reports, and other internal records;
- formal studies or evaluations related to the case that you are studying; and
- news clippings and other articles appearing in the mass media or in community newspapers.

These and other types of documents all are increasingly available through Internet searches. The documents are useful even though they are not always accurate and may not be lacking in bias. In fact, documents must be carefully used and should not be accepted as literal recordings of events that have taken place. Few people realize, for instance, that even the "verbatim" transcripts of official U.S. congressional hearings have been deliberately edited—by the congressional staff and others who may have testified—before being printed in final form. In another field, historians working with primary documents also must be concerned with the validity of a document.

For case study research, the most important use of documents is to corroborate and augment evidence from other sources. First, documents are helpful in verifying the correct spellings and titles or names of people and organizations that might have been mentioned in an interview. Second, documents can provide other specific details to corroborate information from other sources. If the documentary evidence is contradictory rather than corroboratory, you need to pursue the problem by inquiring further into the topic. Third, you can make inferences from documents—for example, by observing the distribution list for a specific document, you may find new questions about communications and networking within an organization. However, you should treat inferences only as clues worthy of further investigation rather than as definitive findings, because the inferences could later turn out to be false leads.

Because of their overall value, documents play an explicit role in any data collection in doing case study research. Systematic searches for relevant documents are important in any data collection plan. For example, prior to doing fieldwork, an Internet search can produce invaluable information. During fieldwork, you should allot time for using local libraries and other reference centers whose documents, such as back issues of periodicals, may not be available electronically. You also should arrange access to examine the files of any organizations being studied, including a review of documents that may have been put into "cold storage" by an organization. The scheduling of such retrieval activities is usually a flexible matter, independent of other data collection activities, and the search can usually be conducted at your convenience. For this reason, there is little excuse for omitting a thorough review of documentary evidence. Among such evidence, news accounts are excellent sources for covering certain topics, such as the two in BOXES 17 and 18.

BOX 17
Combining Personal Participation
with Extensive Newspaper Documentation

Improving educational conditions—especially for urban schools in the United States—has become one of the biggest challenges for the 21st century. How the Houston, Texas, system dealt with constrained fiscal resources, diverse student populations, and local political

(Continued)

(Continued)

constituencies is the topic of an exciting and riveting case study by Donald McAdams (2000). McAdams benefited from having been a member of the system's school board for three elected, 4-year terms. He presents a personal account, not trying to be a social science analyst. At the same time, the book contains numerous references to local news articles to corroborate events. The result is one of the most readable but also well-documented case studies that readers will encounter.

BOX 18
Comparing Evidence from Two Archival Sources to Cover the Same Community Events

One of the most inflammatory community events in the 1990s came to be known as the "Rodney King crisis." White police officers were serendipitously videotaped in the act of beating an African American man, but a year later, they all were acquitted of any wrongdoing. The acquittal sparked a major civil disturbance, in which 58 people were killed, 2,000 injured, and 11,000 arrested.

A case study of this crisis (R. N. Jacobs, 1996) deliberately drew from two different newspapers—the major daily for the metropolitan area and the most significant newspaper for the area's African American community. For the pertinent period surrounding the crisis, the first newspaper produced 357 articles and the second (a weekly, not daily, publication) 137 articles. The case study traces the course of events and shows how the two papers constructed different understandings of the crisis, illustrating the potential biases of documentary evidence and the need to address such biases.

At the same time, many people have been critical of the potential overreliance on documents in case study research. This is probably because the casual researcher may mistakenly assume that all kinds of documents—including proposals for projects or programs—contain the unmitigated truth. In fact, important in reviewing any document is to understand that it was written for some specific purpose and some specific audience *other than* those of the case study being done. In this sense, the case study researcher is a vicarious observer, because the documentary evidence reflects a communication among other parties attempting to achieve some other objectives. By constantly trying to identify these objectives, you are less likely to be misled by documentary evidence and more likely to be correctly critical in interpreting the contents of such evidence.[2]

A newer problem has arisen because of the abundance of materials available through Internet searches. You may get lost in reviewing such materials and actually waste a lot of time on them. Note, however, that the problem is not that different from having an overabundance of numeric data about your case, as might be available from sources such as the U.S. census (also see discussion of archival records, next). In both situations, you need to have a strong sense of your case study inquiry and focus on the most pertinent information. One suggestion is to sort or triage the materials (documents or numeric data) by their apparent centrality to your inquiry. Then, spend more time reading or reviewing what appears central, and leave aside other, less important materials for later reading or review. The procedure will not be perfect, but it will permit you to keep moving forward to other case study tasks.

Archival Records

For many case studies, archival records—often taking the form of computer files and records as in the U.S. census data just mentioned—also may be relevant. Examples of archival records include

- "public use files" such as the U.S. census and other statistical data made available by federal, state, and local governments;
- service records, such as those showing the number of clients served over a given period of time;
- organizational records, such as budget or personnel records;
- maps and charts of the geographical characteristics of a place; and
- survey data produced by others, about your case's employees, residents, or participants.

These and other archival records can be used in conjunction with other sources of information in producing a case study. However, unlike documentary evidence, the usefulness of these archival records will vary from case study to case study. For some studies, the records can be so important that they can become the object of extensive retrieval and quantitative analysis (for example, see the cost data used in a multiple-case study of 20 universities, in Yin, 2012, chap. 11). In other studies, they may be of only passing relevance.

When archival evidence has been deemed relevant, a researcher must be careful to ascertain the conditions under which it was produced, as well as its accuracy. Sometimes, the archival records can be highly quantitative, but numbers alone should not automatically be considered a sign of accuracy. Nearly every social scientist, for instance, is aware of the pitfalls of using the FBI's Uniform Crime Reports—or any other archival records based on crimes reported by law enforcement agencies. The same general word of caution made earlier with documentary evidence therefore also applies to archival evidence: Most archival records were produced for a specific purpose and a specific audience other than your case study, and these conditions must be fully appreciated in interpreting the usefulness and accuracy of the records.

Interviews

One of the most important sources of case study evidence is the interview. You may be surprised by this assertion because of the usual association between interviews and survey research. However, interviews are commonly found in case study research. They will resemble guided conversations rather than structured queries. Although you will be pursuing a consistent line of inquiry, your actual stream of questions in a case study interview is likely to be fluid rather than rigid (Rubin & Rubin, 2011). This type of interview has alternatively been called an "intensive interview," "in-depth interview," or "unstructured interview" (Weiss, 1994, pp. 207–208).

Note that this means you have two jobs throughout the interview process: (a) to follow your own line of inquiry, as reflected by your case study protocol, and (b) to ask your actual (conversational) questions in an unbiased manner that also serves the needs of your line of inquiry (see distinction between "Level 1" and "Level 2" questions in Chapter 3). For instance, you may want (in your line of inquiry) to know "why" a particular process occurred as it did. Becker (1998, pp. 58–60), however, has pointed to the important difference in actually posing a "why" question to an informant (which, in his view, creates defensiveness on the informant's part) in contrast to posing a "how" question—the latter in fact being his preferred way of addressing any "why" question in an actual conversation. Thus, case study interviews require you to operate on two levels at the same time: satisfying the needs of your line of inquiry (Level 2 questions) while simultaneously putting forth "friendly" and "nonthreatening" questions in your open-ended interviews (Level 1 questions).

A common question about doing case study interviews is whether to record them. Using recording devices is a matter of personal preference. Audiotapes certainly provide a more accurate rendition of any interview than taking your own notes. However, a recording device should not be used when (a) an interviewee refuses permission or appears uncomfortable in its presence, (b) there is no specific plan for transcribing or systematically listening to the contents of the electronic record—a process that takes enormous time and energy, (c) a researcher is clumsy enough with mechanical devices that the recording procedure creates distractions during an interview, or (d) a researcher thinks that the recording device is a substitute for "listening" closely throughout the course of an interview.

Given the preceding points, you may want to appreciate that there can be three types of case study interviews: prolonged interviews, shorter interviews, and survey interviews.

Prolonged case study interviews. These interviews may take place over 2 or more hours, either in a single sitting or over an extended period of time covering multiple sittings.

You can ask interviewees about their interpretations and opinions about people and events or their insights, explanations, and meanings related to certain occurrences. You can then use such propositions as the basis for further inquiry, and the interviewee can suggest other persons for you to interview, as well as other sources of evidence.

The more that an interviewee assists in this manner, the more that the role may be considered one of an "informant" rather than a participant. Key informants are often critical to the success of a case study. Such persons can provide you with insights into a matter and also give you access to other interviewees who may have corroboratory or contrary evidence. Such a person, named "Doc," played an essential role in the conduct of the famous case study presented in *Street Corner Society* (Whyte, 1943/1993; see BOX 2A, Chapter 1, p. 8). Similar key informants have been noted in other case studies. Of course, you need to be cautious about becoming overly dependent on a key informant, especially because of the reflexive influence—frequently subtle—that the informant may have over you. A reasonable way of dealing with this pitfall is to rely on other sources of evidence to corroborate any insight by such informants, and to search for contrary evidence as diligently as possible.

Shorter case study interviews. Rather than occurring over an extended period of time or over several sittings, many case study interviews may be more focused and only take about 1 hour or so. In such situations, the interviews may still remain open-ended and assume a conversational manner, but you are likely to be following your case study protocol (or a portion of it) more closely.

For example, a major purpose of such an interview might simply be to corroborate certain findings that you already think have been established, but not to ask about other topics of a broader, open-ended nature. In this situation, the specific questions must be carefully worded, so that you appear genuinely naive about the topic and allow the interviewee to provide a fresh commentary about it; in contrast, if you ask leading questions, the corroboratory purpose of the interview will not have been served. Even so, you need to exercise caution when different interviewees appear to be echoing the same thoughts—corroborating each other but in a conspiratorial way.[3] Further probing is needed. One way is to test the genuineness of the views by deliberately checking with persons known to hold different perspectives. If one of the interviewees fails to comment, even though the others tend to corroborate one another's versions of what took place, you might even jot this down in your notes, citing the fact that a person was asked but declined to comment, as done in good journalistic accounts.

As an entirely different kind of example, your case study protocol might have called for you to pay specific attention to an interviewee's personal rendition of an event. In this case, the interviewee's perceptions and own sense of meaning are the material to be understood (Merton, Fiske, & Kendall, 1990). This type of single interview has a group counterpart, known as a *focus group,* first used to study military morale during World War II and later popularized in doing market research, such as obtaining consumer reactions to prospective radio programs. The focus group procedure calls for you to recruit and convene a small group of persons. You would then moderate a discussion about some aspect of your case study, deliberately trying to surface the views of each person in the group (Krueger & Casey, 2009). To obtain the views of a larger group of persons, you would not enlarge the focus group but would instead assign interviewees to several smaller focus groups.

In both of the preceding examples, whether using an interview to corroborate certain findings or using it to capture an interviewee's own sense of reality, you need to minimize a methodological threat created by the conversational nature of the interview. The conversation can lead to a mutual and subtle influence between you and the interviewee—sometimes referred to as *reflexivity:* Your perspective unknowingly influences the interviewee's responses, but those responses also unknowingly influence your line of inquiry. The result is an undesirable coloring of the interview material.

Whereas you are likely to be aware that prolonged interviews may create a relationship between you and the interviewee—which needs to be monitored—the shorter interviews also pose a reflexive threat. You may not be able to overcome the threat fully, but just being sensitive to its existence should allow you to do better case study interviews.

Survey interviews in a case study. Yet another type of case study interview is in fact the typical survey interview, using a structured questionnaire. The survey could be designed as part of an embedded case study (see Chapter 2) and produce quantitative data as part of the case study evidence (see BOX 19).

BOX 19
A Case Study Encompassing a Survey

Hanna (2000) used a variety of sources of data, including a survey, to conduct a case study of an urban-rural estuarine setting. In this setting, an integrated resource management program was established to help manage environmental and economic planning issues. The case study focused on the estuarine setting, including its description and the policies and public participation that appeared to affect it. Within the case study, participants in the policy process served as an embedded unit of analysis. Hanna surveyed these individuals, and the survey data were presented with statistical tests, as part of the single-case study.

This situation would be relevant, for instance, if you were doing a case study of an urban design project and surveyed a group of designers about the project (e.g., Crewe, 2001) or if you did a case study of an organization that included a survey of workers and managers. This type of survey would follow both the sampling procedures and the instruments used in regular surveys, and it would subsequently be analyzed in a similar manner. The difference would be the survey's role in relation to other sources of evidence. For example, residents' perceptions of neighborhood decline or improvement would not necessarily be taken as a measure of actual decline or improvement but would be considered only one component of the overall assessment of the neighborhood.

Summary. Interviews are an essential source of case study evidence because most case studies are about human affairs or actions. Well-informed interviewees can provide important insights into such affairs or actions. The interviewees also can provide shortcuts to the prior history of such situations, helping you to identify other relevant sources of evidence.

At the same time, when your interviews focus on actions because they are a key ingredient in your case study, the interviews should always be considered *verbal reports* only. As such, even in reporting about such events or explaining how they occurred, the interviewees' responses are subject to the common problems of bias, poor recall, and poor or inaccurate articulation. Again, a reasonable approach is to corroborate interview data with information from other sources.

In other situations, you will be interested in an interviewee's personal views (e.g., opinions, attitudes, and meanings) apart from explaining behavioral events. Corroborating these views against other sources would not be as relevant as when you are dealing with behavioral events. You still may want to get a feeling for the distinctiveness of the views by comparing them with those of others, but the more you do this, the more you are moving toward a conventional survey and should follow survey procedures and precautions.

Direct Observations

Because a case study should take place in the real-world setting of the case, you are creating the opportunity for direct observations. Assuming that the phenomena of interest have not been purely historical, some relevant social or environmental conditions will be available for observation. Such observations serve as yet another source of evidence in doing case study research.

The observations can range from formal to casual data collection activities. Most formally, observational instruments can be developed as part of the case study protocol, and a fieldworker may try to assess the occurrence of certain types of behaviors during certain periods of time in the field (see the two examples in BOX 20). This can involve observations of meetings, sidewalk activities, factory work, classrooms, and the like. Less formally, direct observations might be made throughout your fieldwork, including those occasions during which other evidence, such as that from interviews, is being collected. For instance, the condition of the immediate environment or of work spaces may indicate something about the culture of an organization; similarly, the location or the furnishings of an interviewee's office may be one indicator of the status of the interviewee within an organization.

BOX 20
Using Observational Evidence

20A. Reporting Field Observations

"Clean rooms" are a key part of the manufacturing process for producing semiconductor chips. Among other features, employees wear "bunny suits" of lint-free cloth and handle extremely small components in these rooms. In their case study of high-tech working life, *Silicon Valley Fever,* Rogers and Larsen (1984) used observational evidence to show how employees adapted to the working conditions in these clean rooms, adding that, at the time, most of the employees were women while most of the supervisors were men.

20B. Combining Field Observations with Other Types of Case Study Evidence

Case studies need not be limited to a single source of evidence. In fact, most of the better case studies rely on a variety of sources.

One example of a case study that used such a variety is a book by Gross et al. (1971) covering events in a single school (also see BOX 8, Chapter 2, p. 51). The case study included an observational protocol for measuring the time that students spent on various tasks but also relied on a structured survey of a larger number of teachers, open-ended interviews with a smaller number of key persons, and a review of organizational documents. Both the observational and survey data led to quantitative information about attitudes and behavior in the school, whereas the open-ended interviews and documentary evidence led to qualitative information.

All sources of evidence were reviewed and analyzed together, so that the case study's findings were based on the convergence of information from different sources, not quantitative or qualitative data alone.

Observational evidence is often useful in providing additional information about the topic being studied. If a case study is about a new technology or a school curriculum, for instance, observations of the technology or curriculum at work are invaluable aids for understanding the actual uses of the technology or curriculum and any problems being encountered. Similarly, observations of a neighborhood or of an organizational unit add new dimensions for understanding either the context or the phenomenon being studied.

The observations can be so valuable that you may even consider taking photographs at a fieldwork site. At a minimum, these photographs will help to convey important case characteristics to outside observers (see Dabbs, 1982). Note, however, that in most situations—even in outdoor settings, such as photographing students in a public school playground or people walking on a sidewalk—you will need explicit permission before proceeding.

A common procedure to increase the reliability of observational evidence is to have more than a single observer making an observation—whether of the formal or the casual variety. Thus, when resources permit, case study data collection should allow for the use of multiple observers.

Participant-Observation

Participant-observation is a special mode of observation in which you are not merely a passive observer. Instead, you may assume a variety of roles within a fieldwork situation and may actually participate in the actions being studied (see DeWalt & DeWalt, 2011, chap. 2). In urban neighborhoods, for instance, these roles may range from having casual social interactions with various residents to undertaking specific functional activities within the neighborhood (see Yin, 1982a). The roles for different illustrative studies in neighborhoods and organizations have included

- being a resident in the neighborhood that is the subject of a case study (see BOX 21);
- taking some other functional role in a neighborhood, such as serving as a store-keeper's assistant;
- serving as a staff member in an organizational setting; and
- being a key decision maker in an organizational setting.

BOX 21
Participant-Observation in a Neighborhood
Near "Street Corner Society"

Participant-observation has been a method used frequently to study urban neighborhoods. One such study of subsequent fame was conducted by Herbert Gans, who wrote *The Urban Villagers* (1962), a study about "group and class in the life of Italian-Americans."

Gans's methodology is documented in a separate chapter of his book, titled "On the Methods Used in This Study." He notes that his evidence was based on six approaches: the use of the neighborhood's facilities, attendance at meetings, informal visiting with neighbors and friends, formal and informal interviewing, the use of informants, and direct observation.

(Continued)

(Continued)

Of all these sources, the "participation role turned out to be most productive" (pp. 339–340). This role was based on Gans's being an actual resident, along with his spouse, in the neighborhood he was studying. The result is a classic statement of neighborhood life undergoing urban renewal and change, and a stark contrast to the stability found in a nearby neighborhood, as covered in Whyte's (1943/1993) *Street Corner Society* some 20 years earlier (also see BOX 2A, Chapter 1).

The participant-observation technique has been most frequently used in anthropological studies of different cultural or social groups. The technique also can be used in a variety of everyday settings, such as in a large organization (see BOX 22) or in informal small groups.

BOX 22
A Participant-Observer Study in an "Everyday" Setting

Eric Redman provides an insider's account of how Congress works in his well-regarded case study, *The Dance of Legislation* (1973). The case study traces the introduction and passage of the legislation that created the National Health Service Corps during the 91st Congress in 1970.

Redman's account, from the vantage point of an author who was on the staff of one of the bill's main supporters, Senator Warren G. Magnuson, is well written and easy to read. The account also provides the reader with great insight into the daily operations of Congress—from the introduction of a bill to its eventual passage, including the politics of a lame-duck session when Richard Nixon was president.

The account is an excellent example of participant-observation in a contemporary setting. It contains information about insiders' roles that few persons had been privileged to share. The subtle legislative strategies, the overlooked role of committee clerks and lobbyists, and the interaction between the legislative and executive branches of government were all re-created by the case study, and all add to the reader's general understanding of the legislative process.

Participant-observation provides certain unusual opportunities for collecting case study data, but it also involves major challenges. The most distinctive opportunity is related to your ability to gain access to events or groups that are otherwise inaccessible to a study. In other words, for some topics, there may be no way of collecting evidence other than through participant-observation. Another distinctive opportunity is the ability to perceive reality from the viewpoint of someone "inside" a case rather than external to it. Many have argued that such a perspective is invaluable in producing an accurate portrayal of a case study phenomenon. Finally, other opportunities arise because you may have the ability to manipulate minor events—such as convening a meeting of a group of persons in the case. Only through participant-observation can such manipulation occur, as the use of documents, archival records, and interviews, for instance, assumes a passive researcher. The manipulations will not be as precise as those in experiments, but they can produce a greater variety of situations for the purposes of collecting data.

The major challenges related to participant-observation have to do with the potential biases produced (see Becker, 1958). First, the researcher has less ability to work as an external observer and may, at times, have to assume positions or advocacy roles contrary to the interests of good social science practice. Second, the participant-observer is likely to follow a commonly known phenomenon and become a supporter of the group or organization being studied, if such support did not previously exist. Third, the participant role may simply require too much attention relative to the observer role. Thus, the participant-observer may not have sufficient time to take notes or to raise questions about events from different perspectives, as a good observer might. Fourth, if the organization or social group being studied is physically dispersed, the participant-observer may find it difficult to be at the right place at the right time, either to participate in or to observe important events.

These trade-offs between the opportunities and the challenges have to be considered seriously in undertaking any participant-observation fieldwork. Under some circumstances, this approach to case study evidence may be just the right approach; under other circumstances, the credibility of a whole case study can be threatened.

Physical Artifacts

A final source of evidence is a physical or cultural artifact—for example, a technological device, a tool or instrument, a work of art, or some other physical evidence. Such artifacts may be collected or observed as part of a case study and have been used extensively in anthropological research.

Physical artifacts have less potential relevance in the most typical kind of case study. However, when relevant, the artifacts can be an important component in the overall case. For example, one case study of the use of personal computers in the classroom needed to ascertain the nature of the actual use of the machines. Although use could be directly observed, an artifact—the computer printout—also was available. Students displayed these printouts as the finished product of their work and maintained notebooks of their printouts. Each printout showed the type of schoolwork that had been done as well as the date and amount of computer time used to do the work. By examining the printouts, the case study researchers were able to develop a broader perspective concerning all of the classroom applications over the length of a semester, far beyond that which could be directly observed in the limited time of a classroom visit.

Summary

This section has reviewed six commonly used sources of case study evidence. The procedures for collecting each type of evidence must be developed and mastered independently, to ensure that each source is properly used. Not all sources will be relevant for all case studies. However, the trained case study researcher should be acquainted with the procedures associated with using each source of evidence—or have colleagues who have the needed expertise and who can work as members of the case study team.

Exercise 4.2   Identifying Specific Types of Evidence in Your Case Study

Name a case study topic you would like to study. For some aspect of this topic, identify the specific type of evidence that would be relevant—for example, if a document, what kind of document? If interviews, which interviewees and what questions? If an archival record, what records and what details? If wanting to highlight participants' different perspectives and meanings, what specific participants?

△   FOUR PRINCIPLES OF DATA COLLECTION

The benefits from these six sources of evidence can be maximized if you follow four principles of data collection. These principles are relevant to all six sources and, when used properly, can help to deal with the problems of establishing the construct validity and reliability of the evidence. The four are as follows.

Principle 1: Use Multiple Sources of Evidence

Any of the preceding sources of evidence can and have been the sole basis for entire studies. For example, some studies have relied only on participant-observation but have not examined a single document; similarly, numerous studies have relied on archival records but have not involved a single interview.

This isolated use of sources may be a function of the independent way that sources have typically been conceived—as if a researcher should choose the single most appropriate source or the one with which she or he is most familiar. Thus, on many an occasion, researchers have announced the design of a new study by identifying both the problem to be studied and the prior selection of a *single* source of evidence—such as "interviews"—as the focus of the data collection effort.

Triangulation: Rationale for using multiple sources of evidence. The approach to individual sources of evidence as just described, however, is not recommended when doing case study research. On the contrary, a major strength of case study data collection is the opportunity to use many different sources of evidence (see BOX 23 and—earlier in this chapter—BOX 20B for examples of such studies). Moreover, one analysis of case study methods found that those case studies using multiple sources of evidence were rated more highly, in terms of their overall quality, than those that relied on only single sources of information (see COSMOS Corporation, 1983).

BOX 23
A Case Study Combining Personal Experience
with Extensive Field Research

Most people across the country by now have heard of the federal Head Start program. Its early development and growth into one of the most successful programs is traced by Zigler and Muenchow (1992). Their book is exceptionally insightful, possibly because it is based on Zigler's personal experiences with the program, beginning with his role as its first director. However, the book also calls on other independent sources of evidence, with the coauthor contributing historical and field research, including interviews of more than 200 persons associated with Head Start. All of these multiple sources of evidence are integrated into a coherent if not compelling case study of Head Start. The result is a winning combination: a most readable but also well-documented book.

The need to use multiple sources of evidence far exceeds that in other research methods, such as experiments, surveys, or histories. Experiments, for instance, are largely limited to the measurement and recording of actual behavior in a laboratory and generally do not include the systematic use of survey or verbal information. Surveys tend to be the opposite, emphasizing verbal information but not the measurement or recording of individual behavior. Finally, histories are limited to events in the "dead" past and therefore seldom have any contemporary sources of evidence, such as direct observations of a phenomenon or interviews with key actors.

Of course, each of these strategies can be modified, creating hybrid strategies in which multiple sources of evidence are more likely to be relevant. An example of this is the evolution of "oral history" studies in the past several decades. Such studies can involve extensive interviews with key political leaders who have retired, on the stipulation that the interview information will not be reported until after their death. Later, the historian will join the interview data with the more conventional array of historical evidence. Nevertheless, such a modification of the traditional methods does not alter the fact that case study research inherently deals with a wide variety of evidence, whereas the other methods do not.

The use of multiple sources of evidence in case study research allows a researcher to address a broader range of historical and behavioral issues. However, the most important advantage presented by using multiple sources of evidence is the development of *converging lines of inquiry*. The desired triangulation follows from the principle in navigation, whereby the intersection of different reference points is used to calculate the precise location of an object (Yardley, 2009). Thus, any case study finding or conclusion is likely to be more convincing and accurate if it is based on several different sources of information, following a similar convergence (see BOX 24).

BOX 24
Triangulating from Multiple Sources of Evidence

Basu, Dirsmith, and Gupta (1999) conducted a case study of the federal government's audit agency, the U.S. Government Accountability Office. Their case was theory oriented and examined the relationship between an organization's actual work and the image it presents to external parties (the finding was that the work and image are only loosely coupled). The case study used an impressive array of sources of evidence—an extended period of field observations, with diaries; interviews of 55 persons; and reviews of historical accounts, public records, administrators' personal files, and news articles—all triangulating on the same set of research questions.

Patton (2002) discusses four types of triangulation in doing evaluations—the triangulation:

1. of data sources (*data triangulation*),

2. among different evaluators (*investigator triangulation*),

3. of perspectives to the same data set (*theory triangulation*), and

4. of methods (*methodological triangulation*).

The present discussion pertains only to the first of these four types (*data triangulation*), encouraging you to collect information from multiple sources but aimed at corroborating the same finding. In pursuing such corroboratory strategies, Figure 4.2 distinguishes between two conditions—when you have really triangulated the data (upper portion of Figure 4.2) and when you have multiple sources as part of the same study but that nevertheless address *different* findings (lower portion). When you have really triangulated the data, the case study's findings will have been supported by more than a single source of evidence. In contrast, when you have used multiple sources but analyzed each source of evidence separately, the procedure resembles the comparison of conclusions from separate studies (each based on a different source)—but no data triangulation has taken place.

Figure 4.2   Convergence and Non-convergence of Multiple Sources of Evidence

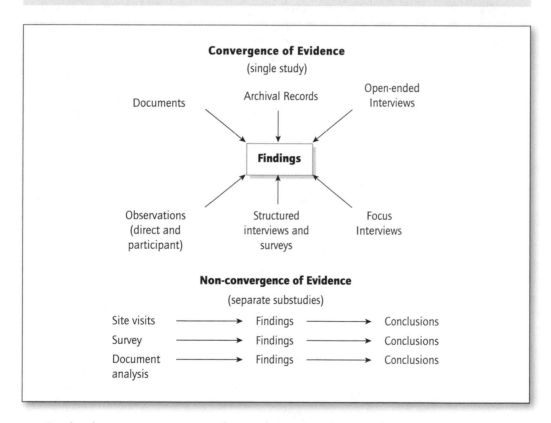

By developing convergent evidence, data triangulation helps to strengthen the *construct validity* of your case study. The multiple sources of evidence essentially provide multiple measures of the same phenomenon. The phenomenon of interest may differ in different kinds of case studies.[4] First, in many case studies, the phenomenon of interest may pertain to a behavioral or social event, with the converged finding implicitly assuming a *single reality.* Use of evidence from multiple sources would then increase confidence that your case study had rendered the event accurately.

In other kinds of case studies, the phenomenon of interest may be a participant's distinctive meaning or perspective—because you have adopted a relativist orientation to appreciate the possibility of *multiple realities.* Triangulation would still be important, to ensure that the case study had rendered the participant's perspective accurately. If nothing else, you should at a minimum have queried the same participant several times or on several occasions—which would then serve in its own way as a set of "multiple" sources.

Prerequisites for using multiple sources of evidence. At the same time, the use of multiple sources of evidence imposes a greater burden, hinted at earlier, on yourself or any other case study researcher. First is that the collection of data from multiple sources is more expensive than if data were only collected from a single source (Denzin, 1978, p. 61). Second and more important, every case study researcher will need to know how to carry out the full variety of data collection techniques. For example, you may have to collect and analyze documentary evidence as in doing history, to retrieve and analyze archival records as in economics, and to design and conduct surveys as in survey research. If any of these techniques is used improperly, the opportunity to address a broader array of issues, or to establish converging lines of inquiry, may be lost. This requirement for mastering multiple data collection techniques therefore raises important questions regarding the training and expertise of a case study researcher.

Unfortunately, many graduate training programs emphasize one type of data collection activity over all others, and the successful student is not likely to have a chance to master the others. To overcome such conditions, you should seek other ways of obtaining the needed training and practice. One such way is to work with a multidisciplinary research team, not necessarily limited to a single academic department. Another way is to analyze the methodological writings of a variety of social scientists (see Hammond, 1968) and to learn of the strengths and weaknesses of different data collection techniques as they have been practiced by experienced scholars. Yet a third way is to design different pilot studies that will provide an opportunity for you to practice the different techniques.

No matter how the experience is gained, every case study researcher should be well versed in a variety of data collection techniques, so that a case study can use multiple sources of evidence. Without such multiple sources, an invaluable advantage of case study research will have been lost. Worse, what started out as a case study may turn into something else. For example, you might overly rely on open-ended interviews for your data, giving insufficient attention to documentary or other evidence to corroborate the interviews. If you then complete your analysis and study, you probably will have done an "interview" study, similar to surveys that are entirely based on verbal reports that come from open-ended interviews—but you would not have done a case study. In this interview study, your text would constantly have to point out the self-reported nature of your data, using such phrases as "as reported by the interviewees," "as stated in the interviews," or "she/he reported that . . ." and the like.

Exercise 4.3 Seeking Converging Evidence

Name a particular incident that occurred recently in your everyday life. How would you go about establishing some facet of this incident, if you wanted now (in retrospect) to demonstrate what had happened? Would you interview any important persons (including yourself)? Would there have been any artifacts or documentation to rely on? Could multiple perspectives be relevant in recalling and defining this facet of the incident?

Principle 2: Create a Case Study Database

A second principle has to do with the way of organizing and documenting the data collected for case studies. Here, case study research has much to borrow from the practices followed by the other research methods defined in Chapter 1. Their documentation commonly consists of two *separate* collections:

1. the data or evidentiary base and

2. the researcher's report, whether in article, report, book, or oral form.

The use of computer files makes the distinction between these two collections even clearer. For example, investigators doing psychological, survey, or economic research may exchange data files and other electronic documentation that contain only the actual database, such as the behavioral responses or test scores in psychology, the itemized responses to various survey questions, or the indicator data in economics. The database then can be the subject of separate, secondary analysis, independent of any reports by the original researcher.

With case study research, the distinction between a separate database and the case study report has only slowly become an everyday but not yet universal practice. Too often in the past, the case study data—mainly taking a narrative form—were embedded in the text presented in a case study report. This left a critical reader no recourse for inspecting the raw data that had led to a case study's conclusions, because the narrative in the case study report was commingled with the author's interpretations of the data.

The needed case study database will be a separate and orderly compilation of all the data from a case study. Such data will go beyond narrative or numeric information and include documents and other materials collected from the field. You may use some computer-*a*ssisted *q*ualitative *d*ata *a*nalysis *s*oftware (CAQDAS) or more routine word-processing tools (e.g., Word or Excel files) to arrange the narrative and numeric data. However, to preserve the other materials as part of the database, you should think of a portfolio contained in a file drawer or set of archival boxes and holding a mixture of folders (with documents and materials). Other persons can then inspect the entire database (electronic files and portfolio) apart from reading your case study report. In this manner, the creation of a case study database markedly increases the *reliability* of your entire case study.

At the same time, the existence of an adequate database does not preclude the need to present sufficient evidence within the case study report itself (to be discussed further in Chapter 6). Every report should still contain enough data so that a reader can second-guess the interpretations and conclusions in your case study, as in reading any other research report. Highly motivated readers can then take the further step of inspecting the database, because it contains the full array of data, not just the evidence that was presented in the report.

Your case study database should be orderly but need not be highly polished. The database's main function is to preserve your collected data in a retrievable form. A well-organized database will not only serve external readers but also will make your own later analysis easier, too.

Unfortunately, the problem of establishing a case study database has not been recognized by most of the books on field methods. Thus, the subsections below represent an extension of the current state of the art. The challenge of developing the database is described in terms of four components: notes, documents, tabular materials, and narratives.

Field notes. For case studies, your own field notes are likely to be the most common component of a database. These notes take a variety of forms. The notes may be a result of your interviews, observations, or document analysis. The notes may be handwritten, typed, audiotaped, or in word-processing or other electronic files. They may have first appeared as jottings in a field diary, on index cards, or recorded in some less organized fashion.

Regardless of their form or content, these field notes must be stored in such a manner that other persons, yourself included, can retrieve them efficiently at some later date. Most commonly, the notes can be organized according to the major topics—as outlined in the case study protocol—covered by a case study; however, any classificatory system will do, as long as the system is usable by an outside party. Only in this manner will the notes be available as part of the case study database.

This identification of the field notes as part of the case study database does not mean, however, that you need to spend excessive amounts of time in rewriting interviews or making extensive editorial changes to polish the notes. Building such a formal case record, by editing and rewriting the notes, may be a misplaced priority. Any such editing should be directed at the case study report itself, not at the notes. The only essential characteristics of the notes are that they be organized, categorized, complete, and available for later access (see BOX 25).

BOX 25
Varieties of Field Notes

Jottings created during actual fieldwork should be converted into more formal field notes on a daily or nightly basis. Both the jottings and formal notes would then become part of a case study database. Four examples follow.

The notes in the first example cover an initial day spent in an urban neighborhood with a community relations officer from the local firehouse (Yin, 2012, chap. 2). The notes focus on the physical condition of the neighborhood and the insights about these conditions from the leaders of three street-level community groups and from the community relations officer's own perceptions and opinions about the neighborhood. Similar notes were then compiled about subsequent days spent in the same neighborhood.

The other three examples come from a single book (DeWalt & DeWalt, 2011, Appendix). Each example happens to cover a different study: a study of women's social power and economic strategies in Manabi, Ecuador; a study of the nutritional strategies of older adults in rural Kentucky; and an evaluation of a community forestry project in Mexico. All of the examples show a high level of detail, reflecting a lot of hard fieldwork.

Case study documents. Many documents relevant to a case study will be collected during the course of a study. Chapter 3 indicated that the disposition of these documents should be covered in the case study protocol and suggested that one helpful way is to have an annotated bibliography of these documents. Besides providing a compact overview of these documents, such an annotated bibliography also can serve as an index, facilitating the documents' storage and retrieval, so that later investigators can inspect or share the database.

The single, unique characteristic of these documents is that they are likely to require a large amount of physical storage space, unless you make portable document format (PDF) copies and store them electronically. In addition, the documents may be of varying importance to the database, and you may want to establish a primary file and a secondary file for such documents. The main objective, again, is to make the documents readily retrievable for later inspection or perusal. In those instances in which a document had been relevant to specific field interviews, an additional cross-reference would be for the interview notes to cite the documents.

Tabular materials. The database may consist of tabular materials, either collected from the site being studied or created by the research team. Such materials also need to be organized and stored to allow for later retrieval.

The materials may include survey and other quantitative data. For example, a survey may have been conducted at a fieldwork site as part of an embedded case study. In such situations, the tabular materials may be stored in computer files. As another example, in dealing with archival or observational evidence, a case study may have called for "counts" of various observed phenomena, commonly known as a *windshield survey* (see Miles & Huberman, 1994). The documentation of these counts, done by the case study team, also should be organized and stored as part of the database.

New narrative compilations. Finally, you may compile your own new narrative material as part of your database. The material can take several forms. The first, already mentioned, would consist of bibliographies, cross-references, or other classifications that help to organize the other materials in the database so you can retrieve them more easily.

A second type of narrative material would compile the evidence dealing with particular themes or ideas that might have caught your attention during or just after data collection. The compilations would help you to sort your evidence more methodically to determine the strength of the empirical support for these themes and ideas. This entire activity may resemble the *memo writing* promoted by researchers practicing *grounded theory* (e.g., Corbin & Strauss, 2007, chap. 6). Although the themes and ideas in these narratives or memos might at first appear to be somewhat isolated from each other, the compilation can provide suggestive first steps for later analyzing your data more fully.

Also potentially moving you toward analysis would be a third type of narrative, which calls for you to compose your own *open-ended answers to the questions in the case study protocol.* Each answer represents your attempt to compile the evidence related to the particular findings in response to one of the protocol's questions. Depending on the nature of any given question, a compilation may either converge on the facts of the matter or strive to appreciate your interviewees' multiple realities and their tentative interpretations. The process is actually an analytic one and is the start of the case study analysis.

The format for the answers may be considered analogous to that of a comprehensive "take-home" exam, used in academic courses. You the researcher are the respondent, and your goal is to cite the relevant evidence—whether from interviews, documents, observations, or archival evidence—in composing an adequate answer. The main purpose of the open-ended answer is to document the connection between specific pieces of evidence and various issues in the case study, generously using footnotes and citations.

The entire set of answers can be considered part of the case study database and can even become the start of the actual case study report (for a single case) or cross-case analysis (for a multiple-case study). However, until the answers actually become part of the case study report, they remain part of the case study database, and you should not spend much time trying to polish the answers. In other words, you need not perform the standard editing and copyediting chores. (However, for an example of a case study that was written entirely in the form of narrative answers to the protocol questions and in which such editing was done, see Yin, 2012, chap. 6.) The most important attribute of good answers is that they indeed connect the pertinent issues—through adequate citations—to specific evidence.

Exercise 4.4 Practicing the Development of a Database

For the topic you covered in Exercise 4.3 (covering some facet of an everyday incident), write a short report (no more than two double-spaced pages) that adheres to the following outline: Start the report by stating a research question that you were attempting to address (about the facet). Now provide your response, citing the evidence you had used (your format should include formal citations and footnotes). Repeat the procedure for a second research question. Envisage how this question-and-response sequence might be one of many in your total case study database.

Principle 3: Maintain a Chain of Evidence

A third principle to be followed, to increase the *reliability* of the information in a case study, is to maintain a chain of evidence. Such a principle is based on a notion similar to that used in forensic investigations.

The principle is to allow an external observer—in this situation, the reader of the case study—to follow the derivation of any evidence from initial research questions to ultimate case study conclusions (see Figure 4.3). Moreover, this external observer should be able to trace the steps in either direction (from conclusions back to initial research questions or from questions to conclusions). As with criminological evidence, the process should be tight enough that evidence presented in "court"—the case study report—is assuredly the same evidence that was collected at the scene of the "crime" during the data collection process. Conversely, no original evidence should have been lost, through carelessness or bias, and therefore fail to receive appropriate attention in considering the findings in a case study. If these objectives are achieved, a case study's evidence also should exhibit heightened construct validity, thereby increasing the overall quality of the case study.

Imagine the following scenario. You have read the conclusions in a case study report and want to know more about the basis for the conclusions. You therefore want to trace the evidentiary process backward.

First, the report itself should have adequately cited or footnoted the relevant sources used to arrive at specific findings—for example, by referring to specific documents, interviews, or observations. Second, these specific sources, upon inspection, should contain the actual evidence, as you might have highlighted the key phrases or words in the documents

Figure 4.3   Maintaining a Chain of Evidence

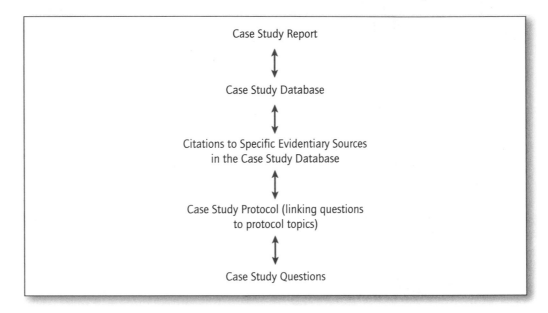

by marking them with a yellow pen. Your methods sections also should have indicated the circumstances under which the evidence had been collected—for example, the time and place of an interview. Third, these circumstances should be consistent with the specific procedures and questions contained in the case study protocol, to show that the data collection had followed the procedures stipulated by the protocol. Finally, a quick review of the protocol should indicate the link between the protocol questions and the original study questions.

In the aggregate, you have therefore been able to move from one part of the case study process to another, with clear cross-referencing to methodological procedures and to the resulting evidence. This is the ultimate "chain of evidence" that is desired.

Exercise 4.5   Establishing a Chain of Evidence

State a hypothetical conclusion that might emerge from a case study you are going to do. Now work backward and identify the specific data or evidence that would have supported such a conclusion. Similarly, work backward and define the protocol question that would have led to the collection of this evidence, and then the study question that in turn would have led to the design of the protocol question. Do you understand how this chain of evidence has been formed and how one can move forward or backward in tracing the chain?

Principle 4: Exercise Care When Using Data from Electronic Sources

A broad array of electronic sources. Most of the six sources of evidence described at the outset of this chapter can be represented by electronic sources, including social media communications. For instance, you can conduct interviews electronically through formal arrangements made with websites such as SurveyMonkey or just by conducting an online chat with another person. Similarly, a cooperative colleague can help you to use a cell phone or tablet to make direct, if remote, observations of worldly events on a real-time basis. Engaging in chat rooms and other online group dialogues offers a kind of participant-observation, and relevant physical artifacts can be depicted in online photographs and videos. In other words, contemporary electronic media and archives open a whole vista of sources of evidence, including access to previous studies and research.

For some case studies, an electronic source may be your actual subject of study (e.g., when you are studying the dialogue and interpersonal interactions taking place over a Skype connection). Under that circumstance, you will be sure to take great care in doing your research. However, when you are using the electronic source not as its own subject of study, but to collect any of the six types of evidence discussed at the outset of this chapter—such as retrieving a document, conducting an online interview, or observing an event remotely—you also need to exercise great caution.

Cautions. The wealth of electronic information can overwhelm you, so the first caution in using electronic sources is to set some limits. Deciding how much time to spend, setting priorities for navigating and drilling into various websites, and having some idea of the centrality of the information to your research all feed into these limits. Of course, your commitment can expand or contract as you gather new information, but try hard not to let matters get out of hand.

A second caution deals with your willingness to cross-check the sources you use and the information you derive from them. For instance, Wikipedia can be an easy starting point for gaining an understanding of a new concept or topic. However, although the website makes every effort to check the accuracy of the information in its postings, specific authors may nevertheless dominate the contributions to any particular concept or topic. As a result, the material is likely to have an interpretive slant, potentially revealed when (and if) you check these authors' other works. Cross-checking online material with other sources would be an important way of understanding a potential slant, incompleteness, or even interpretive bias.

A third caution deals with your use of social media sites, such as Facebook, Twitter, YouTube, and individual blogs. Again, and especially if your case study actually focuses on the ongoing experiences at these sites as the topic of study, you should use the information from such sites with a highly skeptical view—for example, being aware that claims about the authorship, places, or times attributable to the material may not be fully accurate. A final reminder is to inquire about the permission needed to use the materials from these sites, especially photographs, in your case study.

△ SUMMARY

This chapter has reviewed six sources of case study evidence, how evidence can be collected from these sources, and four important principles regarding the data collection process.

The data collection process for case studies is more complex than those used in other research methods. A case study researcher must have a methodological versatility not necessarily required for using other methods and must follow certain formal procedures to ensure quality control during the data collection process. The four principles described in this chapter are steps in this direction. They are not intended to straitjacket the inventive and insightful researcher. They are intended to make the process as explicit as possible, so that the final results—the data that have been collected—reflect a concern for construct validity and for reliability, thereby becoming worthy of further analysis. How such analysis can be carried out is the topic of the next chapter.

△ NOTES TO CHAPTER 4

1. The limited availability of print materials in low-income communities in the United States—even including signage in public places and materials in schools and public libraries—has been the subject of study (Neuman & Celano, 2001). To the extent of such impoverishment, researchers studying such neighborhoods and their community organizations (or schools) may find the use of documentary sources of evidence also limited.

2. Excellent suggestions regarding the ways of verifying documentary evidence, including the nontrivial problem of determining the actual author of a document, are offered by Barzun and Graff (1985, pp. 109–133). An exemplary quantitative study of the authorship problem in relation to the *Federalist Papers* is found in Mosteller and Wallace (1984).

3. Such consistent responses are likely to occur when interviewing members of a "closed" institution, such as the residents of a community drug treatment program or the teachers in a closely knit school. The apparent conspiracy arises because those being interviewed all have previously agreed to the "socially desirable" responses and appear to be providing corroboratory evidence when in fact they are merely repeating their institution's mantra.

4. The author is grateful to reviewers of the fourth edition of this book. They pointed out that the original version of Figure 4.2, depicting the convergence of evidence around a single "fact," implicitly represented a *realist* view. Because no such limited representation had been intended, the revised figure now points to convergence over a set of "findings." The use of this latter term is intended to cover events as well as meanings and perspectives, with case studies and their findings being able to accommodate either realist or relativist orientations.

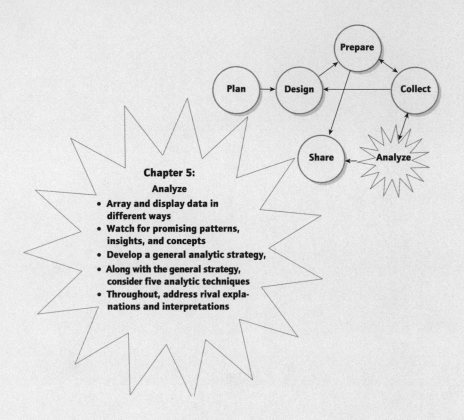

Chapter 5:

Analyze

- Array and display data in different ways
- Watch for promising patterns, insights, and concepts
- Develop a general analytic strategy,
- Along with the general strategy, consider five analytic techniques
- Throughout, address rival explanations and interpretations

ABSTRACT

Data analysis consists of examining, categorizing, tabulating, testing, or otherwise recombining evidence, to produce empirically based findings. Analyzing case study evidence is especially difficult because the techniques still have not been well defined. You can start your own analysis by "playing" with the data and searching for promising patterns, insights, or concepts—the goal being to define your priorities for what to analyze and why. Absent your own strategy, four other general strategies are to rely on theoretical propositions, work your data from the "ground up," develop a case description, and examine rival explanations. Using various computer aids can help to manipulate large amounts of data, but you still will have to define the relevant codes and interpret any observed patterns. In this sense, the computer aids cannot substitute for having a general analytic strategy.

Any of the general strategies then can be used in practicing five specific techniques for analyzing case studies: pattern matching, explanation building, time-series analysis, logic models, and cross-case synthesis. When a case study involves an embedded design and appropriately fine-grained data for the embedded unit of analysis, the analyses can incorporate statistical models for the embedded unit of analysis, but not for the case study as a whole. Throughout, a persistent challenge is to produce high-quality analyses, which require attending to *all* the evidence collected, displaying and presenting the evidence apart from any interpretation, and considering alternative interpretations.

5

ANALYZING CASE STUDY EVIDENCE

How to Start Your Analysis, Your Analytic Choices, and How They Work

AN ANALYTIC STRATEGY: MORE THAN FAMILIARITY △
WITH ANALYTIC TOOLS

Need for an Analytic Strategy

Another challenge. The analysis of case study evidence is one of the least developed aspects of doing case studies. Too many times, researchers start case studies without having the foggiest notion about how the evidence is to be analyzed (despite Chapter 3's recommendation that the analytic approaches be considered when developing the case study protocol). Such case studies easily become stalled at the analytic stage; this author has known colleagues who have simply ignored their case study data for month after month, not knowing what to do with the evidence.

Because of the problem, the experienced case study researcher is likely to have great advantages over the novice at the analytic stage. Unlike statistical analysis, there are few fixed formulas or cookbook recipes to guide the novice. Instead, much depends on a researcher's own style of rigorous empirical thinking, along with the sufficient presentation of evidence and careful consideration of alternative interpretations.

Researchers and especially novices do continue to search for formulas, recipes, or tools, hoping that familiarity with these devices alone will produce the needed analytic result. The tools are important and can be useful, but they are usually most helpful if you know what to look for or have an overall analytic strategy—which unfortunately returns you back to your original challenge, if you hadn't noticed.

Computer-assisted tools. For instance, computer-assisted routines with prepackaged software such as Atlas.ti, HyperRESEARCH, NVivo, or The Ethnograph all are examples of *computer-assisted qualitative data analysis software* (CAQDAS—e.g., Fielding & Lee, 1998). The software has become more diverse and functional over the past decade, covering both text and video-based data. Guidance on coding skills and technique also has improved and become easier to follow (e.g., Auerbach & Silverstein, 2003; Saldaña, 2009). Essentially, the tools and guidance can help you code and categorize large amounts of data. Such data, when taking the form of narrative text, may have been collected from open-ended interviews or from large volumes of written materials, such as documents and newspaper articles.

Key to your understanding of the value of these packages are two words: *assisted* and *tools.* The software will not do the finished analysis on its own, but it may serve as an able assistant and reliable tool. For instance, if you enter your textual data and then define an initial set of codes, one or another of the various software packages will readily locate in the textual data all the words and phrases matching these codes, count the incidence or occurrence of the words or codes, and even conduct Boolean searches to show when and where multiple combinations are found. You can do this process iteratively, gradually building more complex categories or groups of codes. However, unlike statistical analyses, you cannot use the software's outputs themselves as if they were the end of your analysis.

Instead, you will need to study the outputs to determine whether any meaningful patterns are emerging. Quite likely, any patterns—such as the frequency of codes or code combinations—will still be conceptually more primitive (lower) than the initial "how" and "why" research questions that might have led to your case study in the first place. In other words, developing a rich and full explanation or even a good description of your case, in response to your initial "how" or "why" questions, will require much post-computer thinking and analysis on your part.

Backtracking, you also will need to have clarified the reasons for defining the initial codes or subsequent codes, as well as connecting them to your original research design (you, not the software, created them). In what

---

Tip: *How do I start analyzing my case study data?*

You might start with questions (e.g., the questions in your case study protocol) rather than with the data. Start with a small question first, then identify your evidence that addresses the question. Draw a tentative conclusion based on the weight of the evidence, also asking how you should display the evidence so that readers can check your assessment. Continue to a larger question and repeat the procedure. Keep going until you think you have addressed your main research question(s).

Could you have started with the data instead of the questions?

ways do the codes or concepts accurately reflect the meaning of the retrieved words and phrases, and why? Answering these questions requires your own analytic rationale.

Under some circumstances, the computerized functions can nevertheless be extremely helpful (see Tutorial 5-1). The minimal conditions include when (a) the words or verbal reports represent verbatim records and are the central part of your case study evidence, and (b) you have a large collection of such data. Such conditions commonly occur in research using *grounded theory* strategies (e.g., Corbin & Strauss, 2007), where the surfacing of a new concept or theme can be highly valuable. However, even under the best of circumstances, nearly all scholars express strong caveats about any use of computer-assisted tools when dealing with case study data (e.g., Patton, 2002, p. 442): You must still be prepared to be the main analyst and to direct the tools; they are the assistant, not you.

Indeed, most case studies pose a serious challenge in efforts to use computer-assisted tools: Verbatim records such as interviewees' responses are likely to be only part of the total array of case study evidence. The case study will typically be about complex behavior, occurring within a complex, real-world context. Unless you convert all of your evidence—including your field notes and the archival documents you might have collected—into the needed textual form, computerized tools cannot readily handle this more diverse array of evidence. Yet, as emphasized in Chapter 4, such an array should represent an important strength of your case study. For a diverse set of evidence, you therefore need to develop your own analytic strategies.

Starting an analytic strategy. A helpful starting point is to "play" with your data. You are searching for patterns, insights, or concepts that seem promising. These may emerge as you manipulate the data, for instance by juxtaposing the data from two different interviewees. Other manipulations include (see Miles & Huberman, 1994):

- Putting information into different arrays
- Making a matrix of categories and placing the evidence within such categories
- Creating data displays—flowcharts and other graphics—for examining the data
- Tabulating the frequency of different events
- Putting information in chronological order or using some other temporal scheme

Another way of getting started is to write memos or notes to yourself, already mentioned in Chapter 4, about what you might have observed in your data. Scholars practicing *grounded theory* have long promoted the use of such memos (Corbin & Strauss, 2007). Their desired memo writing and diagramming (the graphic form of memo writing) begins during fieldwork and continues into the analysis stage. The memos can contain hints, clues, and suggestions that simply put into writing any preliminary interpretation of any part of your data—basically conceptualizing your data (Lempert, 2011). To start a memo, think of the classic nugget being the idea that you had when you were taking a shower.

Any of these preliminary creations—such as arrays, displays, tabulations, memos, or diagrams—will help to move you toward a general analytic strategy. The needed strategy should follow some cycle (or repeated cycles) involving your original research questions, the data, your defensible handling and interpretation of the data, and your ability to state some findings and draw some conclusions. You actually can try to move backward or forward through this cycle, forcing a strategy to emerge. For instance, you can move backward by asking yourself what you think you might conclude from your case study—and then examine your data fairly to see how they might (or might not) support the conclusion. Once you have made a tentative connection, you may then understand better what you need to do to analyze your data.

The needed strategy should guide you through your analysis. In addition to what you may come up with yourself, consider the four strategies described below, after which five specific techniques for analyzing case study data are reviewed. These strategies and techniques are not mutually exclusive. You can use any of them in any combination. A continued alert is to be aware of these choices *before* collecting your data, to help make sure that your data will be analyzable.

Four General Strategies

Relying on theoretical propositions. One strategy is to follow the theoretical propositions that led to your case study. The original objectives and design of the case study presumably were based on such propositions, which in turn reflected a set of research questions, reviews of the literature, and new hypotheses or propositions.

The propositions would have shaped your data collection plan and therefore would have yielded analytic priorities. As an example, a study of intergovernmental relationships started with the proposition that federal funds have redistributive dollar effects but also create new organizational changes at the local level (Yin, 1980). The basic proposition—the creation of a "counterpart bureaucracy" in the form of local planning organizations, citizen action groups, and other new offices within a local government itself, but all attuned to specific federal programs—was traced in case studies of several cities. For each city, the purpose of the case study was to show how the formation and modification in local organizations occurred *after* changes in related federal programs, and how these local organizations acted on behalf of the federal programs even though they might have been agencies within local government.

The preceding proposition shows how a theoretical orientation guided the case study analysis. The proposition helped to organize the entire analysis, pointing to relevant contextual conditions to be described as well as explanations to be examined (BOX 26 has additional examples).

Working your data from the "ground up." A second strategy contrasts directly with the first. Instead of thinking about any theoretical propositions, pour through your data. Whether as a result of your earlier "playing with the data" or noticing a pattern for the

---

BOX 26
Using Theory to Analyze
Case Studies in Comparative Politics

Case studies in comparative politics show how case study analysis can proceed by addressing preexisting theories. Rogowski (2010) describes five classic case studies, explaining how they benefited from preexisting theories "precise enough to yield implications for single, or for very few observations" (p. 95). Each case study first provided empirical evidence showing important anomalies in the preexisting theory and then proceeded to "conjecture intelligently about a more satisfactory general theory that could avoid such anomalies" (p. 95). Three of the case studies had single cases (the Netherlands and its religious and social cleavages; a single midsized German town and its associational life, such as clubs, societies, and religious groups, prior to World War II; and the development of a central European state into the strongest state in the early modern world). The other two case studies had multiple cases (the economic progress of countries in post-independence Africa; and the success in international markets by several smaller European states).

---

first time, you may now find that some part of your data suggests a useful concept or two. Such an insight can become the start of an analytic path, leading you farther into your data and possibly suggesting additional relationships (see BOX 27).

BOX 27
Emergence of a Case Typology by Working Data
from the Ground Up

A study of residential citizen patrols illustrates the inductive strategy (Yin, 2012, chap. 5). Key concepts emerged by closely examining the data, not from prior theoretical propositions. The study's goal was to understand the circumstances under which patrols could become susceptible to undesired, vigilante-like behavior. The main criteria for selecting cases were that a patrol had to be implemented by a citizens' group (not a private security service) and directed at residential, not commercial, areas. Only after doing case studies of 32 such patrols did three types of patrols become evident: patrols limited to buildings or residential compounds (*building* patrols), patrols overseeing neighborhood streets more generally (*neighborhood* patrols), and patrols offering escort and other community services (*service* patrols). The neighborhood patrols appeared most prone to vigilante-like behavior, because, unlike the other patrols, patrol members could not readily distinguish residents living in the neighborhood from those who were strangers—and were more likely to appear vigilante-like when confronting persons exhibiting seemingly suspicious behavior (even residents belonging to the neighborhood).

This inductive strategy can yield appreciable benefits, with one caveat. More experienced researchers are likely to have relevant concepts in their head because of their richer understanding of their field of study. They also may have followed an inductive strategy in some earlier study. Conversely, novices may be less familiar with the issues in the first place and may be challenged to make useful connections with the data.

In qualitative research, the originators of *grounded theory* (Corbin & Strauss, 2007; Glaser & Strauss, 1967) have provided much guidance over the years for following an inductive approach to data analysis. The procedures assign various kinds of codes to the data, each code representing a concept or abstraction of potential interest. The resulting guidance can be relevant to all case studies, in addition to studies based on *grounded theory*.

For case studies, an inductive strategy offers additional promise if your case study happens to have called for collecting quantitative data, which might have been relevant for at least two reasons. First, the data may cover the behavior and events that your case study is trying to explain—typically, the "outcomes" in an evaluative case study. Second, the data may be related to an embedded unit of analysis within your broader case study. In either situation, your qualitative data then may be critical in explaining or otherwise testing your case study's key propositions. So, imagine a case study about a school, neighborhood, organization, community, medical practice, or other common case study topic. For these topics, the outcomes of an evaluative case study might be, respectively, student achievement (for the case study about the school), housing prices (for the neighborhood), employees' salaries (for the organization), various crime rates (for the community), or the incidence of an illness (for the medical practice). Alternatively, the embedded units might be students (or teachers), census blocks (or single-family housing), employees (for the organization), persons arrested (for the community), or patients (for the medical practice).

All of the illustrative outcomes or embedded units can be the occasion for having collected fine-grained quantitative data. Yet, the main case study questions might have been at a higher level: a single school (not its students), the neighborhood (not its housing units), a business firm (not its employees), a community (not its residents), or a new medical practice (not the patients). To explore, describe, or explain events at this higher level, you would have collected and used qualitative data. Thus, your case study would have deliberately used both qualitative and quantitative data.

Exercise 5.1   Using Quantitative Data in a Case Study

Select one of your own empirical studies—but *not* a case study—in which you analyzed some quantitative data (or choose such a study from the literature). Describe how the data were analyzed in this study. Argue whether this same analysis, virtually in its same form, could be found as one part of a fuller case study analysis. Do you think that quantitative data are less relevant to case studies than qualitative data?

Developing a case description. A third general analytic strategy is to organize your case study according to some descriptive framework (see BOX 28). This strategy is workable in its own right but also serves as an alternative if you are having difficulty using either of the first two strategies. In other words, you may somehow have collected a lot of data without having settled on an initial set of research questions or propositions (disabling your ability to rely on the first strategy) and you also may not have been able to surface any useful concepts from your data (making it difficult to follow the second, or inductive strategy).

BOX 28
Organizing a Case Study
According to a Descriptive Framework

A single case study examined a Tanzanian village council's experience in exercising local control over natural resource management (Nathan, Lund, Gausset, & Andersen, 2007). The policy goal was to promote greater efficiency, equity, and democracy over forest regulation. The findings of the case study were organized according to four topics regarding the council's experience: the council's relation to higher levels of government, to other villages, and to the village's own residents; and the limitations on the council's own capacities. Because the four topics appear to reflect a logical set of policy domains, the use of such a descriptive framework gave credence to the case study's main conclusion—that the devolution of control alone could not overcome all the constraints in natural resource management.

Sometimes, the original and explicit purpose of the case study may have been a descriptive one. This was the objective of the famous sociological study *Middletown* (Lynd & Lynd, 1929), which was a case study of a midwestern city. What is interesting about *Middletown,* aside from its classic value as a rich and historic case, is its compositional structure, reflected by its chapters:

- Chapter I: Getting a Living
- Chapter II: Making a Home
- Chapter III: Training the Young
- Chapter IV: Using Leisure
- Chapter V: Engaging in Religious Practices
- Chapter VI: Engaging in Community Activities

These chapters cover a range of topics relevant to community life in the early 20th century, when Middletown was studied. Note how the descriptive framework organizes the case study analysis but also assumes that data were collected about each topic in the first place. In this sense, you should have thought (at least a little) about your descriptive framework before designing your data collection instruments. As usual, the ideas for your framework should have come from your initial review of literature, which may have revealed gaps or topics of interest to you, spurring your interest in doing a case study. Another suggestion is to note the structure of existing case studies (e.g., by examining in greater detail those cited in the BOXES throughout this book) and at least to observe their tables of contents as an implicit clue to different descriptive approaches.

In other situations, the original objective of the case study may not have been a descriptive one, but a descriptive approach may later help to identify the appropriate explanation to be analyzed—even quantitatively. One notable case study was concerned with the complexity of implementing a local public works program in Oakland, California (Pressman & Wildavsky, 1973). Such complexity, the authors realized, could be *described* in terms of the multiplicity of decisions, by public officials, that had to occur in order for implementation to succeed. This descriptive insight later led to the enumeration, tabulation, and hence quantifying of the various decisions. In this sense, the descriptive approach was used to identify an overall pattern of complexity that the authors then used to "explain" why implementation had failed. The case study came to be regarded as one of the breakthrough contributions to the early research on implementation (Yin, 1982b).

Examining plausible rival explanations. A fourth general analytic strategy, trying to define and test plausible rival explanations, generally works in combination with all of the previous three: Initial theoretical propositions (the first strategy above) might have included rival hypotheses; working from the ground up (the second strategy) may produce rival inductive frameworks; and case descriptions (the third strategy) may involve alternative descriptions of the case.

For instance, the typical hypothesis in an evaluation is that the observed outcomes are the result of a planned intervention. The simple or direct rival explanation would be that the observed outcomes were in fact the result of some other influence besides the planned intervention and that the investment of resources into the intervention may not actually have been needed. Being aware (ahead of time) of this direct rival, your case study data collection should then have included attempts to collect evidence about the possible "other influences." Furthermore, you should have pursued your data collection about them vigorously—as if you were in fact trying to prove the potency of the other influences rather than finding a reason to reject them (Patton, 2002, p. 553; Rosenbaum, 2002, pp. 8–10). Then, if you had found insufficient evidence, you would less likely be accused of stacking the deck in favor of the original hypothesis.

The direct rival—that the original investment was not the reason for the observed outcomes—is but one of several types of plausible rival explanations. Figure 5.1 classifies and lists many types of rivals (Yin, 2000b). For each type, an informal and more understandable descriptor (in the parentheses and quotation marks in Figure 5.1) accompanies the formal social science category, hopefully making the gist of the rival thinking clearer.

Figure 5.1 Brief Descriptions of Different Kinds of Rival Explanations

TYPE OF RIVAL	Description or Examples
Craft Rivals:	
1. The Null Hypothesis	The observation is the result of chance circumstances only
2. Threats to Validity	e.g., history, maturation, instability, testing, instrumentation, regression, selection, experimental mortality, and selection-maturation interaction
3. Investigator Bias	e.g., "experimenter effect"; reactivity in field research
Real-World Rivals:	
4. Direct Rival	An intervention ("suspect 2") other than the target (Practice or Policy) intervention ("suspect 1") accounts for the results (*"the butler did it"*)
5. Commingled Rival	Other interventions and the target intervention both (Practice or Policy) contributed to the results (*"it wasn't only me"*)
6. Implementation Rival	The implementation process, not the substantive intervention, accounts for the results (*"did we do it right?"*)
7. Rival Theory	A theory different from the original theory explains the results better (*"it's elementary, my dear Watson"*)
8. Super Rival	A force larger than but including the intervention accounts for the results (*"it's bigger than both of us"*)
9. Societal Rival	Social trends, not any particular force or intervention, account for the results (*"the times they are a-changin'"*)

SOURCE: Yin (2000b).

The list reminds us of three "craft" rivals that underlie all of our social science research, and textbooks have given much attention to these craft rivals. However, the list also defines six real-world or substantive rivals, which have received virtually no attention by other textbooks (nor, unfortunately, do most texts intensely discuss the challenges and benefits of rival thinking or the use of rival explanations). These real-life rivals are the ones that you should carefully identify prior to your data collection (while not ignoring the craft rivals). Some real-world rivals also may not become apparent until you are in the midst of your data collection, and attending to them at that point is acceptable and desirable.

Overall, the more rivals that your analysis addresses and rejects, the more confidence you can place in your findings.

Rival explanations were a critical part of several of the case studies already contained in the BOXES cited earlier (e.g., refer to BOXES 1 and 11 in Chapters 1 and 2, pp. 7 and 58, respectively). The authors of these case studies used the rivals to drive their entire case study analysis. Additional examples—covering cases of local economic development and of the demise of a *Fortune 50* firm (see also BOX 46, Chapter 6, p. 194) but deliberately focusing on the essence of the evidence about rival explanations—are found in Yin (2012, chap. 10).

Summary. The best preparation for conducting case study analysis is to have a general analytic strategy. The purpose of the analytic strategy is to link your case study data to some concepts of interest, then to have the concepts give you a sense of direction in analyzing the data. You can develop your own strategy but also can consider the four just described: relying on theoretical propositions, working your data from the ground up, developing case descriptions, and examining rival explanations.

Within any general strategy, including one you might develop yourself, you should consider using any of five analytic techniques now to be described in the remainder of this chapter. As will be shown, the techniques are especially intended to deal with the previously noted problems of developing *internal validity* and *external validity* (see Chapter 2) when doing case study research. The specific techniques are (1) pattern matching, (2) explanation building, (3) time-series analysis, (4) logic models, and (5) cross-case synthesis.

Exercise 5.2   Creating a General Analytic Strategy

Assume that you have begun analyzing your case study data but still do not have an overall analytic strategy. Instead of remaining stalled at this analytic step, move to the next step and speculate how you might organize your (later) case study report into separate chapters or sections. Within each chapter or section, create substantive titles and headings (e.g., instead of "introduction," make the title say what the introduction is about, even if more than a few words are needed). Try different sequences of titles and headings, noting how such differences might dictate the creation of different analytic strategies. Now choose one sequence and start sorting your data into the designated chapters or sections. You should be on your way to analyzing your case study data.

△   FIVE ANALYTIC TECHNIQUES

None of the analytic techniques should be considered easy to use, and all will need much practice to be used powerfully. Your objective should be to start modestly, work thoroughly and introspectively, and build your own analytic repertoire over time. The reward will eventually emerge in the form of compelling case study analyses and, ultimately, compelling case studies.

1. Pattern Matching

For case study analysis, one of the most desirable techniques is to use a pattern-matching logic. Such a logic (Trochim, 1989) compares an empirically based pattern—that is, one based on the findings from your case study—with a predicted one made before you collected your data (or with several alternative predictions). In political science research, a technique similar to pattern matching has been called the *congruence method* (see George & Bennett, 2004, chap. 9). If the empirical and predicted patterns appear to be similar, the results can help a case study to strengthen its *internal validity*.

If the case study is an explanatory one, the patterns may be related to the dependent or the independent variables of the study, discussed below. If the case study is a descriptive one, pattern matching is still relevant, as long as the predicted pattern of important descriptive conditions was defined prior to data collection.

Nonequivalent dependent variables as a pattern. The dependent variables pattern may be derived from one of the more potent quasi-experimental research designs, labeled a "nonequivalent, dependent variables design" (Cook & Campbell, 1979, p. 118). According to this design, an experiment or quasi-experiment may have multiple dependent variables—that is, a variety of relevant outcomes. For instance, in public health studies, some outcomes may have been predicted to be affected by a treatment, whereas other outcomes may have been predicted *not* to be affected (Rosenbaum, 2002, pp. 210–211). The pattern matching occurs in the following manner: If, for each outcome, the initially predicted values have been found, and at the same time alternative "patterns" of predicted values (including those deriving from methodological artifacts, or "threats" to validity) have not been found, strong causal inferences can be made.

As a specific example, consider a single case in which you are studying the effects of a newly decentralized office computer system. Your major proposition is that—because each peripheral piece of equipment can work independently of any server—a certain pattern of organizational changes and stresses will be produced. Among these changes and stresses, you specify the following, based on propositions derived from your knowledge of previous decentralization theory:

- employees will create *new applications* for the office system, and these applications will be idiosyncratic to each employee;
- traditional *supervisory links* will be threatened, as management control over work tasks and the use of central sources of information will be diminished;

- *organizational conflicts* will increase, due to the need to coordinate resources and services across the decentralized units; but nevertheless,
- *productivity* will increase over the levels prior to the installation of the new system.

In this example, these four outcomes each represent different dependent variables, and you would assess each with different quantitative or qualitative measures. To this extent, you have a study that has specified *nonequivalent* dependent variables. You also have predicted an overall pattern of outcomes covering each of these variables. If the results are as predicted, you can draw a solid conclusion about the effects of decentralization. However, if the results fail to show the entire pattern as predicted—that is, even if one outcome does not behave as predicted—your initial proposition would have to be questioned (see BOX 29 for another example).

BOX 29
Pattern Matching on Each of Multiple Outcomes

Researchers and politicians alike recognize that U.S. military bases, located across the country, contribute significantly to a local economy's housing, employment, and other markets. When such bases close, a corresponding belief is that the community will suffer in some catastrophic (both economic and social) manner.

To test the latter proposition, Bradshaw (1999) conducted a case study of a closure that had occurred in a modestly sized California community. He first identified a series of sectors (e.g., housing sales, civilian employment, unemployment, population turnover and stability, and retail markets) where catastrophic outcomes might have been feared, and he then collected data about each sector before and after the base closure. A pattern-matching procedure, examining the pre-post patterns of outcomes in every sector and also in comparison to other communities and statewide trends, showed that the outcomes were much less severe than anticipated. Some sectors did not even show any decline. Bradshaw also presented evidence to explain the pattern of outcomes, thereby producing a compelling argument for his conclusions.

Continuing the same example, this first case of office computer systems could then be augmented by a second one, in which another new office system had been installed, but of a centralized nature—that is, the equipment at all of the individual workstations had been networked. Now you would predict a different pattern of outcomes, using the same four dependent variables enumerated above. And now, if the results show that the decentralized system (Case A) had actually produced the predicted pattern and that this first pattern was different from that predicted and produced by the centralized system (Case B), you would be able to draw an even stronger conclusion about the effects of decentralization. In this situation, you have made a *theoretical replication* across cases. (In other situations, you might have sought a *literal replication* by identifying and studying two or more cases of decentralized systems.)

Finally, you might be aware of the existence of certain threats to the validity of this logic (see Cook & Campbell, 1979, for a full list of these threats). For example, as a contextual condition covered by your case study, you found that a new corporate executive had assumed office in Case A, leaving room for a counterargument: that the apparent effects of decentralization were actually attributable to this executive's appointment and not to the newly installed office system. To deal with this threat, you would have to identify some subset of the initial dependent variables and show that the pattern would have been different (in Case A) if the corporate executive had been the actual reason for the effects. If you only had a single-case study, this type of procedure would be essential; you would be using the same data to rule out arguments based on a potential threat to validity. Given the existence of a second case, as in our hypothetical example, you also could show that the claim about the corporate executive would not explain certain parts of the pattern found in Case B (in which the absence of the corporate executive should have been associated with certain opposing outcomes). In essence, your goal is to identify all reasonable threats to validity and to conduct repeated comparisons, showing how such threats cannot account for the dual patterns in both of the hypothetical cases.

BOX 30
Pattern Matching for Rival Explanations and Replicating across Multiple Cases

A common policy problem is to understand the conditions under which new research findings can be made useful to society. This topic was the subject of a multiple-case study of different natural hazards research projects (Yin, 2012, chap. 3, pp. 46–48). The case study first provided definitive evidence that important research findings had indeed been put into practical use in every project, ranging from reducing life loss due to earthquakes to new irrigation methods.

The main research inquiry then dealt with "how" and "why" such outcomes had occurred. The investigators compared three theories ("rivals") from the prevailing literature, that (a) researchers select their own topics to study and then successfully disseminate their findings to the practical world (technology "push"), (b) the practical world identifies

(Continued)

(Continued)

problems that attract researchers' attention and that then leads to successful problem solving (demand "pull"), and (c) researchers and practitioners work together, customizing an elongated process of problem identification and solution testing ("social interaction"). Each theory predicts a different pattern of rival events that should precede the preestablished outcome. For instance, the demand "pull" theory requires the prior existence of a problem as a prelude to the initiation of a research project, but the same condition is not present in the other two theories.

For the nine cases, the events turned out to match best a combination of the second and third theories. The multiple-case study had therefore pattern-matched the events in each case with different theoretical predictions and also used a replication logic across the cases.

Rival independent variables as a pattern. The use of rival explanations, besides being a good general analytic strategy, also provides an example of pattern matching for *inde-pendent* variables. In such a situation (for an example, see BOX 30), several cases may be known to have had a certain type of outcome, and your investigation has focused on how and why this outcome occurred in each case.

The analysis requires the development of rival theoretical propositions, articulated in operational terms. The desired characteristic of these rival explanations is that each involves a pattern of independent variables that is mutually exclusive: If one explanation is to be valid, the others cannot be. This means that the presence of certain independent variables (predicted by your original explanation) precludes the presence of other independent variables (predicted by a rival explanation). The independent variables may involve several or many different types of characteristics or events, each assessed with different measures and instruments. The concern of the case study analysis, however, is with the overall pattern of results and the degree to which the empirically based pattern matches the predicted one.

This type of pattern matching of independent variables also can be done either with a single case or with multiple cases. With a single case, successful matching would be evidence for concluding that the original explanation was the better one (and that the other explanations were less acceptable). Moreover, if this identical result were additionally obtained over multiple cases, *literal replication* of the single cases would have been accomplished, and the cross-case results might be stated even more assertively. Then, if this same result also failed to occur in a second group of cases, due to predictably different circumstances, *theoretical replication* would have been accomplished, and the initial result would stand yet more robustly. Whether dealing with a single or multiple cases, other threats to validity—basically constituting another group of rival explanations—also should be identified and ruled out.

Precision of pattern matching. At this point in the state of the art, the actual pattern-matching procedure involves no precise comparisons. Whether you are predicting a pattern of nonequivalent dependent variables or a pattern based on rival independent variables, the basic comparison between the predicted and the actual pattern may involve no quantitative or statistical criteria. (Available statistical techniques are likely to be irrelevant because each of the variables in the pattern will probably represent a single data point, and none will therefore have the variance needed to satisfy the statistical need.) The most numeric result will likely occur if the study had set preestablished benchmarks (e.g., productivity will increase by 10% or more) and the value of the actual outcome was then compared to this benchmark.

Low levels of precision can allow some interpretive discretion on the part of a researcher, who may be overly restrictive in claiming a pattern to have been violated or overly lenient in deciding that a pattern has been matched. You can make your case study stronger by developing more precise measures. In the absence of such precision, an important suggestion is to avoid postulating very subtle patterns, so that your pattern matching deals with gross matches or mismatches whose interpretation is less likely to be challenged.

2. Explanation Building

A second analytic technique is in fact a special type of pattern matching, but the procedure is more difficult and therefore deserves separate attention. Here, the goal is to analyze the case study data by building an explanation about the case. (Again, a counterpart to explanation building in political science research has been called *process tracing*— see Bennett, 2010; George & Bennett, 2004.)

As used in this chapter, the procedure is mainly relevant to explanatory case studies. A parallel procedure, for exploratory case studies, has been commonly cited as part of a hypothesis-generating process (see Glaser & Strauss, 1967), but its goal is not to conclude a study but to develop ideas for further study.

Elements of explanations. To "explain" a phenomenon is to stipulate a presumed set of causal links about it, or "how" or "why" something happened. The causal links may be complex and difficult to measure in any precise manner (see BOX 31).

In most case studies, explanation building occurs in narrative form. Because such narratives cannot be precise, the better case studies are the ones in which the explanations reflect some theoretically significant propositions, whose magnitudes might start to offset the lack of precision. For example, the causal links may reflect critical insights into public policy process or into social science theory. The public policy propositions, if

---

BOX 31

Explanation Building in a Single-Case Study

Why businesses succeed or fail continues to be a topic of popular as well as research interest. Explanations are definitely needed when failure occurs with a firm that, having successfully grown for 30 years, had risen to become the number two computer maker in the entire country and, across all industries, among the top 50 corporations in size. Edgar Schein's (2003) single-case study assumed exactly that challenge and contains much documentation and interview data (also see BOX 46, Chapter 6, p. 194).

Schein, a professor at MIT, had served as a consultant to the firm's senior management during nearly all of its history. His case study tries to explain how and why the company had a "missing gene"—one that appeared critical to the business's survival. The author argues that the gene was needed to overcome the firm's other tendencies, which emphasized the excellent and creative quality of its technical operations. Instead, the firm should have given more attention to its business and marketing operations. The firm might then have overcome its inability to address layoffs that might have pruned deadwood in a more timely manner and set priorities among competing internal projects (for instance, the firm developed three different PCs, not just one).

---

correct, could lead to recommendations for future policy actions (see BOX 32A for an example); the social science propositions, if correct, could lead to major contributions to theory building, such as the transition of countries from agrarian to industrial societies (see BOX 32B for an example).

BOX 32

Explanation Building in Multiple-Case Studies

32A. A Study of Multiple Communities

In a multiple-case study, one goal is to build a general explanation that fits each individual case, even though the cases will vary in their details. The objective is analogous to creating an overall explanation, in science, for the findings from multiple experiments.

Martha Derthick's (1972) *New Towns In-Town: Why a Federal Program Failed* is a book about a housing program under President Lyndon Johnson's administration. The federal government was to give its surplus land—located in choice inner-city areas—to local governments for housing developments. But after 4 years, little progress had been made at the seven sites—San Antonio, Texas; New Bedford, Massachusetts; San Francisco, California; Washington,

(Continued)

(Continued)

D.C.; Atlanta, Georgia; Louisville, Kentucky; and Clinton Township, Michigan—and the program was considered a failure.

Derthick's (1972) account first analyzes the events at each of the seven sites. Then, a general explanation—that the projects failed to generate sufficient local support—is found unsatisfactory because the condition was not dominant at all of the sites. According to Derthick, local support did exist, but "federal officials had nevertheless stated such ambitious objectives that some degree of failure was certain" (p. 91). As a result, Derthick builds a modified explanation and concludes that "the surplus lands program failed both because the federal government had limited influence at the local level and because it set impossibly high objectives" (p. 93).

32B. A Study of Multiple Societies

An analytic approach similar to Derthick's is used by Barrington Moore (1966) in his history on the *Social Origins of Dictatorship and Democracy*. The book serves as another illustration of explanation building in multiple-case studies, even though the cases are actually historical examples.

Moore's (1966) book covers the transformation from agrarian to industrial societies in six different countries—England, France, the United States, China, Japan, and India—and the general explanation of the role of the upper classes and the peasantry is a basic theme that emerges and that became a significant contribution to the field of history.

Iterative nature of explanation building. The explanation-building process, for explanatory case studies, has not been well documented in operational terms. However, the eventual explanation is likely to be a result of a series of iterations:

- Making an initial theoretical statement or an initial explanatory proposition
- Comparing the findings of *an initial case* against such a statement or proposition
- Revising the statement or proposition
- Comparing other details of the case against the revision
- Comparing the revision to the findings from *a second, third, or more cases*
- Repeating this process as many times as is needed

In this sense, the final explanation may not have been fully stipulated at the beginning of a study and therefore differs from the pattern-matching approaches previously described. Rather, as the case study evidence is examined, explanatory propositions are revised, and the evidence is examined once again from a new perspective in this iterative mode. If you were only doing a single-case study, the procedure would not end conclusively, but it could become more compelling if you could apply the revised explanation to additional cases, as part of a multiple-case study.

The gradual building of an explanation is similar to the process of refining a set of ideas, in which an important aspect is again to entertain other *plausible or rival explanations*. As before, the objective is to show how these rival explanations cannot be supported, given the actual set of case study findings.

Potential problems in explanation building. Others have pointed to the challenges and pitfalls of this iterative process, as in Diane Vaughan's apt, thoughtful, and helpful rendition of her notion of "theory elaboration" (Vaughan, 1992). As a general matter, you should be forewarned that this approach to case study analysis is fraught with dangers. Much analytic insight and sensitivity are demanded of the explanation builder. As the iterative process progresses, for instance, a researcher may slowly begin to drift away from the original topic of interest. Worse, an unwanted selective bias may creep into the process, leading to an explanation that glosses over some key data.

To reduce the threats, you should check frequently with the original purpose of the inquiry, use external colleagues as "critical friends," and continually examine possible alternative explanations. Other safeguards already have been covered by Chapters 3 and 4—that is, using a case study protocol (indicating what data were to be collected), establishing a case study database for each case (formally storing the entire array of data that were collected, available for inspection by a third party), and following a chain of evidence.

Exercise 5.3   Constructing an Explanation

Identify some observable changes that have been occurring in your neighborhood (or the neighborhood around your campus). Develop an explanation for these changes and indicate the critical set of evidence you would collect to support or challenge this explanation. If such evidence were available, would your explanation be complete? Compelling? Useful for investigating similar changes in another neighborhood?

---

3. Time-Series Analysis

A third analytic technique is to conduct a time-series analysis, directly analogous to the time-series analysis conducted in experiments and quasi-experiments. Such analysis can follow many intricate patterns, which have been the subject of several major textbooks in experimental and clinical psychology with single *subjects* (e.g., see Kratochwill, 1978); the interested reader is referred to such works for further detailed guidance. The more intricate and precise the pattern, the more that the time-series analysis also will lay a firm foundation for the conclusions of the case study.

Simple time series. Compared to the more general pattern-matching analysis, a time-series design can be much simpler in one sense: In time series, there may only be a single dependent or independent variable. In these circumstances, when the single variable is nevertheless represented by a large number of time data points, statistical tests can even be used to analyze the data (see Kratochwill, 1978).

However, the pattern can be more complicated in another sense because the appropriate starting or ending points for this single variable may not be clear. As one possible consequence, the available data points may only be a truncated segment of a broader (and opposing) trend. Despite this problem, the ability to trace changes over time is a major strength of case studies—which are not limited to cross-sectional or static assessments of a particular situation. If the events over time have been traced in detail and with precision, some type of time-series analysis always may be possible, even if the case study analysis involves some other techniques as well (see BOX 33).

BOX 33
Using Time-Series Analysis in a Single-Case Study

In New York City, and following a parallel campaign to make the city's subways safer, the city's police department took many actions to reduce crime in the city more broadly. The actions included enforcing minor violations ("order restoration and maintenance"), installing computer-based crime-control techniques, and reorganizing the department to hold police officers accountable for controlling crime.

Kelling and Coles (1997) first describe all of these actions in sufficient detail to make their potential effect on crime reduction understandable and plausible. The case study then presents time series of the annual rates of specific types of crime over a 7-year period. During this period, crime initially rose for a couple of years and then declined for the remainder of the period. The case study explains how the timing of the relevant actions by the police department matched the changes in the crime trends. The authors cite the plausibility of the actions' effects, combined with the timing of the actions in relation to the changes in crime trends, to support their explanation for the reduction in crime rates in the New York City of that era.

The essential logic underlying a time-series design is the match between the observed (empirical) trend and either of the following: (a) a theoretically significant trend specified before the onset of the investigation or (b) some rival trend, also specified earlier. Within the same single-case study, for instance, two opposing time patterns may have been hypothesized. This is what Campbell (1969) did in his now-famous study of the change in Connecticut's speed limit law, reducing the limit to 55 miles per hour in 1955. The predicted time-series pattern was based on the proposition that the new law (an "interruption" in the time series) had substantially reduced the number of fatalities, whereas the other time-series pattern was based on the proposition that no such effect had occurred. Examination of the actual data points—that is, the annual number of fatalities over a period of years before and after the law was passed—then determined which of the alternative time series best matched the empirical evidence. Such comparison of "interrupted time series" within the same case can be used in many different situations.

The same logic also can be used in doing a multiple-case study, with contrasting time-series patterns postulated for different cases. For instance, a case study about economic development in cities may have examined the reasons that a manufacturing-based city had more negative employment trends than those of a service-based city. The pertinent outcome data might have consisted of annual employment data over a pre-specified period of time, such as 10 years. In the manufacturing-based city, the predicted employment trend might have been a declining one, whereas in the service-based city, the predicted trend might have been a rising one. Similar analyses can be imagined with regard to the examination of youth gangs over time within individual cities, changes in health status (e.g., infant mortality), trends in college rankings, and many other indicators. Again, with appropriate time data, the analysis of the trends can be subjected to statistical analysis. For instance, you can compute "slopes" to cover time trends under different conditions (e.g., comparing student achievement trends in schools with different kinds of curricula) and then compare the slopes to determine whether their differences are statistically significant (see Yin, Schmidt, & Besag, 2006). As another approach, you can use regression discontinuity analysis to test the difference in trends before and after a critical event, such as the passing of a new speed limit law (see Campbell, 1969).

Complex time series. The time-series designs can be more complex when the trends within a given case are postulated to be more complex. For instance, you can postulate not merely a rising or declining (or flat) trend but some rise followed by some decline within the same case. This type of mixed pattern, across time, would be the beginning of a more complex time series. The relevant statistical techniques would then call for using nonlinear models. As always, the strength of case study research would not merely be in assessing this type of time series (with or without statistics) but in developing a rich explanation for the complex time series.

Greater complexities also arise when a multiple set of variables—not just a single one—are relevant to a case study and when each variable may be predicted to have a different pattern over time. Such conditions can especially be present in embedded case studies: The case study may be about a single case, but extensive data also cover an embedded unit of analysis (see Chapter 2, Figure 2.3). BOX 34 contains two examples.

The first (see BOX 34A) was a single-case study about one school system, but hierarchical linear models were used to analyze a detailed set of student achievement data. The second (see BOX 34B) was about a single neighborhood revitalization strategy taking place in several neighborhoods; the authors used statistical regression models to analyze time trends for the sales prices of single-family houses in the targeted and comparison neighborhoods and thereby to assess the outcomes of the single strategy.

BOX 34
More Complex Time-Series Analyses:
Using Quantitative Methods

When Single-Case Studies Have an Embedded Unit of Analysis

34A. Evaluating the Impact of Systemwide Reform in Education

Supovitz and Taylor (2005) conducted a case study of Duval County School District in Florida, with the district's students serving as an embedded unit of analysis. A quantitative analysis of the students' achievement scores over a 4-year period, using hierarchical linear models adjusted for confounding factors, showed "little evidence of sustained systemwide impacts on student learning, in comparison to other districts."

The case study includes a rich array of field observations and surveys of principals, tracing the difficulties in implementing new systemwide changes prior to and during the 4-year period. The authors also discuss in great detail their own insights about systemwide reform and the implications for evaluators—that such an "intervention" is hardly self-contained and that its evaluation may need to embrace more broadly the institutional environment beyond the workings of the school system itself.

34B. Evaluating a Neighborhood Revitalization Strategy

Galster, Tatian, and Accordino (2006) do not present their work as a case study. The aim of their study was nevertheless to evaluate a single neighborhood revitalization strategy (as in a single-case study) in Richmond, Virginia. The article presents the strategy's rationale and some of its implementation history, and the main conclusions are about the revitalization strategy. However, the distinctive analytic focus is on what might be considered an embedded unit of analysis: the sales prices of single-family homes. The overall evaluation design is highly applicable to a wide variety of embedded case studies.

To test the effectiveness of the revitalization strategy, the authors used regression models to compare pre- and postintervention (time-series) trends between housing prices in targeted and comparison neighborhoods. The findings showed that the revitalization strategy had "produced substantially greater appreciation in the market values of single-family homes in the targeted area than in comparable homes in similarly distressed neighborhoods."

In general, although a more complex time series creates greater problems for data collection, it also leads to a more elaborate trend (or set of trends) that can lead to a stronger analysis. Any match of a predicted with an actual time series, when both are complex, will produce better evidence for an initial theoretical proposition.

Chronological sequences. The compiling of chronological events is a frequent technique in case studies and may be considered a special form of time-series analysis. The chronological sequence again focuses directly on the major strength of case studies cited earlier—that case studies allow you to trace events over time.

You should not think of the arraying of events into a chronology as a descriptive device only. The procedure can have an important analytic purpose—to investigate presumed causal events—because the basic sequence of a cause and its effect cannot be temporally inverted. Moreover, the chronology is likely to cover many different types of variables and not be limited to a single independent or dependent variable. In this sense, the chronology can be richer and more insightful than general time-series approaches. The analytic goal is to compare the chronology with that predicted by some explanatory theory—in which the theory has specified one or more of the following kinds of conditions:

- Some events must always occur before other events, with the reverse *sequence* being impossible.
- Some events must always be followed by other events, on a *contingency* basis.
- Some events can only follow other events after a prespecified *interval of time*.
- Certain *time periods* in a case study may be marked by classes of events that differ substantially from those of other time periods.

If the actual events of a case study, as carefully documented and determined by a researcher, have followed one predicted sequence of events and not those of a compelling, rival sequence, the single-case study can again become the initial basis for causal inferences. Comparison to other cases, as well as the explicit consideration of threats to internal validity, will further strengthen this inference.

Summary conditions for time-series analysis. Whatever the stipulated nature of the time series, the important case study objective is to examine some relevant "how" and "why" questions about the relationship of events over time, not merely to observe the time trends alone. An interruption in a time series will be the occasion for postulating potential causal relationships; similarly, a chronological sequence should contain causal postulates.

On those occasions when the use of time-series analysis is relevant to a case study, an essential feature is to identify the specific indicator(s) to be traced over time, as well as the specific time intervals to be covered and the presumed temporal relationships among events, *prior to* collecting the actual data. Only as a result of such prior specification are the relevant data likely to be collected in the first place, much less analyzed properly and with minimal bias.

In contrast, if a study is limited to the analysis of time trends alone, as in a descriptive mode in which causal inferences are unimportant, a non–case study strategy is probably more relevant—for example, the economic analysis of consumer price trends over time. Note, too, that without any hypotheses or causal propositions, chronologies risk becoming *chronicles*—descriptive renditions of events that lack any explanatory value.

Exercise 5.4 Analyzing Time-Series Trends

Identify a simple time series—for example, the number of students enrolled at your university for each of the past 20 years. How would you compare one period of time with another within the 20-year period? If the university's admissions policies had changed during this time, how would you compare the effects of such policies? How might this analysis be considered part of a broader case study of your university?

---

4. Logic Models

This fourth technique has become increasingly useful in recent years, especially in doing case study evaluations (e.g., Mulroy & Lauber, 2004) and in studying theories of change (e.g., Funnell & Rogers, 2011). The logic model stipulates and operationalizes a complex chain of occurrences or events over an extended period of time. The events are staged in repeated cause-effect-cause-effect patterns, whereby a dependent variable (event) at an earlier stage becomes the independent variable (causal event) for the next stage (Peterson & Bickman, 1992; Rog & Huebner, 1992). Researchers also have demonstrated the benefits when logic models are developed collaboratively—that is, when researchers and the officials implementing a program being studied work together to define a program's logic model (see Nesman, Batsche, & Hernandez, 2007). The process can help a group define more clearly its vision and goals, as well as how the sequence of programmatic actions will (in theory) accomplish the goals.

As an analytic technique, the use of logic models consists of matching empirically observed events to theoretically predicted events. Conceptually, you therefore may consider the logic model technique to be another form of pattern matching. However, because of their sequential stages, logic models deserve to be distinguished as a separate analytic technique from pattern matching.

Joseph Wholey (1979) was at the forefront in developing logic models as an analytic technique. He first promoted the idea of a program logic model, tracing events when a public program intervention was intended to produce a certain outcome or sequence of outcomes. The *intervention* could initially produce activities with their own *immediate* outcomes; these immediate outcomes could in turn produce some *intermediate* outcomes; and in turn, the intermediate outcomes were supposed to produce final or *ultimate* outcomes.

To illustrate Wholey's (1979) framework with a hypothetical example, consider a school intervention aimed at improving students' academic performance. The hypothetical intervention involves a new set of classroom activities during an extra hour in the school day (*intervention*). These activities provide time for students to work with their peers on joint exercises (*immediate outcome*). The result of this immediate outcome is evidence of increased understanding and satisfaction with the educational process, on the part of the participating students, peers, and teachers (*intermediate outcome*). Eventually, the exercises and the satisfaction lead to the increased learning of certain key concepts by the students, and they demonstrate their knowledge with higher test scores (*ultimate outcome*).

The entire example shows how a logic model helps to explain the ultimate outcome, exceeding the capability of the common experimental design, which essentially (but only) tests the relationship between the presence of the school intervention and the occurrence of the higher test scores. Because of the inability to explain how the intervention produced the ultimate outcome, such an experimental design is commonly considered a "black box" evaluation (e.g., Rogers, 2000, p. 213). By using logic models, case study research can "open" the black box.

Going beyond Wholey's (1979) approach and using the strategy of plausible rival explanations espoused throughout this book, an analysis also could entertain rival chains of events, as well as the potential importance of spurious external events. Now returning to the preceding example, if the data supported the role of the extra hour of schooling, and if no rivals could be substantiated, the analysis could claim a causal effect between the initial school intervention and the later test scores. Alternatively, the conclusion might be reached that the specified series of events was *illogical*—for instance, that the school intervention had involved students during the semester prior to the one when learning had been assessed. In this situation, the logic model would have helped to explain a spurious finding.

Program logic models can apply to a variety of situations, such as research on organizational change (e.g., Burke, 2007) or on community and economic development (e.g., Phillips & Pittman, 2009), not just those where an intervention is the topic of a case study. The key ingredient is the claimed existence of a repeated cause-and-effect sequence of events, linked together. Depending upon the number of cases in your own case study, you may analyze the links qualitatively *or* quantitatively.

A qualitative analysis would first compare the consistency between the observed and the originally stipulated sequence for each case, affirming (or rejecting or modifying) the original sequence. The complete analysis would then proceed to provide additional qualitative data, explaining in a fair manner why the sequence had been affirmed (or rejected or modified). A quantitative analysis would follow the same analytic strategy but would be based on a large number of cases. With the large number of cases, the initial comparison could be made by using a path model, such as a structural equation model (e.g., Bryk, Bebring, Kerbow, Rollow, & Easton, 1998). After having affirmed (or rejected or modified) the original sequence, the analysis would again add new data, potentially assuming the form of different variables being added to the initial structural equation model, to explain why the sequence had been affirmed (or rejected or modified).

These qualitative and quantitative analytic strategies both apply to the three types of logic models described next. The three types vary according to the type of case in your case study—that is, its unit of analysis.

For illustrative purposes, all of the graphics depict a linear sequence or progression of events over time. Such a straightforward rendition can graphically serve the needs of most case studies, even though real-world events are certainly more complex. However, for those who want to press further into the graphic complexities, Tutorial 5-2 depicts a more complicated, nonlinear logic model. More important than the graphics per se is the increasing appreciation that a case study analysis can examine nonlinear interdependencies and interrelationships, as described in using case studies in both health care (e.g., Anderson, Crabtree, Steele, & McDaniel, 2005; Anaf, Drummon, Sheppard, 2007) and business (e.g., Dubois & Gadde, 2002).

Individual-level logic model. The first type assumes that your case study is about an individual person, with Figure 5.2 depicting the behavioral course of events for a hypothetical youth. The events flow across a series of boxes and arrows reading from left to right in the figure. It suggests that the youth may be at risk for becoming a member of a gang, may eventually join a gang and become involved in gang violence and drugs, and even later may participate in a gang-related criminal offense. The logic model also has a set of 11 numbers associated with the various arrows in the figure. Each of the 11 represents an opportunity, through some type of planned intervention (e.g., community or public program), to prevent an individual youth from continuing on the course of events. For instance, community development programs (number 1) might bring jobs and better housing to a neighborhood and reduce the youth's chances of becoming at risk in the first place.

Disregarding the interventions for a moment, your case study might simply have tracked a youth's path through the stipulated sequence of boxes in Figure 5.2, ending with the youth committing a gang-related offense (you might have tracked the sequence backwards, collecting retrospective data about a youth who had already committed such an offense). Your case study might have found that the sequence was not accurate, and after analyzing the paths taken by several different youths (i.e., replications), your case study might have arrived at a new sequence. If it provided new insights into youth development, your findings would have made a contribution to new knowledge, for either research or practical purposes.

Alternatively, your case study might have focused on the 11 interventions in Figure 5.2. The analysis would have examined how a particular youth might have encountered and

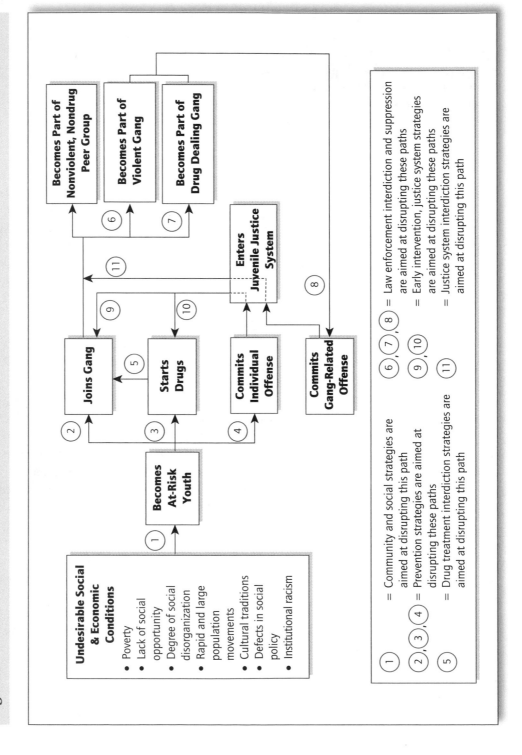

Figure 5.2 Youth Behavior and 11 Possible Interventions

dealt with them, either confirming or reaching new conclusions about the role of these interventions. Whether dealing with a youth's path through the sequence of boxes alone or also with the interventions, you can see how the logic model represents an initial theory about your case(s) and then provides a framework for analyzing your data.

Firm- or organizational-level logic model. A second type of logic model traces events taking place in a single organization, such as a manufacturing firm. Figure 5.3 shows how changes in a firm (Boxes 5 and 6 in Figure 5.3) are claimed to lead to improved manufacturing (Box 8) and eventually to improved business performance (Boxes 10 and 11). The flow of boxes also reflects a hypothesis—that the initial changes were the result of external brokerage and technical assistance services (Boxes 2 and 3). Given this hypothesis, the logic model therefore also contains rival or competing explanations (Boxes 12 and 13). The data analysis for this case study would then consist of tracing the actual events over time, at a minimum giving close attention to their chronological sequence. The data collection also should have tried to identify ways in which the boxes were actually linked in real life, thereby corroborating the layout of the arrows connecting the boxes.

Program-level logic model. Figure 5.4 contains a third type of logic model. Here, the model depicts the rationale underlying a public program, aimed at reducing the incidence of HIV/AIDS by supporting community planning and prevention initiatives. The depicted program provides funds and technical assistance to 65 state and local health departments across the United States. The model was used to organize and analyze data from eight case studies, including the collection of data on rival explanations, whose potential role also is shown in the model (see Yin, 2012, chap. 15, for the entire multiple-case study). In like manner, you could develop a program-level logic model to study any other public program in any other country.

Sharpening your use of logic models. The examples thus far have provided you with the basic principles for using logic models as analytic tools, going beyond their common role in designing new studies (texts devoted solely to logic models may emphasize the beginning of a new study and only give fleeting attention to the analytic phase—e.g., Knowlton & Phillips, 2009). The following two topics, illustrated by Figures 5.5 and 5.6, now may sharpen your use of logic models to an even greater degree.

The two portions of Figure 5.5 illustrate the first topic: highlighting *the transitions, not just the activities,* in logic models. Both portions of the figure repeat the same logic model, which stipulates how the work of an education partnership might support appropriate activities that eventually could produce desirable K–12 student outcomes. However, the bottom portion of Figure 5.5 accentuates the "arrows" between the boxes, alerting you to the need for case studies to offer actual explanations for how events transition from one stage to another. In other words, the data from most case studies tend to address only the "boxes," treating the occurrence of the events in a correlational manner but overlooking the transitions.

Figure 5.3 Changes in Performance in a Manufacturing Firm

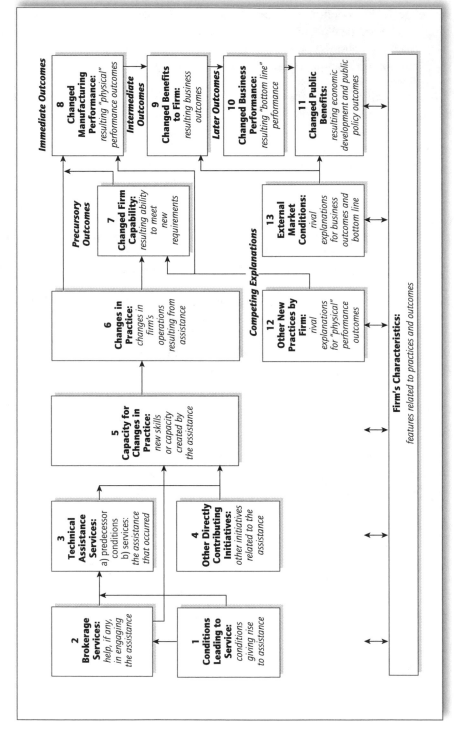

SOURCE: Yin and Oldsman (1995).

Figure 5.4 Improving Community Planning for HIV/AIDS Prevention

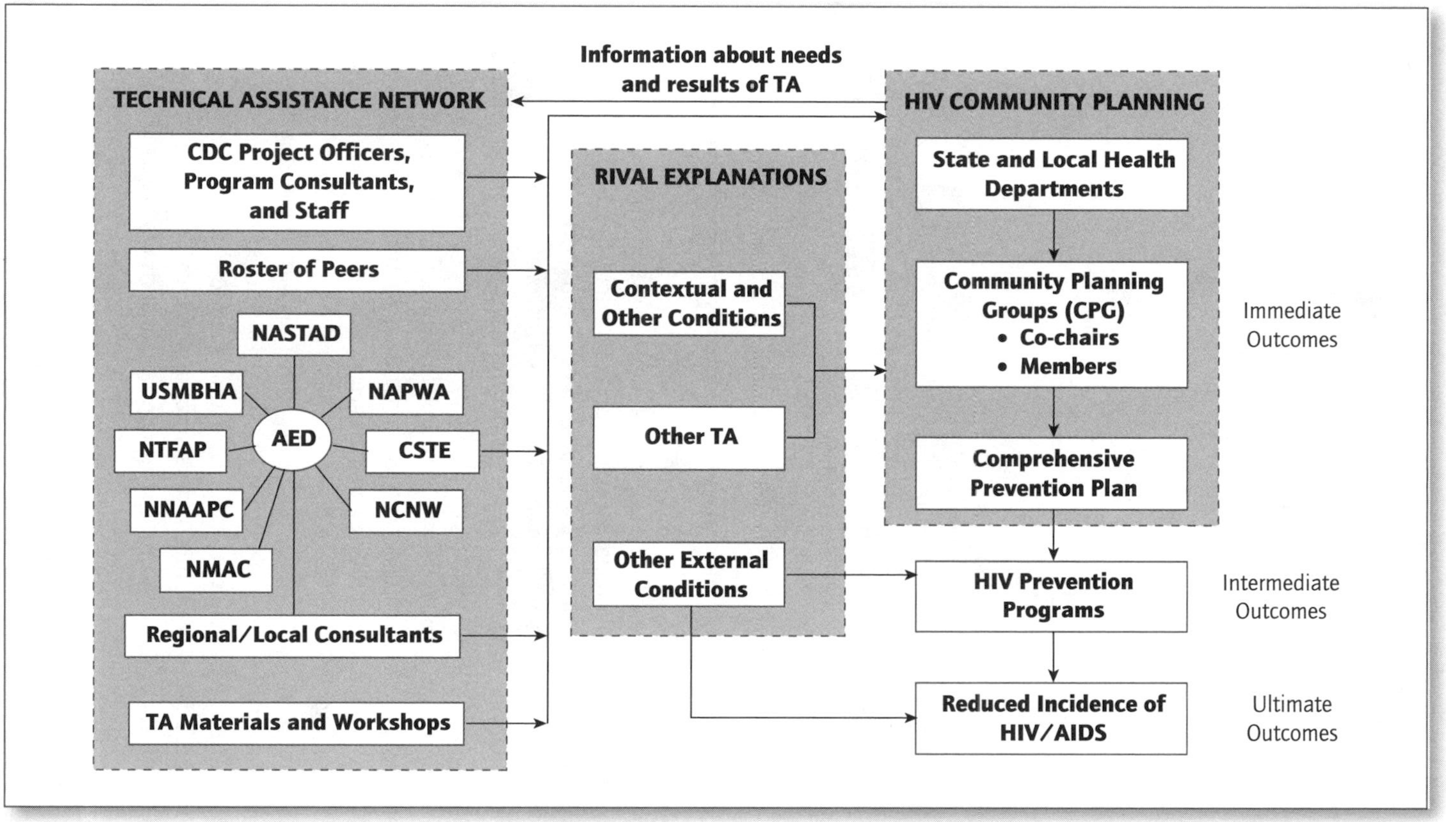

SOURCE: Yin (2003, chap. 8).

Figure 5.5 Highlighting Transitions, Not Just Activities

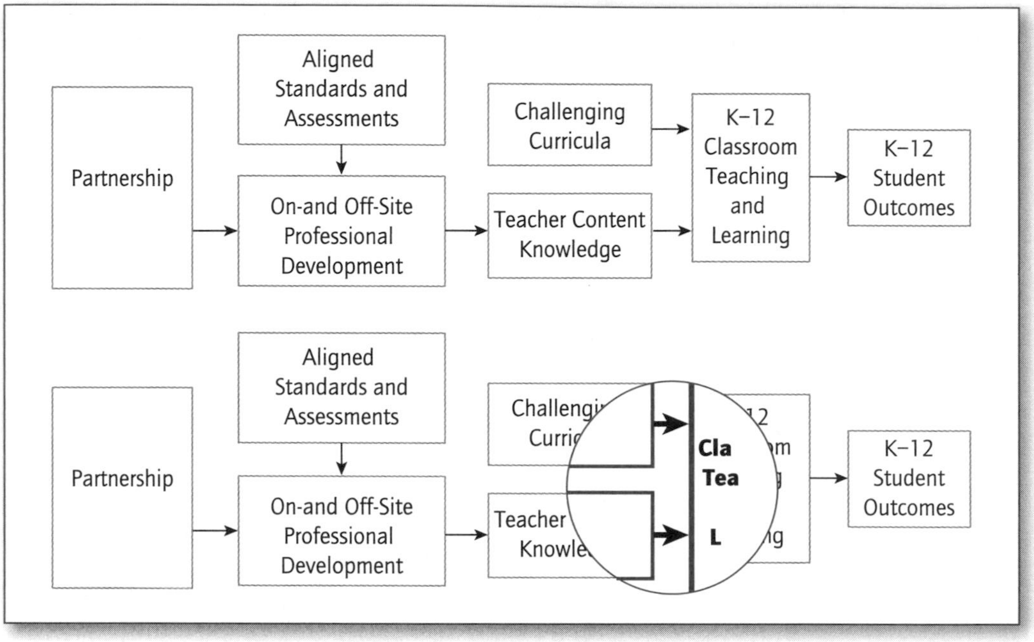

For instance, qualitative data might have covered the chronological sequence of events, which might then have been found to match (or not) the sequence in the original logic model. Quantitatively, a structural equation model similarly might have assessed the strength and sequence among the boxes. However, neither the qualitative nor quantitative situations may have tried to explain the transitions—for example, how and why an event (in one box) appeared to have produced a subsequent event (in the next box). Such explanations produce a more compelling and stronger test of a logic model, so the lesson here is to collect and present data about the transitions, not just the events.[1]

Figure 5.6 illustrates the second topic: attending to *contextual conditions* as an integral part of logic models. Many logic models, such as the ones presented previously, only barely attend to contextual conditions. Not only are these conditions likely to be an important part of every case study, in some situations, they may overwhelm the "case" being studied. Neglecting those conditions therefore may yield a case study with an incomplete if not misleading understanding of the case.

For instance, the logic model in Figure 5.6 portrays a generic intervention with an assumed progression from the investment of "resources" to the occurrence of "outcomes." Such an intervention might serve as the case in a case study, and—with one exception—the logic model shares a similar structure with the logic models previously presented in Figures 5.1 and 5.2. The exception is that, unlike the earlier logic models,

Figure 5.6 Attending to Contextual Conditions and Rivals

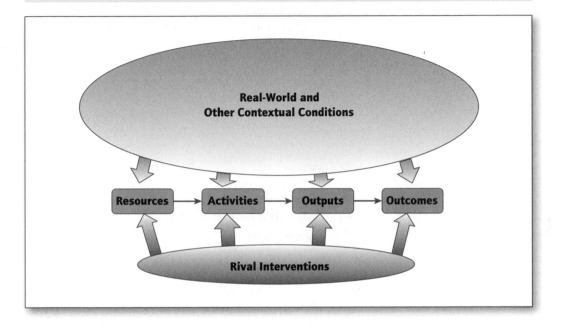

the one in Figure 5.6 purposely expands the potential scope of the case study by calling explicit attention to the possibility of a whole host of relevant real-world and other contextual conditions, including rival interventions. Though external to the case, such conditions and rivals might in fact be found to influence strongly the intervention's outcomes, possibly outweighing the effects of the resources and activities supported by the intervention.

The specific contextual conditions needing to be specified and then monitored in a case study will vary from case to case. For instance, case studies of individual people should be wary of family, peer, and community conditions—all of which might have enriched an understanding of the hypothetical youth's progression in Figure 5.1. Similarly, case studies of organizations such as businesses should be wary of the role of competitors, conditions in the industry at large, and regulatory conditions—again barely hinted at in Figure 5.2.

Summary. Using logic models, whether to examine a theory of change (that is, a presumed sequence of events as in a neighborhood revitalization process) or to assess an intervention, represents a fourth technique for analyzing case study data. The analysis can use qualitative or quantitative data (or both), and three types of illustrative models have been discussed. Each differs in relation to the type of case being studied (an individual, an organization, or a program).

5. Cross-Case Synthesis

A fifth technique only applies to the analysis of multiple cases (the previous four techniques can be used with either single- or multiple-case studies). The technique is especially relevant if, as encouraged in Chapter 2, a case study consists of at least two cases (for a synthesis of six cases, see Ericksen & Dyer, 2004). The analysis is likely to be easier and the findings likely to be more robust than having only a single case. BOX 35 presents an excellent example of the important research and research topics that can be addressed by having a "two-case" case study. Again, having more than two cases could strengthen the findings even further.

BOX 35
Using a "Two-Case" Case Study
to Test a Policy-Oriented Theory

The international marketplace of the 1970s and 1980s was marked by Japan's prominence. Much of its strength was attributable to the role of centralized planning and support by a special governmental ministry—considered by many to be an unfair competitive edge, compared to other countries. For instance, the United States was considered to have no counterpart support structures. Gregory Hooks's (1990) excellent case study points to a counterpart frequently ignored by advocates: the role of the U.S. defense department in implementing an industrial planning policy within defense-related industries.

Hooks (1990) provides quantitative data on two cases—the aeronautics industry and the microelectronics industry (the forerunner to the entire computer chip market and its technologies, such as the personal computer). One industry (aeronautics) has traditionally been known to be dependent upon support from the federal government, but the other has not. In both cases, Hooks's evidence shows how the defense department supported the critical early development of these industries through financial support, the support of R&D, and the creation of an initial customer base for the industry's products—thereby showing that the U.S. had a competitive edge like that of Japan. The existence of both cases, and not the aeronautics industry alone, makes the author's entire argument powerful and persuasive.

Cross-case syntheses can be performed whether the individual case studies have previously been conducted as independent research studies (authored by different persons) or as a predesigned part of the same study. In either situation, the technique treats each individual case study as a separate study. In this way, the technique does not differ from other research syntheses—aggregating findings across a series of individual studies (see BOX 36). If there are large numbers of individual case studies available, the synthesis can incorporate quantitative techniques common to other research syntheses (e.g., Cooper & Hedges, 1994) or meta-analyses (e.g., Lipsey, 1992). In addition, Tutorial 5-3 discusses two techniques developed specifically for case studies with large numbers of cases. However, if only a modest number of case studies are available, alternative tactics are needed.

BOX 36
Eleven Program Evaluations and a Cross-Case Analysis

Dennis Rosenbaum (1986) collected 11 program evaluations as separate chapters in an edited book. The 11 evaluations had been conducted by different investigators, had used a variety of methods, and were not case studies. Each evaluation was about a different community crime prevention intervention, and some presented ample quantitative evidence and employed statistical analyses. The evaluations were deliberately selected because nearly all had shown positive results. A cross-case analysis was conducted by the present author (Yin, 1986), treating each evaluation as if it were a separate "case." The analysis dissected and arrayed the evidence from the 11 evaluations in the form of word tables. Generalizations about successful community crime prevention, independent of any specific intervention, were then derived by using a replication logic, given that all of the evaluations had shown positive results.

One possibility starts with the creation of word tables that display the data from the individual cases according to one or more uniform categories. Figure 5.7 has a simplified example of such a word table, capturing the findings from 14 organizational centers (COSMOS Corporation, 1998). Of the 14 centers, 7 had received programmatic support and were considered "intervention" centers; the other 7 were selected as "comparison" centers.

For each of the centers, the important category addressed the center's co-location arrangement (or sharing of facilities) with its partnering organization(s). Such co-location had been one of several outcomes of interest in the original study: The centers with programmatic support were hypothesized to undertake a shared co-location whereas the comparison centers had not been expected to show any co-location. The results in Figure 5.7 showed no strong differences between the two groups, so the programmatic support did not appear to have been associated with any impact on this outcome. Additional word tables, addressing how and why the 14 centers had (or had not) formed any co-locations, were examined in the same way. A qualitative analysis of the entire collection of word tables then enabled the study to draw cross-case conclusions about

Figure 5.7   Co-location of Interorganizational Partners (14 Centers and
Their Counterpart Organizations)

ORGANIZATION CENTERS (n = 14)	Characteristics of Co-location with Partnering Center
Intervention Centers (n = 7):	
1	Partnering staff are located in the same facility as Center 1 and follow Center 1's policies that were in place prior to the partnership. Center 1 receives $25,000 annually from the partnership budget for software and peripherals, and communication and supplies.
2	As a business unit of Center 2, the partnering staff are housed within Center 2's offices. Center 2's parent organization contributes $2,500 for space and $23,375 for indirect expenses annually to the partnership budget.
3	Five partnership offices are co-located with Center 3's staff.
4	Center 4 and its partner share office space.
5	Center 5 staff and the partnering staff are located in the same building, but do not share office space.
6	The two organizations are not co-located.
7	Partnering staff are located in Center 7's offices.
Comparison Centers (n = 7):	
8	Center 8 and its partner share office space in eight locations statewide.
9	Some sites are co-located.
10	Center 10 and its partner are not co-located.
11	The partnering and center staff share office space.
12	Center 12 and its partner's staff are located in the same building.
13	Center 13 and its partner's staff are located in the same office.
14	Center 14 shares office space with three regional partners.

SOURCE: COSMOS Corporation (1998).

the two groups of centers, and in particular why the centers with programmatic support failed to develop a shared co-location.

Your case study might not have started with any predefined groupings, such as the two groups of organizational centers. Moreover, you might have created more complex word tables, going beyond single categories, by arraying a whole set of categories or features, effectively profiling each case—still on a case-by-case basis. Such an array now permits your analysis to probe whether different cases appear to share similar profiles and deserve to be considered instances (replications) of the same "type" of general case. Alternatively, the profiles may be sufficiently different that the cases deserve to be considered as contrasting cases. A predicted similarity or contrast might have been part of the original design of the case study. If so, the findings based on the observed profiles will either confirm or disconfirm the original expectations and connect well to the prior research that had been reviewed in developing the original design.

The preceding example illustrates the conduct of a cross-case synthesis when a case study tries to explore whether the cases being studied had replicated or contrasted with each other. An important caveat in conducting this kind of cross-case synthesis is that the examination of word tables for cross-case patterns will rely strongly on argumentative interpretation, not numeric tallies. Chapter 2 has previously pointed out, however, that this method is directly analogous to cross-*experiment* interpretations, which also have no numeric properties when only a small number of experiments are available for synthesis. A challenge you must be prepared to meet in doing a case study is therefore to know how to develop strong, plausible, and fair arguments that are supported by the data.

Cross-case syntheses have at least one other variation: Unlike the preceding discussion, a case study may have been designed to extend to a higher level—that is, beyond the cross-case synthesis. In this situation, the main case study may be about a broader or larger case or unit of analysis, with the multiple case studies (and the cross-case synthesis) serving as embedded units. The findings and conclusions would then require separate data from the broader or larger unit of analysis that serves as the main case, in addition to cross-case data from the multiple case studies (still analyzed in the replicating pattern as previously discussed). The data from both levels (larger unit of analysis and the embedded cases) would feed into the final case study (see BOX 37).

BOX 37
Case Studies within a Case Study

In some multiple-case studies, a cross-case synthesis is only part of the picture. In an evaluation conducted by the United Nations (United Nations Development Programme, 2010), four countries—Botswana, Paraguay, Togo, and Saudi Arabia—were the topics of separate case studies. The aim was to evaluate how these countries had addressed their national development goals. However, these four case studies in fact served as embedded units of analyses, because the broader case study was about the role played by a single organization—the United Nations Development Programme (UNDP)—in providing development assistance to individual countries. Because of the dual-level inquiry, the final analysis therefore included data about the individual countries but also included separate, single-case data about the policies, practices, and staffing at the UNDP as the assisting organization. The final product was in reality a case study of UNDP, based (only) in part on a cross-case synthesis from the four countries.

The concluding section of this chapter offers some ideas for you to consider, regardless of whether you are doing a cross-case synthesis or following any of the other analytic techniques discussed in this chapter. These ideas may help to boost the quality of your entire case study analysis.

△   PRESSING FOR A HIGH-QUALITY ANALYSIS

No matter what specific analytic strategy or techniques have been chosen, you must do everything to make sure that your analysis is of the highest quality. At least four principles underlie all good social science research (Yin, 1994a, 1994b, 1997, 1999) and deserve your attention.

First, your analysis should show that you attended to *all the evidence.* Your analytic strategies, including the development of rival hypotheses, must exhaustively cover your key research questions (you can now appreciate better the importance of defining sharp as opposed to vague questions). Your analysis should show how it sought to use as much evidence as was available, and your interpretations should account for all this evidence and leave no loose ends. Without achieving this standard, your analysis may be vulnerable to alternative interpretations based on the evidence that you had (inadvertently) ignored.

Second, your analysis should address, if possible, *all plausible rival interpretations.* If someone else has an alternative interpretation for one or more of your findings, make this alternative into a rival. Is there evidence to address the rival? If so, what are the results? If not, should the rival be restated as a loose end to be investigated in future studies?

Third, your analysis should address *the most significant aspect* of your case study. Whether it is a single- or multiple-case study, you will have demonstrated your best analytic skills if the analysis focuses on the most important issue (whether defined at the outset of the case study or by working with your data from the "ground up"). By avoiding excessive detours to lesser issues, your analysis will be less vulnerable to the accusation that you diverted attention away from the main issue because of potentially contrary findings.

Fourth, you should use your own *prior, expert knowledge* in your case study. The strong preference here is for you to demonstrate awareness of current thinking and discourse about the case study topic. If you know your subject matter as a result of your own previous research and publications, so much the better.

The case study in BOX 38 was done by a research team with academic credentials as well as strong and relevant practical experience. In their work, the authors demonstrate a care of empirical investigation whose spirit is worth considering in all case studies. The care is reflected in the presentation of the cases themselves, not by the existence of a stringent methodology section whose tenets might not have been fully followed in the actual case study. If you can emulate the spirit of these authors, your case study analysis also will receive appropriate respect and recognition.

BOX 38
Analytic Quality in a Multiple-Case Study
of International Trade Competition

The quality of a case study analysis is not dependent solely on the techniques used, although they are important. Equally important is that the investigator demonstrate expertise in carrying out the analysis. This expertise was reflected in Magaziner and Patinkin's (1989) book, *The Silent War: Inside the Global Business Battles Shaping America's Future.*

The authors organized their nine cases in excellent fashion. Across cases, major themes regarding America's competitive advantages (and disadvantages) were covered in a replication design. Within each case, the authors provided extensive interview and other documentation, showing the sources of their findings. (To keep the narrative reading smoothly, much of the data—in word tables, footnotes, and quantitative tabulations—were relegated to footnotes and appendices.) In addition, the authors showed that they had extensive personal exposure to the issues being studied, as a result of numerous domestic and overseas visits.

Technically, a more explicit methodological section might have been helpful. However, the careful and detailed work, even in the absence of such a section, helps to illustrate what all investigators should strive to achieve (also see BOX 5, Chapter 2, p. 30).

Exercise 5.5   Analyzing the Analytic Process

Select and obtain one of the case studies described in the BOXES in this book. Find one of the case study's chapters (usually in the middle of the study) in which evidence is presented, but conclusions also are being made. Describe how this linkage—from cited evidence to conclusions—occurs. Are data displayed in tables or other formats? Are comparisons being made?

SUMMARY △

This chapter has presented several ways of analyzing case studies. First, the potential analytic difficulties can be reduced if you have a general strategy for analyzing the data— whether such a strategy is based on theoretical propositions, working with your data from the ground up, using descriptive frameworks, or checking on rival explanations. In the absence of such strategies, you may have to "play with the data" in a preliminary sense, as a prelude to developing a systematic sense of what is worth analyzing and how it should be analyzed.

Second, given a general strategy, several specific analytic techniques are relevant. Of these, five (pattern matching, explanation building, time-series analysis, logic models, and cross-case syntheses) can be effective in laying the groundwork for high-quality case studies. For all five, a similar replication logic should be applied if a study involves multiple cases. Attending to rival propositions and threats to internal validity also should be made within each individual case.

None of these techniques is easy to use. None can be applied mechanically, following any simple cookbook procedure. Not surprisingly, case study analysis is the most difficult stage of doing case studies, and novice researchers are likely to have a troublesome experience. Again, one recommendation is to begin with a simple and straightforward case study (or, more preferably, a "two-case" design), even if the research questions are not as sophisticated or innovative as might be desired. Experience gained in completing such straightforward case studies will lead to the ability to tackle more difficult topics in subsequent case studies.

△ NOTE TO CHAPTER 5

1. The lack of attention to the transitions has possibly arisen because of the graphic confusion between a logic model and a flowchart. In a flowchart, the lines merely indicate that one box is followed by another. In a logic model, the lines presuppose a trigerring relationship—that one box *produces* the next one. How the trigerring occurs is then the transition requiring an explanation when using logic models.

Tutorial 5.1:
More on Using CAQDAS Software to Analyze Case Study Data

Chapter 5 already should have provided sufficient support but also forewarning about using CAQ-DAS tools. If you plan to use these tools, distinguishing among three CAQDAS functions can be helpful (Yin, 2011): (1) *compiling data* (retrieving and tallying specific words and terms from your notes); (2) *disassembling data* (moving methodically to a higher conceptual level by assigning codes to like words and terms); and (3) *reassembling data* (interpreting the relationships among codes, their combinations, and conceptually higher patterns). Regarding the three functions, different tools have different strengths. However, beware that, although most tools can help you to compile and to disassemble your data (e.g., Saldaña, 2009), you are likely to have to closely direct the tools in reassembling the data. Also be aware that the final result may not justify the extensive time and effort you spend in compiling or disassembling the data.

To preview possible problems, you might take a portion of your data and practice the three functions manually, before using any software tool. If you then decide to use a CAQDAS tool (especially if you have a lot of data), closely consult a comprehensive guide (e.g., Hahn, 2008; Lewins & Silver, 2007) that can help you to select a specific software tool and use it efficiently. Then check specialized guidances covering the more popularly used tools (e.g., Friese, 2012).

Possibly inflated expectations about CAQDAS tools come as a result of everyone's experiences with computer-assisted *quantitative* analysis. In those situations, computer routines follow complex and pre-established statistical algorithms, with the analyst providing a set of input data and the computer arriving at the output, or result. In contrast, with CAQDAS tools, you must define the complex algorithms yourself, including the level of granularity (e.g., whether to code single words, utterances, sentences, or paragraphs), the combinations worthy of attention, and the analytic routine for compiling the final results (Fielding & Warnes, 2009, p. 278). Without your explicit guidance, and contrary to the experience with quantitative analysis, the computer alone cannot arrive at any usable output.

Briefly Annotated References for Tutorial 5.1

Fielding, N., & Warnes, R. (2009). Computer-based qualitative methods in case study research. In D. Byrne & C. C. Ragin (Eds.), *The Sage handbook of case-based methods* (pp. 270–288). London: Sage. Provides a conceptual overview—but not specific steps as in the following three works—on how CAQDAS tools and functions apply to case study data.

Friese, S. (2012). *Qualitative data analysis with ATLAS.ti*. London: Sage. Covers *ATLAS.ti*.

(Continued)

(Tutorial 5.1, Continued)

Hahn, C. (2008). *Doing qualitative research using your computer: A practical guide.* Thousand Oaks, CA: Sage. Gives step-by-step guidance for using three common tools: *Word, Excel,* and *Access.*

Lewins, A., & Silver, C. (2007). *Using software in qualitative research: A step-by-step guide.* London: Sage. Discusses three leading CAQDAS packages individually: *ATLAS.ti5, MAXqda2,* and *NVivo7.*

Saldaña, J. (2009). *The coding manual for qualitative researchers.* London: Sage. Presents a wide array of coding choices and practices.

Yin, R. K. (2011). *Qualitative research from start to finish.* New York: Guilford. Gives operational guidance for compiling, disassembling, and reassembling qualitative data.

Tutorial 5.2:
Depicting a Nonlinear Logic Model

The logic models in Chapter 5 all depict linear sequences of events. However, real-world events vacillate and intertwine in a more complex manner. The linear logic model may still have merit, because a sequence can be linear in the long run, smoothing over any short-term vacillations. However, Figure 5-A might help if you want to depict the nonlinear complexity explicitly (Yin & Davis, 2006, 2007).

The figure has four panels, each with a title at the top and a time interval, *t1* to *t4,* in the lower right-hand corner. In each panel, the group of concentric circles represents an organization whose reform status fluctuates vertically from panel to panel. Thus, at *t1,* the circles are at their lowest, representing an organization at its lowest reform status, whereas *t3* shows the organization at its highest status. The flexibility along the vertical dimension permits the reform status to be represented nonlinearly, so for illustrative purposes, a regressive reform status is shown at *t4.* In this manner, the progressive and regressive shifts can be depicted over any amount of time and even shown in motion, graphically.

In this example, the organization is a school system. The various elements within the school system appear as lettered objects within each group of concentric circles (the lettered objects are decoded in the "key" at the bottom of Figure 5-A). The theory of education reform posits that system reform will advance as the elements become aligned (depicted by their shifting from the periphery to the center of the concentric circles over time). The vertical scale is student performance, with the theory claiming greater reform to be associated with improved student performance. As a result, the theory also stipulates that the desired reform needs to affect an increasing number of units within the organization, in this case the schools (represented by the flags) within the school system.

A similar nonlinear logic model can represent a business or any other organization undergoing coordinated operational changes aimed at transforming the organization and its culture—and in business, even its name (see Yin, 2012, chaps. 9 and 12 for a case study of a single firm and then the cross-case analysis of a group of transformed firms).

Figure 5.A Hypothetical States of an Education K–12 Reforming System

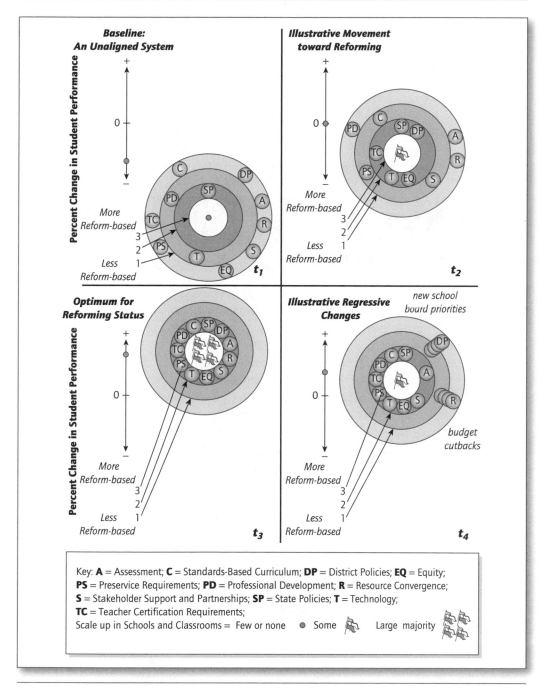

Key: **A** = Assessment; **C** = Standards-Based Curriculum; **DP** = District Policies; **EQ** = Equity; **PS** = Preservice Requirements; **PD** = Professional Development; **R** = Resource Convergence; **S** = Stakeholder Support and Partnerships; **SP** = State Policies; **T** = Technology; **TC** = Teacher Certification Requirements;

Scale up in Schools and Classrooms = Few or none ● Some 🚩 Large majority 🚩🚩🚩

SOURCE: Yin and Davis (2007).

(Continued)

(Tutorial 5.2, Continued)

Briefly Annotated References for Tutorial 5.2

Yin, R. K. (2012). *Applications of case study research* (3rd ed.). Thousand Oaks, CA: Sage. Contains case studies on comprehensive transformation within business firms.

Yin, R. K., & Davis, D. (2006). State-level education reform: Putting all the pieces together. In K. Wong & S. Rutledge (Eds.), *Systemwide efforts to improve student achievement* (pp. 1–33). Greenwich, CT: Information Age Publishing. Describes comprehensive education reform.

Yin, R. K., & Davis, D. (2007). Adding new dimensions to case study evaluations: The case of evaluating comprehensive reforms. In G. Julnes & D. J. Rog (Eds.), *Informing federal policies for evaluation methodology* (New Directions in Program Evaluation, No. 113, pp. 75–93). San Francisco: Jossey-Bass. Discusses the education issues related to the illustrative nonlinear logic model.

Tutorial 5.3:
When a Case Study Has Many Cases

Most case studies will only have a few or even a single case. However, having a case study with many cases—for example, 15 to 20 or more—makes additional analytic strategies possible, other than those already highlighted in Chapter 5. Should you have such a large number of cases, you may consider at least two analytic strategies.

The first is to decompose each case into a set of common variables. Unlike a regression or other multivariate statistical analysis, in which the data are grouped by variable (and therefore across cases), the desired array preserves the integrity of each case and its potentially unique combination of variables—including important ones that were not necessarily part of the common set of variables. Only then can such within-case patterns be tracked across the set of cases, as in Charles Ragin's "qualitative comparative analysis" (QCA) technique (Ragin, 1987; Rihoux & Lobe, 2009). Each case's combination of variables can be tallied, creating a quantitative cross-case analysis. At the same time, you need to proceed with caution: The unique aspects of each case also need to be taken into account through some qualitative (e.g., replication) analysis that will complement any quantitative tallies and that may lead to caveats about them. Using the replication logic, each case could sequentially build support for the appropriate theoretical proposition (e.g., Small, 2009).

The second strategy assumes an even larger number of cases—usually more than 100 case studies that may have been previously conducted by different researchers (e.g., Wolf, 1997; Yin & Yates, 1975). The analytic method reverts to a strictly quantitative approach—a "survey" of the case studies (e.g., Yin, Bingham, & Heald, 1976; Yin & Heald, 1975). Such a survey requires you to develop and use a formal questionnaire in which you query each case study to produce coded, closed-ended responses. In this "case survey" method, you would then analyze the coded data as you would any other survey database.

Briefly Annotated References for Tutorial 5.3

Ragin, C. C. (1987). *The comparative method: Moving beyond qualitative and quantitative strategies.* Berkeley: University of California Press. Describes qualitative comparative analysis (QCA) as a new method.

Rihoux, B., & Lobe, B. (2009). The case for qualitative comparative analysis (QCA): Adding leverage for thick cross-case comparison. In D. Byrne & C. C. Ragin (Eds.), *The Sage handbook of case-based methods* (pp. 222–242). London: Sage. Describes and explains QCA procedures.

Small, M. L. (2009). "How many cases do I need?" On science and the logic of case selection in field-based research. *Ethnography, 10,* 5–38. Poses a thoughtful article on key issues in designing field-based research, including the challenge of generalizing from field situations.

Wolf, P. (1997). Why must we reinvent the federal government? Putting historical developmental claims to the test. *Journal of Public Administration Research and Theory, 3,* 358–388. Analyzes 170 case studies of federal agencies.

Yin, R. K., Bingham, E., & Heald, K. (1976). The difference that quality makes. *Sociological Methods and Research, 5,* 139–156. Examines 140 case studies of technological innovation in local services, highlighting the differences between high- and low-quality case studies.

Yin, R. K., & Heald, K. (1975). Using the case survey method to analyze policy studies. *Administrative Science Quarterly, 20,* 371–381. Describes the techniques used in the case survey method.

Yin, R. K., & Yates, D. T. (1975). *Street-level governments: Assessing decentralization and urban services.* Lexington, MA: Lexington Books. Analyzes 269 case studies of neighborhood services.

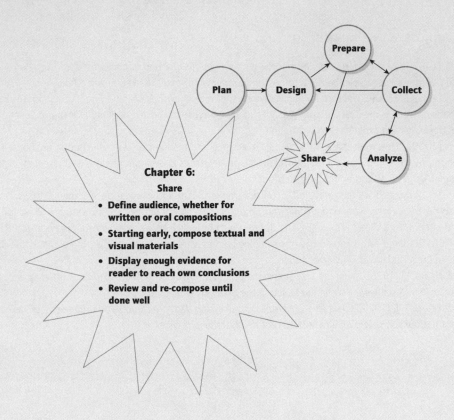

Chapter 6:

Share

- Define audience, whether for written or oral compositions
- Starting early, compose textual and visual materials
- Display enough evidence for reader to reach own conclusions
- Review and re-compose until done well

ABSTRACT

Sharing the conclusions from a case study, whether in writing or orally, means bringing its results and findings to closure. Regardless of the form of the report, similar steps underlie the sharing process, including identifying the audience for the report, defining its compositional format, and having drafts reviewed by others. However, going beyond the typical procedural reminders that you can find in other guidances about report writing, this chapter also discusses the specific choices that you might face in creating your case study.

For instance, six alternative compositional structures specific to case studies are suggested: linear-analytic, comparative, chronological, theory-building, "suspense," and unsequenced structures. Also described are the portions of your report devoted to methodology and reviewing the literature.

The final case study may appear independently or as part of a larger, mixed methods study. In either situation, creating a case study report is one of the most rewarding aspects of doing case studies. The best general advice is to start drafting preliminary portions of your case study early (four possibilities are identified), rather than waiting until the end of the data analysis process. A case study report also presents a choice regarding the disclosure or anonymity of case identities. A final set of suggestions tries to define what might make your case study exemplary, and not just run-of-the-mill.

6

REPORTING CASE STUDIES

How and What to Compose

Having a Flair

As a general rule, the reporting phase makes great demands on a case study researcher. A case study does not follow any stereotypic form, such as a journal article in psychology. Because of this uncertain nature, researchers who do not like to compose may want to question their interest in doing case studies in the first place. Most of the notable case study scholars have been ones who liked to compose and also actually had a flair for writing or for presenting results orally. Do you?

Of course, most researchers can eventually learn to compose easily and well, and inexperience in composing should not be a deterrent to doing case studies. However, much practice will be needed. Furthermore, to do good case studies, you should want to become good at composing—and not merely to put up with it. One indicator of success at this phase of the craft is whether you found term papers easy or difficult to do in high school or college. The more difficult they were, the more difficult it will be to compose a case study. Another indicator is whether composing is viewed as an opportunity or as a burden. The successful researcher usually perceives the compositional phase as an opportunity—to make a significant contribution to knowledge or practice and to share this contribution with others.

What "Composing" Covers

This chapter is about "composing," not just writing, because a case study report can include textual and nontextual forms. The most obvious nontextual forms would be tables, figures, charts, drawings, and other graphics. You may create a slide show, for instance, to communicate an entire case study (e.g., Naumes & Naumes, 1999, chap. 10). Other case studies might have an audiovisual component—though you will be taking a great risk if you try to report your first case study on the same occasion as your first audiovisual product.

Preceding the compositional activity is a cognitive one: *thinking*. Without some specific ideas in your head, you will have difficulty composing. Such a mundane observation nevertheless comes with a useful insight: When you know you have nothing much going on cognitively, if you try at that moment to start composing (e.g., to meet some external deadline), you may experience great frustration. In actuality, you need to get your mind going first. One way is to read a key research study directly related to your case study. Another is to review your notes. Hopefully, as a practiced scholar, you probably know other ways that will best get your ideas rolling before you can expect to do any composing.

A further comment about composing case study reports: Although this chapter will encourage you to compose creatively and with some flair, you should not think or talk about composing case studies as if you were writing a novel. Any reference to "storytelling," "dramatizing," or other features of good fiction—however couched—may lead readers to question the soundness if not validity of your research and interpretations. Instead, think about *nonfiction* writing as the counterpart craft. There are many works on creative and effective nonfiction writing (e.g., Caulley, 2008), and you can check that literature for additional guidance about composing.

Similarly, you should feel comfortable consulting other textbooks that cover the composing of research reports in the social sciences more generally (e.g., Barzun &

> **Tip: *What's the best way of getting my case study finished, with the least trouble and time?***
>
> Every researcher differs, so you have to develop your own style and preferences. Improvement occurs with each case study you produce. Thus, don't be surprised if your first one is more difficult. One possible strategy is to think about composing "inside-out" and "backwards." *Inside-out:* Start creating your final product (written or oral) with a table, exhibit, vignette, or quotation to be cited in the text of your case study (but don't try to write the accompanying text yet). In the same manner, now amass all of the tables, exhibits, vignettes, or quotations for your entire case study, arraying them in the sequence that they might appear in the final text. *Backwards:* Now start by composing the narrative for the final portion of the case study before the rest, then compose the analytic narrative that led to the final portion, and so on.
>
> If you successfully follow the preceding suggestions, would you be finished, or would you have but a first draft that now needs to be recomposed so that it blends better?

Graff, 1985; Becker, 1986; Wolcott, 2009). Such texts offer invaluable reminders about taking notes, making outlines, using plain words, writing clear sentences, establishing a schedule for composing, and combating the common urge not to compose. Hopefully, these all will help you to improve your composing and to avoid "writer's cramps."

As a final comment, the purpose of this chapter is not to repeat these general lessons. They are applicable to all forms of research compositions, including case studies. However, the general works all tend to emphasize "when" and "where" to compose most comfortably. The works tend not to provide concrete ideas about "what" you might consider composing, as well as other issues that might arise, when specifically producing a case study report. To fill this void, the present chapter consists of the following sections:

- audiences for case study reports;
- varieties of case study compositions;
- procedures for composing a case study report; and, in conclusion,
- speculations on the characteristics of an exemplary case study (extending beyond the report itself and covering the design and content of the case).

One reminder from Chapter 4 is that the case study report should not be the main way of recording or storing the evidentiary base of your case study. Rather, Chapter 4 advocated the use of a case study database for this purpose (see Chapter 4, Principle 2), and the compositional efforts described in this chapter are primarily intended to serve reporting, not documentation, objectives.

Exercise 6.1   Reducing the Barriers to Composition

Everyone has difficulties in composing reports, whether case studies or not. To succeed at composing, researchers must take specific steps during the conduct of a study to reduce barriers to composition. Name five such steps that you would take—such as starting on a portion of the composition at an early stage. Have you followed any of these five steps in the past?

AUDIENCES FOR CASE STUDY REPORTS △

Potential Audiences

Giving some initial thought to your likely or preferred audience and reporting formats serves as a good starting point for composing your case study. Sharing a case study and its findings can involve a more diverse set of potential audiences than most other types of research. The potential case study audiences include (1) academic colleagues; (2) policy makers, practitioners, community leaders, and other professionals who do not specialize in case study or other social science research; (3) special groups such as a dissertation or thesis committee; and (4) funders of research.[1]

In sharing the results of research based on other methods, such as experiments, the second audience is not typically relevant, as few would expect the findings from a laboratory experiment to be directed at nonspecialists. However, for case studies, this second audience may be a frequent target of a case study report. Similarly, the third audience also is a frequent consumer of the case study report, due to the large number of theses and dissertations in the social sciences that rely on case studies.

Because case studies have more potential audiences than other types of research, one of your essential tasks in designing the overall case study report is to identify the specific audience for the report. Each audience has different needs, and no single report will serve all audiences simultaneously.

As examples, for *academic colleagues,* the relationships among the case study, its findings, and previous theory or research are likely to be most important (see BOX 39). For *nonspecialists,* the descriptive elements in portraying some real-world situation, as well as the implications for action, are likely to be more important. For a *thesis committee,* mastery of the methodology and theoretical issues, along with an indication of the care with which the research was conducted, is important. Finally, for *research funders,* the significance of the case study findings, whether cast in academic or practical terms, is probably more important than how you describe your research methods. Successful communication with more than one audience may mean the need for more than one version of a case study report. Researchers have and can consider catering to such a need (see BOX 40).

BOX 39
Famous Case Study Reprinted

For many years, Philip Selznick's *TVA and the Grass Roots* (1949/1980) has stood as a classic about public organizations. The case has been cited in many subsequent studies of federal agencies, political behavior, and organizational decentralization.

Fully 30 years after its original publication, this case was reprinted in 1980 as part of the Library Reprint Series by the University of California Press, the original publisher. This type of reissuance allowed numerous other researchers to have access to this famous case study and reflected its substantial contribution to the field.

BOX 40
Two Versions of the Same Case Study

The city planning office of Broward County, Florida, implemented an office automation system beginning in 1982 ("The Politics of Automating a Planning Office," Standerfer & Rider, 1983). The implementation strategies were innovative and significant—especially in relation to tensions with the county government's computer department. As a result, the case study is interesting and informative, and a popularized version—appearing in a practitioner journal—is fun and easy to read.

Because this type of implementation also covers complex technical issues, the authors made supplementary information available to the interested reader. The popularized version provided a name, address, and telephone number, so that such a reader could obtain the additional information. This type of dual availability of case study reports is but one example of how different reports of the *same* case study may be useful for communicating with different audiences.

Exercise 6.2   Defining the Audience

Name the alternative audiences for a case study you might compose. For each audience, indicate the features of the case study report that you should highlight or de-emphasize. Would the same report serve all the audiences, and why?

Orienting a Case Study Report to an Audience's Needs

Overall, the preferences of the potential audience should dictate the form of your case study report. Although the research procedures and methodology should have followed other guidelines, suggested in Chapters 1 through 5, your final composition should reflect emphases, details, compositional forms, and even a length suitable to the needs of the potential audience. The importance of the audience suggests that you might want to collect formal information about what the audiences need and their preferred styles of information sharing (Morris, Fitz-Gibbon, & Freeman, 1987, p. 13). Along these lines, this author has frequently called the attention of thesis or dissertation students to the fact that the thesis or dissertation committee may be their *only* audience. The ultimate case study, under these conditions, should attempt to communicate directly with this committee. A recommended tactic is to integrate the committee members' previous research into the thesis or dissertation, creating greater conceptual (and methodological) overlap and thereby increasing the thesis or dissertation's potential communicability with that particular audience.

Whatever the audience, the greatest error you can make is to compose a case study from an egocentric perspective. This error will occur if you complete your case study without identifying a specific audience or without understanding the specific needs of such an audience. To avoid this error, you should identify the audience, as previously noted. A second and equally important suggestion is to examine other case studies that have successfully shared their findings with this audience. These other case studies may offer helpful clues for composing a new case study. For instance, consider again the thesis or dissertation student. The student should consult previous dissertations and theses that have passed the academic regimen successfully—or are known to have been exemplary works. The inspection of such works may yield insights regarding the departmental norms (and reviewers' likely preferences) for designing a new thesis or dissertation.

Communicating with Case Studies

One additional difference between the case study and other types of research is that your case study report can itself be a significant communication device. For many nonspecialists, exposure to a cogent and compelling single-case study can raise awareness, provide insight, or even suggest solutions to a given situation. Such a case study may be enhanced by simple but appealing nontextual materials, such as vignettes, pictures, and graphics. All this information can help others to understand a phenomenon when a dense or abstract array of statistics—no matter how compelling to a research audience—cannot do the trick.

A related situation, often overlooked, occurs with testimony before a legislative committee. If an elderly person, for instance, testifies about her or his health services before such a committee, its members may assume that they have acquired initial insights into health care for the elderly more generally—based on this "case." Only then might the members be willing to review broader statistics about the prevalence of similar cases. Later, the committee may inquire about the representative nature of the initial case, before proposing new legislation. However, throughout this entire process, the initial "case"—represented by a witness—may have been the essential stimulus that drew attention to the health care issue in the first place.

In these and other ways, your case study can communicate research-based information about a phenomenon to a variety of nonspecialists. The usefulness of a case study therefore can go far beyond the role of the typical research report, which is generally addressed to research colleagues rather than nonspecialists. Obviously, descriptive as well as explanatory case studies can be important in this role, and you should not overlook the potential descriptive impact of a well-presented case study (see BOX 41).

BOX 41
Using a Metaphor to Organize
Both Theory and Presentation in Another Field

Whether four "countries"—the American colonies, Russia, England, and France—all underwent similar courses of events during their major political revolutions is the topic of Crane Brinton's (1938) famous historical study, *The Anatomy of a Revolution.* Tracing and analyzing these events is done in a descriptive manner, as the author's purpose is not so much to explain the revolutions as to determine whether they followed similar courses (also see BOX 44B, later in this chapter).

The "cross-case" analysis reveals major similarities: All societies were on the upgrade, economically; there were bitter class antagonisms; the intellectuals deserted their governments; government machinery was inefficient; and the ruling class exhibited immoral, dissolute, or inept behavior (or all three). However, rather than relying solely on this "factors" approach to description, the author also develops the metaphor of a human body suffering from a fever as a way of describing the pattern of events over time. The author adeptly uses the cyclic pattern of fever and chills, rising to a critical point and followed by a false tranquility, to describe the ebb and flow of events in the four revolutions.

VARIETIES OF CASE STUDY COMPOSITIONS △

Case study reports can embrace many compositional forms. Some of these forms may resemble those used in reports based on other research methods. However, when you are composing a case study, you will encounter a useful array of choices specifically related to case studies, falling under the categories covered in the remainder of this section: (1) reporting formats; (2) illustrative overall structures for case study compositions; (3) the methods and research literature portions of a case study report; and (4) case studies as part of larger, mixed methods studies.

Reporting Formats

Case study reporting formats fall into four categories.

Single-case study. The first is the classic single-case study. A single text is used to describe and analyze the case. You may augment the text with tables as well as with charts, graphics, pictures, and maps. Depending upon the depth of the case study, these classic single-case studies sometimes may expand to the length of a book, seemingly limiting your publishing options. At the same time, many academic journals, including the best discipline-based ones, do now publish articles of sufficient length to accommodate well-conceived case studies. You should check the journals in your field before assuming that your case study can only be published in book form.

Recall, too, that a single-case study could have followed an embedded design (see Chapter 2, Figure 2.4). Following this design, you may have collected data about an embedded unit of analysis by using other methods (e.g., surveys or quantitative analyses of archival data such as health status indicators). In this situation, your completed case study report would incorporate the reporting of the data from these other methods (e.g., see Chapter 4, BOX 19, p. 112).

Multiple-case study. A second reporting format is the multiple-case version of the classic single-case study. Your full multiple-case report will consist of the single cases, usually presented as separate chapters or sections. In addition to these individual cases, your full report will contain an additional chapter or section covering the cross-case analysis and results. As another common variant, the cross-case material can form the bulk of the main report (especially suitable for a journal-length article), with the individual cases presented as a set of appendices (or made separately available by you if related to a journal-length article). In a more expansive format, a multiple-case study report may call for several cross-case chapters or sections, creating a sufficiently large cross-case portion to justify an entire volume, separate from a second volume that then has the individual cases (see BOX 42).

BOX 42
A Multiple-Case Report

Multiple-case studies often contain both the individual case studies and some cross-case chapters. The composing of such a multiple-case study also may be shared among several authors.

This type of arrangement was used in a study of eight innovations in mathematics and science education, edited by Raizen and Britton (1997). The study, titled *Bold Ventures,* appears in three separate and lengthy volumes (about 250, 350, and 650 pages, respectively). The individual case studies appear in the last two volumes, while the seven chapters in Volume 1 all cover cross-case issues. Many different and multiple authors conducted both the individual case studies and the cross-case chapters, although the entire study was orchestrated and coordinated as a single undertaking.

Option for either a single- or multiple-case study. A third reporting format covers either a single or multiple case but does not use the conventional text. Instead, the composition for each case follows a series of questions and answers, based on the questions and answers in your case study database (see Chapter 4). For reporting purposes, you would shorten the content of the original database and now edit it for readability, with the final product still assuming the format, analogously, of a comprehensive examination. (In contrast, the conventional case study text may be considered similar to the format of a term paper.) The question-and-answer format may not reflect your full creative talent, but the format helps to reduce the problems of writer's cramps. This is because you can proceed immediately to answer the required set of questions. (Again, the comprehensive exam has a similar advantage over a term paper.)

If you use this question-and-answer format to report a multiple-case study, repeating the same set of questions in covering each individual case study, the advantages are potentially enormous: Your reader(s) need only examine the answers to the same question or questions within each case study to begin making her or his own cross-case comparisons. Because each reader may be interested in different questions, the entire format facilitates the development of a cross-case analysis tailored to the specific interest of each reader (see BOX 43). Yin (2012, chap. 6) contains a complete case study demonstrating this format.

BOX 43
A Question-and-Answer Format:
Case Studies without the Traditional Narrative

Case study evidence does not need to be presented in the traditional narrative form. An alternative format for presenting the same evidence is to write the narrative in question-and-answer form. A series of questions can be posed, with the answers taking some reasonable space—for example, three or four paragraphs each. Each answer can contain all the relevant evidence and can even be augmented with tabular presentations and citations.

This alternative was followed in 40 case studies of community organizations produced by the U.S. National Commission on Neighborhoods (1979), *People, Building Neighborhoods.* The same question-and-answer format was used in each case, so that the interested reader could do her or his own cross-case analysis by following the same question across all of the cases. The format allowed hurried readers to find exactly the relevant portions of each case. For people offended by the absence of the traditional narrative, each case also called for a summary, unconstrained in its form (but not longer than several pages), allowing the author to exercise her or his more literary talents.

Option for multiple-case study only. The fourth and last format applies to multiple-case studies only. In this situation, there may be *no* separate chapters or sections devoted to the individual cases. Rather, your entire report may consist of the cross-case analysis, whether purely descriptive or also covering explanatory topics. In such a report, each chapter or section would be devoted to a separate cross-case issue, and the information from the individual cases would be dispersed throughout each chapter or section. With this format, summary information about the individual cases, if not ignored altogether (see BOX 44 as well as Chapter 1, BOX 3B), might be presented in abbreviated vignettes. Especially for oral versions of your multiple-case study, such vignettes, embedded in the main presentation covering the cross-case issues, work well.

BOX 44
Writing a Multiple-Case Report

In a multiple-case study, the individual case studies need not always be presented in the final manuscript. The individual cases, in a sense, serve only as the evidentiary base for the study and may be cited sporadically in the cross-case analysis (also see BOX 3B, Chapter 1).

44A. An Example in Which No Single Cases Are Presented

This approach was used in a book about six federal bureau chiefs, by Herbert Kaufman (1981), *The Administrative Behavior of Federal Bureau Chiefs.* Kaufman spent intensive periods of time with each chief to understand his day-to-day routine. He interviewed the chiefs, listened in on their phone calls, attended meetings, and was present during staff discussions in the chiefs' offices.

The book's purpose, however, was not to portray any single one of these chiefs. Rather, the book synthesizes the lessons from all of them and is organized around such topics as how chiefs make decisions, how they receive and review information, and how they motivate their staffs. Under each topic, Kaufman draws appropriate examples from the six cases, but none of the six is presented as a single-case study.

44B. Another Example (from Another Field) in Which No Single Cases Are Presented

A design similar to Kaufman's is used in another field—history—in a famous book by Crane Brinton (1938), *The Anatomy of a Revolution.* Brinton's book is based on four revolutions: the English, American, French, and Russian revolutions (also see BOX 41, earlier in this chapter). The book is an analysis and theory of revolutionary periods, with pertinent examples drawn from each of the four "cases"; however, as in Kaufman's book, there is no attempt to present the single revolutions as individual cases.

As a final note, the specific type of case study composition, involving a choice among at least these four alternatives, should be identified during the *design* of the case study. Your initial choice always can be altered, as unexpected conditions may arise, and a different type of format may become more relevant than the one originally selected. However, early selection will facilitate both the design and the conduct of the case study. Such an initial selection should be part of the case study protocol, alerting you to the likely nature of the final format and its requirements.

Illustrative Overall Structures for Case Study Compositions

Within a single report, the chapters, sections, subtopics, and other components must be organized in some way, and this constitutes your case study report's compositional structure. Attending to such structure has been a topic of attention with other methodologies. For instance, Kidder and Judd (1986, pp. 430–431) write of the "hourglass" shape of a report for quantitative studies. In ethnography, John Van Maanen (1988) has identified a variety of ways of reporting fieldwork results, which he defines as covering realist, confessional, impressionist, critical, formal, literary, and jointly told perspectives. These different types may be used in different combinations in the same report.

Alternatives also exist for structuring case study reports. This section suggests six illustrative structures (see Figure 6.1). The illustrations are described mainly in relation to the composition of a single-case study, although the principles are readily transferable to multiple-case reports. As a further note and as indicated in Figure 6.1, the first three are all applicable to descriptive, exploratory, and explanatory case studies. The fourth is applicable mainly to exploratory and explanatory case studies, the fifth to explanatory cases, and the sixth to descriptive cases.

Figure 6.1 Six Structures and Their Application to Different Purposes of Case Studies

TYPE OF COMPOSITIONAL STRUCTURE	Purpose of Case Study		
	Explanatory	Descriptive	Exploratory
1. **LINEAR-ANALYTIC**	X	X	X
2. **COMPARATIVE**	X	X	X
3. **CHRONOLOGICAL**	X	X	X
4. **THEORY-BUILDING**	X		X
5. **"SUSPENSE"**	X		
6. **UNSEQUENCED**		X	

Linear-analytic structures. This is a standard approach for composing research reports. The sequence of subtopics starts with the issue or problem being studied and a review of the relevant prior literature. The subtopics then proceed to cover the methods used, the data collected, and the data analysis and findings, ending with the conclusions and their implications for the original issue or problem that had been studied.

Most journal articles in experimental science reflect this type of structure, as do many case studies. The structure is comfortable to most researchers and probably is the most advantageous when research colleagues or a thesis or dissertation committee comprise the main audience for a case study. Note that the structure is applicable to explanatory, descriptive, or exploratory case studies. For example, an exploratory case may cover the issue or problem being explored, the methods of exploration, the findings from the exploration, and the conclusions (for further research).

Comparative structures. A comparative structure repeats the same case study material two or more times, comparing alternative descriptions or explanations of the same case. As a distinctive advantage, this structure can apply equally well to case studies based on either realist or relativist inquiries.

Graham Allison's (1971) famous case study on the Cuban missile crisis (see Chapter 1, BOX 1) illustrates a realist application. In this book, the author repeats the single set of "facts" of the crisis three times. However, each repetition takes place in relation to a different conceptual model. The purpose of each repetition is to show the degree to which the same facts fit each model. The repetitions and their interpretations, appearing in three separate chapters of the book, actually illustrate a pattern-matching technique at work.

The relativist application arises when a case study repeats a similar set of episodes, but from the perspective of different participants, accommodating relativist or constructivist approaches and the presentation of multiple realities. A book by Frederick Wertz and his coauthors (Wertz et al., 2011) illustrates an analogous situation, whereby separate chapters are used to present five different interpretations of a single intensive interview. In the interview, a young woman describes an extremely unfortunate illness and how she survived it. Each interpretation subsequently and purposely illustrates a different way of analyzing the same interview data.

Note that both the realist and relativist case studies can be used whether a case study is serving a descriptive or explanatory purpose. For instance, the same case can be described repeatedly, from different points of view or with different models, to understand how the same case (i.e., reality) might be categorized in multiple ways—whether the aim is to converge on a single interpretation or not. The main feature is that the same case (or its interpretation) is repeated two or more times, in an explicitly comparative mode.

Chronological structures. Because case studies generally cover events over time, a third approach is to present the case study evidence in chronological order. Here, the sequence of chapters or sections might follow the early, middle, and late phases of a case. This approach can serve an important purpose in doing explanatory case studies because presumed causal sequences must occur linearly over time. If a presumed cause of an event occurs after the event has occurred, one would have reason to question the initial causal proposition.

Whether used for explanatory, descriptive, or exploratory case studies, a chronological approach has one pitfall to be avoided: giving disproportionate attention to the early events and insufficient attention to the later ones. Most commonly, a researcher will expend too much effort in composing the introduction to a case, including its early history and background, and leave insufficient time to write about the current status of the case. Yet, much of the interest in the case may be related to the more recent events. Thus, one recommendation when using a chronological structure is to *draft* the case study *backward*. Those chapters or sections that are about the current status of the case should be drafted first, and only after these drafts have been completed should the background to the case be drafted. Once all drafts have been completed, you can then return to the normal chronological sequence in refining the final version of the case study.

Theory-building structures. In this approach, the sequence of chapters or sections will follow some theory-building logic. The logic will depend on the specific topic and theory, but each chapter or section should reveal a new part of the theoretical argument being made. If structured well, the entire sequence and its unfolding of key ideas can produce a compelling and impressive case study.

The approach is relevant to both explanatory and exploratory case studies, both of which can be concerned with theory building. Explanatory cases will be examining the various facets of a causal argument; exploratory cases will be debating the value of further investigating various hypotheses or propositions.

Suspense structures. This structure inverts the linear-analytic structure described previously. The main outcome of a case study and its substantive significance is, paradoxically, presented in the initial chapter or section. The remainder of the case study—and its most suspenseful parts—are then devoted to the development of an explanation of the outcome, with alternative explanations considered in the ensuing chapters or sections.

This type of approach is relevant mainly to explanatory case studies, as a descriptive case study has no especially important outcome. When used well, the suspense approach is often an engaging compositional structure.

Unsequenced structures. An unsequenced structure is one in which the sequence of sections or chapters assumes no particular importance. This structure is often sufficient for descriptive case studies, as in the example of *Middletown* (Lynd & Lynd, 1929). Basically, one could change the order of that book's six chapters, as listed earlier in Chapter 5, and not alter its descriptive value.

Descriptive case studies of organizations often exhibit the same characteristic. Such case studies use separate chapters or sections to cover an organization's genesis and history, its ownership and employees, its product lines, its formal lines of organization, and its financial status. The particular order in which these chapters or sections is presented is not critical and may therefore be regarded as an unsequenced approach (see BOX 45 for another example).

BOX 45
Unsequenced Chapters, but in a Best-Selling Book

A best-selling book, appealing to both popular and academic audiences, was Peters and Waterman's (1982) *In Search of Excellence*. Although the book is based on more than 60 case studies of America's most successful large businesses, the text contains only the cross-case analysis, each chapter covering an insightful set of general characteristics associated with organizational excellence. However, the particular sequence of these chapters is alterable. The book would have made a significant contribution even if the chapters had been in some other order.

If an unsequenced structure is used, the researcher does need to attend to one other problem: a test of completeness. Thus, even though the order of the chapters or sections may not matter, their overall collection does. If certain key topics are left uncovered, the description may be regarded as incomplete. A researcher must know a topic well enough—or have related models of case studies to reference—to avoid such a shortcoming. If a case study fails to present a complete description, the researcher can be accused of having assembled a skewed version of the case—even though the case study was only descriptive.

Methods and Research Literature Portions of a Case Study Report

As part of the compositional structures just described, every case study report will cover at least two other topics, whether in a comprehensive or even informal manner: the methods used and the related research literature. You can consult other general works for relevant guidelines for covering these two topics, because case study reports do not usually demand any nonconventional styles or forms. However, case studies can raise a few additional issues, discussed next.[2]

Description of methods. Most outside readers will not have a detailed knowledge of the specific methods used in any given research study. However, and not uncommon in case study research, some readers also may not be familiar with case study methods *in general*. For this latter reason, the description of your methods may assume a more than routine function in convincing a reader about the quality of your methods. You therefore should make sure to use a thoughtful, balanced, and transparent tone: You would like readers to know what you did and that you conducted your case study with great care and methodological awareness, while minimizing pitfalls and aiming for high-quality results.

Your description can be long or short, depending upon your audience's preferences. For instance, as discussed earlier, some audiences may be more interested in your findings and not very interested in your methods. If so, you should still consider composing a more thorough methods section that can be offered as a side document. If well executed, the side document even can lead to an additional publication (see Tutorial 6-1).

Regardless of the length, the composition should cover several subtopics (see Figure 6.2). In them, you should make sure that key case study issues stand out, such as:

(a) a careful wording of your research questions, showing how they led logically to the need for conducting a case study rather than using some other method (see Item 2, Figure 6.2);

(b) the definition and selection of your cases (see Item 3);

(c) a data collection profile convincingly portraying the data as yielding up-close and in-depth information about the case (Item 5); and

(d) an explicit and clear analytic strategy (Item 6).

Figure 6.2 Outline for a Methodology Section in a Case Study Report

METHODOLOGICAL TOPIC	Illustrative Content
1. **OVERALL TONE**	• a thoughtful, balanced, and transparent tone; methodic but also attractively written
2. **RESEARCH QUESTIONS**	• should suit case study research: e.g., dominated by "how" and "why" questions
3. **DESIGN**	• definition of the case(s) and how selected; • the (logical) connection between the research question(s) and the data to be collected; • rivals that were considered

(Continued)

(Continued)

4. OVERVIEW OF REST OF METHODOLOGY SECTION	• a brief summary of the data collection and analysis methods (enables reader to avoid reading the rest of methodology section, if the reader so desires)
5. DATA COLLECTED	• emphasis on how the data provided an "up close" and "in depth" coverage of the case(s) • presentation of the case study protocol and how it was used • list of sources in order of importance; further detail about specific items within each source (e.g., numeric profile of interviewees in tabular form or an appended list of documents reviewed) • how the data were verified (e.g., triangulation methods) • unexpected difficulties that were encountered and how they might have affected the data collection
6. ANALYSIS METHODS	• description of the analytic approach: e.g., pattern-matching, explanation building, etc.; • identification of any CAQDAS software and how used
7. CAVEATS ABOUT STUDY	• inherent shortcomings in the design and analysis and how the shortcomings might have influenced the findings

You should set high standards in describing your methods, as if you were describing the most important part of your report rather than a routine and necessarily dull one. Readability, credibility, and concern with confirmability all matter. Strive to customize your description with exceptional features. For instance, if your case study report contains vignettes and anecdotes, most methods sections do not identify or describe the larger pool from which these were chosen (e.g., Bachor, 2002). In a similar vein, readers will especially appreciate your efforts to make their work easier, such as an overview allowing readers to skip many details if desired (see Item 4, Figure 6.2) and even a glossary of the acronyms, abbreviations, and any specialized terms (i.e., "jargon") appearing in your case study.

Coverage of research literature. Describing the relevant research literature has two purposes—to show your mastery over the topic of study and to use the literature to support the importance of your research questions and case study. Again, the length of your description will vary and may not attain the formal status of a literature review, depending upon your audience's circumstances.

Two suggestions should complement the guidance you might obtain if you check other sources about how to describe relevant research literatures. First, do not equate mastery with a lengthy literature review that wanders all over the place or that has a huge number of citations. Rather, do your best to identify the key citations and to treat them fairly. Second, in using the literature to support your case study work, do not hesitate to discuss previous research that might have used alternative methods. Show an appreciation for the other methods but also indicate how their findings might have left a void that only a good case study was likely to fill.

Case Studies as Part of Larger, Mixed Methods Studies

A totally new situation arises when your case study has been deliberately designed to be part of a larger, mixed methods study (Yin, 2006b). In this situation, *the larger study encompasses the case study.* The larger study will contain your completed case study but also should report separately the findings about the data from the other methods. The larger study's overall report would then be based on the pattern of evidence from both the case study and the other methods.

This mixed methods situation deserves a bit more attention so that you will understand its implications for your case study, even though you might not compose your case study report any differently than if it had been a "stand-alone" report. At least three different rationales might have motivated the larger study to use mixed methods.

First, the larger study may have called for mixed methods simply to determine whether converging evidence (triangulation) might be obtained when different methods had been used (Datta, 1997). In this scenario, your case study would have shared the same initial research questions as those driving the other methods, but you would likely have conducted, analyzed, and reported your case study independently. Part of the larger study's assessment would then be to compare the case study results with those based on the other methods.

Second, the larger study may have been based on a survey or quantitative analysis of archival data—for example, a study of households' financial situations under different income tax conditions. The larger study might then have wanted case studies to illustrate, in greater depth, the experiences of individual families. In this scenario, the questions for your case study might only have surfaced *after* the survey or archival data had been analyzed, and the selection of cases might come from the pool of those surveyed or contained within the archival records. The main implications for your case study effort are that both its timing and direction may depend on the progress and findings of the other inquiries.

Third, the larger study might knowingly have called for case studies to elucidate some underlying process and used another method (such as a survey) to define the prevalence or frequency of such processes. In this scenario of complementarity as opposed to convergence, the case study questions are likely to be closely coordinated with those of the other methods, and the complementary inquiries can occur simultaneously or sequentially. However, the initial analysis and reports from each inquiry should be conducted independently (even though the final analysis may merge findings from all the different methods). BOX 46 contains two examples of larger studies done under this third scenario.

BOX 46
Integrating Case Study and Survey Evidence:
Complementarity of Findings

Multimethod studies can pose complementary questions that are to be addressed by different methods. Most commonly, case studies are used to gain insight into explanatory processes, whereas surveys provide an indication of the prevalence of a phenomenon. Two studies illustrate this combination.

The first was a study of educational projects funded by the U.S. Department of Education (Berman & McLaughlin, 1974–1978). The study combined case studies of 29 projects with a survey of 293 projects, revealing invaluable information on the implementation process and its outcomes. The second study (Yin, 1981c) combined case studies of 19 sites with a survey of 90 other sites. The findings contributed to understanding the life cycle of technological innovations in local public services.

These three different situations show how your case study and its reporting may have to be coordinated within some broader context. Beware that when your case study is not independent, you may have to coordinate deadlines and technical directions, and your case study report may not proceed as you might have expected initially. Also assess carefully your willingness and ability to be part of a larger team before making any commitments.

△ PROCEDURES IN COMPOSING A CASE STUDY REPORT

Every researcher should have a well-developed set of procedures for composing an empirical report. Numerous texts, cited throughout this chapter, offer good advice on how you can develop your own customized procedures. One common warning is that writing means rewriting—a function not commonly practiced by students and therefore underestimated during the early years of research careers (Becker, 1986, pp. 43–47). The more rewriting, especially in response to others' comments, the better a report is likely to be. In this respect, the case study report is not much different from other research reports.

However, three important procedures pertain specifically to case studies and deserve further mention. The first deals with the specific tactics for starting a composition, the second covers the problem of whether to leave the case identities anonymous, and the third describes a review procedure for increasing the *construct validity* of a case study.

When and How to Start Composing

The first procedure is to start composing during the early stages of your case study. Developing such a practice will help you to compose any social science report but especially a case study. Because case study compositions do not follow any preset patterns, your freedom in customizing your composition—as in adopting any of the six structures discussed in the preceding section—correspondingly comes with a high risk of encountering writer's block. The general reminder that "you cannot begin writing too early" (Wolcott, 2009, p. 20) therefore has extra meaning when you are doing a case study.

Following such advice, your goal is to begin drafting certain portions of your report even before you have completed data collection, much less analysis. Although you may have to leave the portions incomplete until a later time, the drafting itself will serve as an important accomplishment, because you will have started to compose.

Let's take some examples of where and when you might start. For instance, your initial research activities will include reviewing the literature and designing your case study. After these activities, you already can start defining several portions of the case study report: the bibliography, methods, discussion of previous research, and initial case descriptions.

Your initial *bibliography* can be augmented later, with new references if necessary, but by and large the main set of references will have been covered in relation to your having reviewed the relevant research literature. This is therefore the time to formalize the references, to be sure that they are complete, and to construct a draft bibliography. If some references are incomplete, you can track them down while the rest of the case study proceeds. Such multitasking will avoid the usual practice among researchers who only attend to their bibliographies at the end of a case study and who therefore spend much clerical time at that final stage rather than doing the more important (and pleasurable!) tasks of writing, rewriting, and editing the substance of their reports.

Similarly, you can start describing your *methods* at this early stage because the anticipated procedures for data collection and possibly even analysis should have been part of your case study design. You won't be able to complete the description until after you have neared the end of your analysis, but by starting the draft, you will remember some of the design and data collection procedures with greater precision. One possibility, depending upon your experience with review and approval by your institutional review board (IRB—see Chapter 3), would be to start drafting the methods portion just after having received IRB approval. You will be surprised how well you will remember some of the methodological details, at least as you intend to implement them, at this juncture!

A third early portion would discuss the *research literature* and how it led to or complemented your research questions and the propositions being studied. Because your case study design will have settled on these questions and propositions in order to proceed with protocol development and data collection, you will have given serious thought to your case study's connectivity to the literature. Although you may again need to revisit this earlier version after completing your data collection and analysis, having a preliminary draft never hurts.

You can start yet a fourth portion after data collection but before analysis begins, covering the *descriptive data about the case(s)* you have studied. Whereas the methods should have included the issues regarding the selection of the case(s), the descriptive data should now cover each case's description or profile. You still may not have finalized your ideas about the type of case study format you will use or the type of composition structure you will follow. However, the descriptive profiles are likely to be useful regardless of the format or structure. Furthermore, drafting the initial case descriptions, even in preliminary form, may stimulate your thinking about the overall format and structure.

If you can draft these four portions before analysis has been completed, you will have made a major advance. These portions also may call for substantial documentation (e.g., copies of your final case study protocol as part of your methodology), and therefore an opportune time to put such documentation into presentable form (that is, "camera ready") occurs at this stage of the research. You also will be at an advantage if, during data collection, you have accurately recorded all details—citations, references, organizational titles, and spellings of people's names and titles—related to your study (Wolcott, 2009, pp. 52–53).

At this same stage—that is, before analysis has been completed—you can add more information to your earlier draft methods section. You will know more details about the data collection procedures as they actually occurred, and you may know more about your planned analysis strategies. This information will readily enhance the initial methodology that you drafted.

If you start the drafting process early and continue to add to your drafts as your case study progresses, you may find that you can focus your thoughts more clearly on the analysis itself, as well as on the tentative findings and conclusions. In other words, having an ongoing picture of where you've been might help you to see more clearly where you are going. To begin composing early also serves another important psychological function: You may get accustomed to the composing process as an ongoing (possibly even daily) practice and have a chance to routinize it before the task becomes truly awesome. Thus, if you can identify other portions to be drafted at these early stages, you should draft them as well.

Case Identities: Real or Anonymous?

Nearly every case study presents a researcher with a choice regarding the anonymity of the case: Should the case study and its informants be accurately identified, or should the names of the entire case and its participants be disguised? Note that the anonymity issue can be raised at two levels: that of the entire case (or cases) and that of an individual person within a case (or cases).

The most desirable option is to disclose the identities of both the case and the individuals, within the constraints for protecting human subjects, discussed in Chapter 3. Disclosure produces two helpful outcomes. First, the reader has the opportunity to recollect any other previous information he or she may have learned about the same case—from previous research or other sources—in reading and interpreting your case study. This ability to become familiar with a new case study in light of prior knowledge is invaluable, similar to the ability to recall previous experimental results when reading about a new set of experiments. Second, the absence of disguised names will make the entire case easier for you to review, so that footnotes and citations can be checked, if necessary, and appropriate external comments can be solicited about the published case.

Nevertheless, anonymity is necessary on some occasions. The most common rationale occurs when a case study has been on a controversial topic. Anonymity then serves to protect the real case and its real participants. A second occasion occurs when the issuance of the final case report may affect the subsequent actions of those that were studied. This rationale was used in Whyte's (1943/1993) original case study, *Street Corner Society,* which was about an anonymous neighborhood, "Cornerville" (although the neighborhood's true identity was divulged years later). As a third illustrative situation, the purpose of the case study may be to portray an "ideal type," and there may be no reason for disclosing the true identities. This rationale was used by the Lynds in their study *Middletown* (Lynd & Lynd, 1929), in which the names of the small town, its residents, and its industries all were disguised (although again divulged years later).

On those occasions when anonymity may appear justifiable, however, other compromises should still be sought. First, you should determine whether the anonymity of the individuals alone might be sufficient, thereby leaving the case itself to be identified accurately.

A second compromise would be to name the individuals as part of a longer list of all your sources, but to avoid attributing any particular point of view or comment to any single individual. However, the lack of attribution may not always be completely protective—you also may have to disguise the comments so that no case participant (or other reader) can infer the likely source.

For multiple-case studies, a third compromise would be to avoid composing any single-case reports and to report only a cross-case analysis. This last situation would be roughly parallel to the procedure used in surveys, in which the individual responses are not disclosed and in which the published survey report is limited to the aggregate evidence.

Only if these compromises are impossible should you consider making the entire case study and its informants anonymous. However, anonymity is not to be considered a desirable choice. Not only does it eliminate some important background information about the case, but it also makes the mechanics of composing the case difficult. The case and its components must be systematically converted from their real identities to fictitious ones, and you must make a considerable effort to keep track of the conversions. The cost of undertaking such a procedure should not be underestimated.

Exercise 6.3   Maintaining Anonymity in Case Studies

Identify a case study whose "case" has been given a fictitious name (or check some of the boxes in this book for an example). What are the advantages and disadvantages of using such a technique? What approach would you use in reporting your own case study, and why?

Reviewing the Draft Case Study: A Validating Procedure

A third procedure to be followed in doing the case study report will boost the overall quality of the study. The procedure is to have the draft report reviewed, not just by peers (as would be done for any research manuscript) but also by the informants and participants in the case. When comments are exceptionally helpful, researchers even have included them as part of the entire case study (see BOX 47).

BOX 47
Reviewing Case Studies—and Printing the Comments

A major way of improving the quality of case studies and ensuring their construct validity is to have the draft cases reviewed by those who have been the subjects of study. This procedure was followed to an exemplary degree in a set of five case studies by Alkin, Daillak, and White (1979).

Each case study was about a school district and the way that the district used evaluative information about its students' performance. As part of the analytic and reporting procedure, the draft for each case was reviewed by the informants from the relevant district. The comments were obtained in part as a result of an open-ended questionnaire devised by the investigators for just this purpose. In some instances, the responses were so insightful and helpful that the investigators modified their original material and also printed the responses as part of their book.

With such presentation of supplementary evidence and comments, any reader can reach her or his own conclusions about the adequacy of the cases—an opportunity that has occurred, unfortunately, all too seldom in traditional case study research.

Such review is more than a matter of professional courtesy. The procedure has been correctly identified as a way of corroborating the essential findings and evidence presented in a case report (Schatzman & Strauss, 1973, p. 134). The informants and participants may cling to their own perspectives and disagree with your conclusions and interpretations, but these readers should have the opportunity to challenge a study's key findings. If disagreement emerges during the formal review process, you may have to regard the case study report as being unfinished until the disagreement has been settled through a search for further evidence. Often, the opportunity to review the draft itself produces further evidence, as the informants and participants may remember new materials that they had forgotten during the initial data collection period.

This type of review should be followed even if the case study or some of its components are to remain anonymous. Some earlier but still recognizable version of the draft must be shared with the case study informants or participants. After they have reviewed this earlier draft, and after any differences in facts have been settled, you can disguise the identities so that only the informants or participants will know the true identities. When Whyte (1943/1993) first completed *Street Corner Society,* he followed this procedure by sharing drafts of his book with "Doc," his major informant. He notes,

> As I wrote, I showed the various parts to Doc and went over them with him in detail. His criticisms were invaluable in my revision. (p. 341)

From a methodological standpoint, the corrections made through this process will enhance the accuracy of the case study, hence increasing the *construct validity* of the study. The likelihood of falsely reporting an event or of misrepresenting a relativist perspective should be reduced. In addition, when differences persist, the procedure should help to identify the various perspectives, which can then be represented in the case study report. At the same time, you need not respond to all the comments made about the draft. For example, you are entitled to your own interpretation of the evidence and should not automatically incorporate your informants' reinterpretations. In this respect, your discretionary options are no different from how you might respond to comments made in the conventional peer review process.

The review of the draft case study by its informants will clearly extend the period of time needed to complete the case study report. Informants, unlike academic reviewers, may use the review cycle as an opportunity to begin a fresh dialogue about various facets of the case, thereby extending the review period even further. You must anticipate these extensions and not use them as an excuse to avoid the review process altogether. When the process has been given careful attention, the potential result is the production of a high-quality case study (see BOX 48).

BOX 48
Formal Reviews of Case Studies

As with any other research product, the review process plays an important role in enhancing and ensuring the quality of the final results. For case studies, such a review process should involve, at a minimum, a review of the draft case study.

One set of case studies that followed this procedure, to an exemplary degree, was sponsored by the U.S. Office of Technology Assessment (1980–1981). Each of 17 case studies, which were about medical technologies, was "seen by at least 20, and some by 40 or more, outside reviewers." Furthermore, the reviewers reflected different perspectives, including those of government agencies, professional societies, consumer and public interest groups, medical practice, academic medicine, and economics and decision sciences.

In one of the case studies, a contrary view of the case—put forth by one of the reviewers—was included as part of the final published version of the case, as well as a response by the case study authors. This type of open printed interchange adds to the reader's ability to interpret the case study's conclusions and therefore to the overall quality of the case study evidence.

Exercise 6.4   Anticipating the Difficulties of the Review Process

Case study reports are likely to be improved by having some review by informants—that is, those persons who were the most involved participants in the case study. Discuss the pros and cons of having such reviews. What specific advantage, for quality control purposes, is served? What disadvantages are there? On balance, are such reviews worthwhile?

△ WHAT MAKES AN EXEMPLARY CASE STUDY?

In all of case study research, one of the most challenging tasks is to define an exemplary case study. Although no direct evidence is available, some speculations seem an appropriate way of concluding this book.[3]

The exemplary case study goes beyond the methodological procedures already highlighted throughout this book. Even if you, as a case study researcher, have followed most of the basic procedures—using a case study protocol, maintaining a chain of evidence, establishing a case study database, and so on—you still may not have produced an *exemplary* case study. The mastering of these procedures makes you a good technician but not necessarily an esteemed social scientist. To take but one analogy, consider the difference between a chronicler and a historian: The former is technically correct but does not produce the insights into human or social processes provided by the latter.

Five general characteristics of an exemplary case study are described below. They are intended to help your case study to be a lasting contribution to research.

Exercise 6.5 Defining a Good Case Study

Select a case study that you believe is one of the best you know (again, the selection can be from the BOXES in this book). What makes it a good case study? Why are such characteristics so infrequently found in other case studies? What specific efforts might you make to emulate such a good case study?

The Case Study Must Be Significant

The first general characteristic may be beyond the control of many researchers. If a researcher has access to only a few "cases," or if resources are extremely limited, the ensuing case study may have to be on a topic of only marginal significance. This situation is not likely to produce an exemplary case study. However, where choice exists, the exemplary case study is likely to be one in which

- the individual case or cases are unusual and of general public interest (see BOX 49),
- the underlying issues are nationally important—either in theoretical terms or in policy or practical terms, or
- your case study meets both of the preceding conditions.

BOX 49
Examining Significant World Events

The Eastern European revolutions of 1989, ending with the demise of the Soviet Union, became significant world events, especially altering the relationships among the major powers. Why the Soviet Union did not intervene militarily in the 1989 revolutions remains

(Continued)

(Continued)

a pressing question in search of explanation. Andrew Bennett (2010) summarizes and considers the most prominent explanations, including the Soviet Union's then-recent military losses in Afghanistan; a decline in the Soviet Union's economic growth rates; and the domestic politics within the Soviet Union's ruling coalition. Bennett's report, while not composed as a formal case study, shows how case study methods can address these kinds of significant world events.

For instance, a single-case study may have been chosen because it was a revelatory case—that is, one reflecting some real-world situation that social scientists had not been able to study in the past. This revelatory case is in itself likely to be regarded as a discovery and to provide an opportunity for doing an exemplary case study. Alternatively, a critical case may have been chosen because of the desire to compare two rival propositions; if the propositions are at the core of a well-known debate in the literature—or reflect major differences in public beliefs—the case study is likely to be significant. Finally, imagine the situation in which both discovery and theory development are found within the same case study, as in a multiple-case study in which each individual case reveals a discovery but in which the replication across cases also adds up to a significant theoretical breakthrough. This situation would truly lend itself to the production of an exemplary case study.

In contrast to these promising situations, many students select nondistinctive cases or outmoded theoretical issues as the topics for their case studies. This situation can be avoided, in part, by doing better homework with regard to the existing body of research. Prior to selecting a case study, you should describe, in detail, the contribution to be made, assuming that the intended case study were to be completed successfully. If only a weak answer is forthcoming, you might want to plan an alternative case study.

The Case Study Must Be "Complete"

This characteristic is extremely difficult to describe operationally. However, a sense of completeness is as important in doing a case study as it is in defining a complete series of laboratory experiments (or in completing a symphony or finishing a painting). All have the problem of defining the desired end points of the effort, but few guidelines are available.

For case studies, completeness can be characterized in at least three ways. First, the complete case is one in which a researcher gives clear attention to the boundaries of the case—that is, the distinction between the phenomenon being studied and its context.

Sample boundaries might include your designating time and geographic (or organizational) limits for the case, the activities to be included in the case, and explicit notations about the contextual conditions that lie outside of the case (Baxter & Jack, 2008). If you define the boundaries of your case only mechanically—for example, by limiting the scope of your case to a few field participants who happened to make themselves available to you even though other people should have been included as participants—a nonexemplary case study is likely to result. The best way to defend your designated boundaries is to show, either through logical argument or the presentation of evidence, that as an analytic periphery is reached, information is of decreasing relevance to the case. Such testing of the boundaries can occur throughout the analytic and reporting steps of doing case studies.

A second way involves the collection of evidence. The complete case study should demonstrate convincingly that the researcher made an exhaustive effort to collect all the relevant evidence. The documentation of such evidence need not be placed in the text of the case study, thereby dulling its content. Footnotes, appendices, and the like will do. The overall goal, nevertheless, is to convince the reader that little relevant evidence remained untouched, given the boundaries of the case study. This does not mean that you should literally collect all available evidence—an impossible task—but that you have given complete attention to the critical pieces. Such critical pieces, for instance, would be those representing rival propositions.

A third way concerns the absence of certain artifactual conditions. A case study is not likely to be complete if the study ended only because resources were exhausted, because you ran out of time (that is, when the semester ended), or because you faced other, nonresearch constraints. When a time or resource constraint is known at the outset of a study, the responsible researcher should design a case study that can be comfortably completed within such constraints, rather than being artificially limited by them. This type of design requires much experience and some good fortune. Nevertheless, these are the conditions under which an exemplary case study is likely to be produced. Unfortunately, if in contrast a severe time or resource constraint suddenly emerges in the middle of a case study, it is unlikely that the case study will become exemplary.

The Case Study Must Consider Alternative Perspectives

For explanatory case studies, one valuable approach is the consideration of rival propositions and the analysis of the evidence in terms of such rivals (see Chapter 5). The citing of rival claims or alternative perspectives also should be part of a good abstract for your case study (Kelly & Yin, 2007). Even in doing an exploratory or a descriptive case study, the examination of the evidence from different perspectives will increase the chances that a case study will be exemplary.

For instance, a descriptive case study that fails to account for different perspectives may raise a critical reader's suspicions. The researcher may not have collected all the relevant evidence and only may have attended to the evidence supporting a single point of view. Even if the investigator was not purposefully biased, different descriptive interpretations might not have been entertained, thereby presenting a one-sided case. To this day, this type of problem persists whenever studies of organizations appear to represent the perspectives of management and not workers, when studies of social groups appear to be insensitive to issues of gender or multiculturalism, or when studies of youth programs appear to represent adult perspectives and ignore those of youths.

To represent different perspectives adequately, an investigator must seek those alternatives that most seriously challenge the assumptions of the case study. These perspectives may be found in alternative cultural views, different theories, variations among the stakeholders or decision makers who are part of the case study, or some similar contrasts. If sufficiently important, the alternative perspectives can appear as alternative renditions covering the same case, using the comparative structure of composition described earlier in this chapter as one of six possible structures. Less prominent but still invaluable would be the presentation of alternative views as separate chapters or sections of the main case study (see BOX 50).

BOX 50
Adding Alternative Perspectives, Written by a Case Study's Participants, as Supplements to a Case Study

Edgar Schein's (2003) single-case study tried to explain the demise of a computer firm that had been among the country's top 50 corporations in size (see BOX 31, Chapter 5, p. 148). The contemporary nature of the case study meant that the firm's former executives were still available to offer their own rendition of the firm's fate. Schein supported his own explanation with much documentation and interview data, but he made his case study distinctive in another way: He also included supplementary chapters, each giving one of the key executives the opportunity to present his own rival explanation.

Many times, if a researcher describes a case study to a critical listener, the listener will immediately offer an alternative interpretation of the findings of the case. Under such circumstances, the researcher is likely to become defensive and to argue that the original interpretation was the only relevant or correct one. In fact, the exemplary case study anticipates these "obvious" alternatives, even advocates their positions as forcefully as possible, and shows—empirically—the basis upon which such alternatives might be rejected.

The Case Study Must Display Sufficient Evidence

Although Chapter 4 strongly urged you to create a case study database, the critical pieces of evidence for a case study must still be contained within the case study report. The exemplary case study judiciously and effectively presents the most relevant evidence, including "how the investigation was conducted and how collected evidence was handled and interpreted" (Bachor, 2002, p. 21). In other words, the desired presentation should enable a reader of the case study report (without referring to the database) to reach an independent judgment regarding the merits of your case study and its findings.

This selectiveness does not mean that the evidence should be cited in a biased manner—for example, by including only the evidence that supports your conclusions. On the contrary, the evidence should be presented neutrally, with both supporting and challenging data. The reader should then be able to arrive at an independent conclusion about the validity of a particular interpretation. An acceptable selectiveness may limit the report to the most salient evidence (including rivals) and not clutter the presentation with supportive but secondary information. Such selectiveness takes a lot of discipline among novices, who usually want to display their entire evidentiary base, in the (false) hope that sheer volume or weight will sway the reader. (In fact, sheer volume or weight will bore the reader.)

Another goal is to present enough evidence to gain the reader's confidence that the researcher "knows" her or his subject. In doing a field study, for instance, the evidence presented should convince the reader that the researcher has indeed spent quality time in the field, made penetrating inquiries while there, and become steeped in the issues about the case. A parallel goal exists in multiple-case studies: The report should show the reader that all of the single cases have been treated fairly and that the cross-case conclusions have not been biased by undue attention to one or a few of the entire array of cases.

Finally, the display of adequate evidence should be accompanied by some indication that the researcher attended to the validity of the evidence—in maintaining a chain of evidence, for example. This does not mean that all case studies need to be burdened with methodological treatises. A few judicious footnotes will serve the purpose. Alternatively, some words in the preface of a case study can cover the critical validating steps. Notes to a table or figure also will help. As a negative example, a figure or table that presents evidence without citing its source is an indication of sloppy research and cautions the reader to be more critical of other aspects of the case study. This is not a situation that produces exemplary case studies.

The Case Study Must Be Composed in an Engaging Manner

One last global characteristic has to do with the composition of the case study report. Regardless of the medium used (a written report, an oral presentation, or some other form), the report should be engaging.

For written reports, this means a clear writing style, but one that constantly entices the reader to continue reading. A good manuscript is one that "seduces" the eye. If you read such a manuscript, your eye will not want to leave the page, and you will continue to read paragraph after paragraph, page after page, until exhaustion sets in. Anyone reading good fiction has had this experience. This type of seduction, as might be applied to nonfiction, should be the goal in composing any case study report.

The production of such seductive writing calls for talent and experience. Challenge yourself to "open with text that is vivid and vital" (Caulley, 2008, p. 424)—and even to make the text "action-packed." Clarity also increases with rewriting, which is highly recommended.

Engagement, enticement, and seduction—these are unusual characteristics of case studies. To produce such a case study requires a researcher to be enthusiastic about the research and to want to communicate the results widely. In fact, the good researcher might even think that the case study contains earth-shattering conclusions. This sort of inspiration should pervade the entire investigation and will indeed lead to an exemplary case study.

Δ   NOTES TO CHAPTER 6

1. Ignored here is a frequent audience for case studies: students taking a course using case studies as a curriculum material. Such use of case studies, as indicated in Chapter 1, is for teaching and not research purposes, and the entire case study strategy might be defined and pursued differently under these conditions.

2. Much of the information comes from my experience in reviewing numerous case study manuscripts over the years, as well as providing written comments to dozens of doctoral students since 2010, each of whom had to compose a dissertation prospectus that included methodology and literature review sections.

3. The speculations also are based on some empirical findings. As part of an earlier investigation, 21 prominent social scientists were asked to name the best qualities of case studies (see COSMOS Corporation, 1983). Some of these qualities are reflected in this discussion of exemplary case studies.

Tutorial 6.1:
Reporting Your Case Study Methodology as an Independent Research Article

As discussed in Chapter 6, the formal case study report will include some description of your case study methods. Even if your audience is only likely to want an abbreviated version of this description, you could consider composing a more extended version, which might then appear as an appendix to the report or, better yet, be submitted for publication as a separate research article. Such an effort would produce a welcome benefit, both contributing to the work of other researchers and preserving the detailed procedures for your own future reference. Your reputation for doing quality case study work would not suffer, either.

Christine Benedichte Meyer (2001) produced one such methodological treatise that appeared in the journal *Field Methods*. Meyer embedded a discussion of her own methods—used in a case study of two mergers in the financial industry in Norway—within the broader range of methodological choices and concerns that arise when doing a case study. In other words, she used her cases to illustrate important methodological principles, thereby justifying the work as an independent article.

For instance, Meyer discussed the advantages of using the case study method because it enabled her inquiry to explore issues such as the power struggles between the merging organizations, the complexity of the process of integrating the merging organizations, and the cultural integration occurring over an extended period of time. None of these topics would have been easily addressed by using other methods. She also discussed how she "bounded" the cases, including her decision to concentrate on the core businesses and her exclusion of the business units that were less affected by the merger, as well as her detailed criteria for defining the persons to be interviewed within the merging firms. Analytically, Meyer showed how she used analytic generalization to interpret the significance of the findings, also acknowledging that some findings "could not be explained either by the merger and acquisition literature or the four theoretical perspectives" [that had been presented as part of her study] (p. 343). Not overlooked were the problems she encountered, including her inability to gain access to all the documents that she had requested. In all, the general issues raised by the article, along with the concrete illustrative experiences, contribute to a valuable and highly readable methodological article.

Briefly Annotated Reference for Tutorial 6.1

Meyer, C. B. (2001). A case in case study methodology. *Field Methods, 13*, 329–352. Illustrates how the methods used in a case study can become the topic of a separate research article.

Appendix A

A NOTE ON THE USES OF CASE STUDY RESEARCH IN PSYCHOLOGY

In psychology as in other fields, all case study research starts from the same compelling feature: the desire to derive a(n) (up)close or otherwise in-depth understanding of a single or small number of "cases" (Bromley, 1986, p. 1). In addition to assuming such a proximal perspective, case study research focuses on the wholeness or integrity of a case, also setting it within its real-world context. Because the contextual conditions may interact in subtle ways with the case, a good case study should therefore lead to an insightful understanding of a case and its internal as well as external complexity.

Clarifying the Niche for Case Study Research: Three Comparisons

1. Case study research compared to other uses of case studies. The case study as a research method differs from the popular use of case studies as teaching tools. The teaching tools are invaluable, but a teaching case's data can be manipulated for instructional purposes, and the cases are not part of the research literature. In contrast, case study research must adhere to formal methodological procedures, linking all findings to explicit evidence. For examples of teaching cases in psychology, see Golden (2004) and Dunbar (2005). For a broad discussion of teaching cases in business, law, and medicine, see Garvin (2003).

The case study as a research method also differs from case records—sometimes used or referred to as "case studies"—that are maintained by service agencies. Bromley (1986) noted that such records, although otherwise appearing to be case studies, could be influenced by service providers' "expectations regarding accountability rather than factual data" (p. 69) and were therefore "liable to a variety of accidental or deliberate omissions and distortions" from a research perspective (p. 90).

2. Case study research compared to other social science methods. Among social science research methods, Chapter 1 of this book has identified case study research as one of a group of methods that includes experiments, quasi-experiments (also known as "observational studies"—see Rosenbaum, 2002), surveys, archival analyses, and histories. Although all the methods overlap to a certain extent, Chapter 1 claims that case study research, like the others, is a separate method with its own design, data collection, and analysis techniques. For example, and as discussed in Chapter 2, case studies should not be considered a strand of some other research method, such as quasi-experiments (see p. 32).

In psychology, case study research also may be considered apart from qualitative research—evidenced by the fact that psychology textbooks on qualitative research have generally ignored case study research. Two of them both devote the bulk of their texts to a variety of "qualitative research methods" in psychology, such as discourse analysis, grounded theory, phenomenological analysis, and narrative research (see Forrester, 2010; Wertz et al., 2011). Despite this broad coverage, one book ignores case studies in its array of contemporary methods, even though it recognizes the prominence of case studies in its lengthy history of psychological methods; the other book refers fleetingly to single cases but not to case study research at all.

Another two textbooks each consists of an edited collection of articles on doing qualitative research in psychology (Camic, Rhodes, & Yardley, 2003; Smith, 2008). In the first textbook, one of the articles refers to psychoanalytic therapy as a case study, but none of the articles discusses case study research. In the second textbook, each article covers a different strand of qualitative research (e.g., phenomenology, grounded theory, narrative psychology, conversation analysis, discourse analysis, focus groups, and action research). Case study research is not mentioned anywhere and does not appear in the textbook's index, much less having a chapter of its own.

Consistent with the preceding four textbooks, Bromley's landmark work (1986) on case study research, cited several times in this appendix, conversely offers little discussion of qualitative research. Overall, the absence of any attempt to integrate qualitative research and case study research in psychology appears to attest further to the separateness of case study research from the other social science methods.

3. Case study research compared to three other research methods in psychology. Also pertinent to psychology is the contrast between case study research and three other research methods, the first two of which have like-sounding names:

(A) *single-subject research,* found in neuropsychology and in behavioral research more generally (e.g., see Barlow & Nock, 2009; Kazdin, 1982, 2003; Kratochwill, 1978; Morgan & Morgan, 2009), as well as in special education (e.g., Tawney & Gast, 1984);

(B) *case control studies,* frequently used in epidemiological research (e.g., see Schlesselman, 1982); and

(C) *experiments,* whose group designs are the basis for the most frequently used method in psychological research (e.g., see Murray, 1998).

Figure A-1 depicts the relationships among all four methods, although—as with all research methods—the four choices also can overlap, so that the depiction in Figure A-1 represents an ideal classification. The relationships are shown by attending to two dimensions: (1) whether a study is based on data from a group of subjects or from a single subject, and (2) whether a study involves an intervention—that is, a behavioral manipulation.

Figure A.1 Case Study Research Compared to Three Other Kinds of Behavioral Research

	Intervention(s) Manipulated by a Researcher	
	YES	NO
GROUPED DATA	Conventional Experimental Designs	Case-Control Studies
INDIVIDUAL DATA	Single-Subject Research	Case Study (single or multiple)

Examining Figure A-1 horizontally, and between the two types of methods emphasizing individual data (row 2), *single-subject research* differs from case study research by employing formal interventions, such as a repeated-trial type of pattern using different combinations of stimuli (including the absence of any stimuli). The researcher can deliberately design such a pattern to develop a strong basis for inferring causal relationships, and case studies do not have such a capability. At the same time, single-subject research bears some resemblance to case study research by involving single- or multiple-cases— that is, a single-subject research study also can include multiple single subjects (e.g., Chassan, 1960).

Examining Figure A-1 vertically, and between the two types of methods each having the ability to create an intervention (column 1), *conventional experimental designs* may provide a firmer evidentiary base than *single-subject research*—as long as there are a sufficient number of subjects to form a group of the needed size (Robertson, Knight, Rafal, & Shimamura, 1993). Unfortunately for researchers, some important psychological phenomena are too rare to support the needed sized group.

More relevant to case study research is the comparison between the two types of methods that do not have the ability to intervene (column 2). *Case control studies* differ from case study research by covering grouped data, usually a group of individuals who already have exhibited a behavioral condition of interest (e.g., tobacco users). The studies then proceed to estimate the differences between the group's mean and the mean of a retrospectively selected control group (e.g., nontobacco users). In principle, case study research also could make such a comparison—that is, if a single case study contained two sufficiently large groups of multiple cases. However, and except in unusual situations—either where a case study has sacrificed much of the "in-depth" inquiry of each single case or where a case study involves an extensive amount of resources and time—the number of cases is not likely to be large enough to support a meaningful comparison between the two groups.

In summary, given the two dimensions in Figure A-1, case study research occupies the distinctive cell whereby a study focuses on individual (not grouped) data and is limited by the inability to manipulate any intervention.

Case Studies: Conditions That Lead to Having More Variables Than Data Points

Assuming that each case is a single data point, Chapter 1 of this book has earlier offered one part of the definition of case study research as involving inquiries where the number of variables of interest will far outstrip the number of available data points (see p. 18). Three conditions lead to the large number of variables in any given case study: making an in-depth inquiry, studying conditions over time, and covering contextual conditions. Case studies in psychology aptly illustrate all three conditions.

In-depth inquiry. First, a case study involves an in-depth inquiry into the case. The multiple features of a case translate into a large number of variables.

In psychology, the case is likely to focus on some individual's behavior. In an earlier era in psychological research, such an individual might have served as both the investigator and the subject of study, producing the famous studies on memory, perception, and learning by Ebbinghaus, Stratton, and Galton, respectively (see Garmezy, 1982) as well as the legacy created by the Phase I safety trials in medicine, during which medical scientists' first commitment has been to test newly created medical remedies on their own bodies. These kinds of studies, in which the individuals were either the researchers or their medical research colleagues (Jadad, 1998, p. 14), also appear to have been an integral part of the tradition in doing case study research in applied linguistics (Duff, 2008, p. 37).

In contemporary settings, the individuals of interest can come from a wide range of situations, including clinical cases, studies of individual development or learning as in a Piagetian study of cognitive development, and single animal preparations in comparative psychology.[1] One of the most notable case studies in neurology, referenced by one analyst as "the most famous neurological case in the world" (Rolls, 2005, p. 51), involved the case of "H.M.," about whom more than 30 articles had been published between 1957 and 1968 alone (Scoville & Milner, 1957; Sidman, Soddard, & Mohr, 1968)—also see BOX A-1.

BOX A.1
Classic Case Studies in Psychology

Over the years, psychologists have studied many unusual individuals. Some have behaved distinctively as a result of unique brain injuries (e.g., the cases of H.M. and of Phineas Gage). Other people have suffered from psychiatric disorders, such as the multiple personality disorder represented by the three faces of Eve. Yet other people had the misfortune of encountering strange environmental or social conditions, such as the case of Kitty Genovese in Queens, New York, or of the so-called wild boy of Aveyron, France. All of these cases have been the subject of formal psychological study, and some have drawn attention from the mass media and therefore have become well-known outside of psychology.

In a compact book entitled *Classic Case Studies in Psychology*, Geoff Rolls (2005) has compiled 16 of these cases into a series of individual case studies. Each case study has a minimum of technical jargon but is accompanied by key references to related research. Should a reader want to learn more about a case, the references help to uncover the research literature.

Alternatively, other subfields in psychology (e.g., social, educational, management, occupational, environmental, and community psychology), as well as related fields outside of psychology, may focus on organizations or other entities, rather than on individuals (see BOX A-2). The in-depth study of such entities also will translate into a large number of variables.

BOX A.2
Case Studies of Organizational Entities in Psychology

Case studies within and outside of psychology can focus on organizations, events such as decisions, and other entities—not just individual people. A clinical setting such as a hospital, clinic, or psychologist's office might serve as the case in a case study.

As an example, one type of collaborative care clinic deals with the challenge of integrating mental health and primary care services. Such clinics were therefore the subject of a collection of over 30 research articles contributing to the redesign of health care, attempting to create "more effective, efficient, patient-involved, and cost-sensitive health care" (Kessler & Stafford, 2008, p. 4). Several of the articles present case studies of specific clinics. One of these describes a longstanding program first started in 1994. The case study uses qualitative and quantitative data—the latter represented by measures involving patient functioning as well as the responses to a patient satisfaction survey (Kates, 2008).

Conditions over time. A second common condition comes from the fact that interest in a case usually covers multiple conditions extending over time. Analyzing the temporal pattern can be the explicit subject of a case study, as in the unfolding of key events that might explain some culminating event—or as in a development case study that traces human or animal behavior over a specified period of time (e.g., Denenberg, 1982).

Even if a temporal pattern is not a direct topic of inquiry or is fairly short (e.g., Bromley, 1986, p. 5), the pattern can create a continuous flow of variables that may be relevant and that cannot be ignored. In this sense, and regardless of the brevity of the time period, case studies rarely serve as literal snapshots—as if everything occurred at the same exact moment. Important events, including the repetition of seemingly-like (but not precisely alike) behavior, occur at different points in time. These events bring another large group of variables that can be an essential part of understanding a case.

Contextual conditions. A third set of conditions comes from outside of the case. Thus, in addition to investigating a case in depth and over time, a case study will include data about the contextual conditions surrounding the case. Indeed, one of the strengths of case study research is its ability to examine contextual conditions to the fullest extent that might appear relevant. For instance, if the case is an individual, data about the individual's family, work, and peer environments could be common components of a full case study. If the case is a small group or an organization, data about cultural, economic, social, and political conditions and trends would be counterpart components.

Moreover, the boundary between a case and its context may not be sharp because real-world affairs do not readily fall into clear-cut categories. The ability to appreciate any such blurring as part of a case study is considered a strength of case study research. The contextual conditions even can lead to an entirely new understanding of a case—an understanding that was not necessarily appreciated at the outset of the case study.

By comparison, other methods will likely treat any blurring between the focus of study and its context as, at best, an annoyance. In fact, other methods do not address contextual conditions with any great ease. For instance, other than a small number of covariates, experiments try to minimize the role of contextual conditions by controlling them out. Similarly, surveys cannot include too many questions about the context because of a similar limitation on the degrees of freedom. With these methods, adequate degrees of freedom are essential for carrying out statistical analyses—that is, having multiple data points for any given variable.

Summary of three conditions. In sum, three conditions help to explain why the number of variables of interest in a case study is likely to be enormous. In contrast, the number of data points, as represented by the individual cases, is likely to be small. As a practical matter, no single case study, even if consisting of multiple cases, will be able to have the number of cases that would match, much less exceed in any realistic multiple, the number of variables.

This situation has far-reaching implications for case study design and analysis. The designs belong to a family of their own and cannot be considered part of some other family of designs, such as quasi-experimental or qualitative research designs. Likewise, the analytic methods cannot employ most of the statistical methods conventionally used with other types of methods, because the case study's data points will have little or no variance.

Motives for Using Case Study Research in Psychology

Given the preceding constraints, case study research might at first appear to have limited value. In fact, however, case studies have been a common part of research in psychology and related fields for a long time. Why is this?

Exploration. A quick but overly narrow response considers case study research as only serving an *exploratory* purpose—for example, to collect some data to determine whether a topic is worthy of further investigation, and if so, the research questions or the data collection procedures that might be most relevant in the subsequent research. In this exploratory mode, the only role for case study research is to serve as a prelude to a subsequent study, which may use a different method, such as a survey or an experiment.

Such an outdated hierarchy of research methods is surely incorrect (e.g., Bromley, 1986, p. 15). Among other problems with the hierarchical view is the fact that surveys and experiments also have exploratory modes. Conversely, case study research can be used in *descriptive, explanatory,* and *evaluative* modes, in addition to its use in an exploratory mode. Case study research can therefore produce its own findings and conclusions, without appealing to or engaging any other methods.

Description and explanation. Descriptive case studies can serve many purposes, such as presenting a rarely encountered situation or one not normally accessible to researchers. For instance, referring again to clinical and neurological studies, a frequent type of descriptive case study that appears in the literature will focus on a single individual who has exhibited some unusual syndrome or behavior worthy of note and continued investigation (see BOX A-3).

BOX A.3
Descriptive Case Studies of People
Who Are Unable to Recognize Human Faces

Especially valued in psychology are case studies of persons with unusual syndromes, such as *prosopagnosia*—a condition, usually induced by an unusual brain injury, whereby a person is

(Continued)

(Continued)

unable to recognize or differentiate among the faces of different people. Not many more than 20 persons with prosopagnosia have been the subjects of published case studies over the past several decades (Busigny, Graf, Mayer, & Rossion, 2010).

One challenge of the case studies has been to show whether prosopagnosia is a specific disability or whether it is simply part of a more general inability to perform visual recognition tasks. The most common finding of the case studies, while still being descriptive, has been to demonstrate that patients with prosopagnosia can nevertheless carry out other recognition tasks (e.g., Busigny & Rossion, 2011). These case studies, along with research using the experimental method with normal adults and patients with penetrating brain injuries (Yin, 1978), in contemporary brain-imaging studies (McKone, Kanwisher, & Duchaine, 2007), and with nonhuman subjects such as monkeys (Leopold, Bondar, & Giese, 2006), have begun to support the possibility of a neurologically based capability that is face specific and not part of a broader syndrome. At the same time, researchers have not yet addressed how face recognition works, and why such a special capability might exist.

As for the explanatory mode of case studies, a common example comes from the field of educational psychology. The example also points to the complementary relationships among different research methods (see BOX A-4).

BOX A.4
Using Case Studies in an Explanatory Mode

In K–12 education, the effectiveness of a curriculum can be studied by using an experimental (or quasi-experimental) design that compares two groups of students, under treatment and control conditions. The successful completion of such a study would address the statistical significance of the differences between the two groups. However, the data are not likely to explain how and why the treatment actually produced the observed results. To seek such an explanation would require a case study (National Research Council, 2004, pp. 167–168).

The desired case study would carefully examine how the treatment had worked in actual classroom settings. The study would cover the relevant events, including the implementation of the treatment and how the treatment appeared to have altered classroom teaching and learning. Covering such a breadth of topics would likely require a variety of field-based evidence, such as classroom observations, teacher interviews about their instructional strategies, student interviews about their learning strategies, and data about potentially relevant school and community conditions. The needed explanation would be especially invaluable for later replicating the original experimental study or for disseminating the curriculum practice to other schools.

Many other examples of descriptive and explanatory case studies can be cited, whether the subjects of study are individuals, small groups, organizations, or more abstract entities such as "decisions."

Evaluation. Evaluation may be considered a fourth motive for doing case study research in psychology (also see Appendix B of this book). One case study evaluated different teaching strategies in working with students with a special type of disability. The case study consisted of multiple cases and therefore was a multiple-case study (see BOX A-5).

BOX A.5
An Evaluative Case Study
Based on a Multiple-Case Study

One multiple-case study in psychology evaluated the effectiveness of teaching strategies by studying seven pairs of teachers and students (Miyahara & Wafer, 2004). The teaching strategies were intended to deal with a behavioral condition among the students, *developmental coordination disorder,* and each teacher-student pair was defined as a separate case. The case study used a between-pair replication logic to determine the relationship between systematically alternating teaching strategies and a student's performance. The students' performance was assessed quantitatively—with a variety of psychometric measures over time.

On another evaluation topic, case study methods are frequently emulated in assessing academic environments, although the efforts are not formally organized or labeled as case study research (e.g., Wilson, 1982). These case studies take the form of the assessments conducted by visiting committees, such as accreditation teams and state coordinating boards, who periodically review individual academic departments. The visiting committee focuses on the well-being and progress being made by a department and collects a variety of evidence (observations, interviews, and reviews of pertinent documents such as the department's publications) to arrive at both formative and summative judgments.

The preceding illustrations show how using case studies in any of these exploratory, descriptive, explanatory, or evaluative modes highlights the potential value of case study research as an important part of a researcher's full methodological repertoire.

Caveats and Concerns in Doing Case Study Research

Despite its apparent applicability for studying many relevant real-world situations and addressing important research questions, case study research nevertheless has not achieved widespread recognition as a method of choice in psychology. Some people actually think of it as a method of last resort. Why is this?

Part of the notoriety comes from a lack of trust in the credibility of a case study researcher's procedures, which do not seem to protect sufficiently against such biases as a researcher seeming to find what she or he had set out to find. For instance, a researcher might have started a case study on the basis of a certain design, only to find it either unworkable or less promising than originally thought, following some initial data collection. As with laboratory experiments, the remedy would be to cease collecting data under the original design and to revise it, then to restart data collection afresh. The common criticism of case studies, unfortunately, is that the original data might not have been discarded but might have been reused, thereby creating an unwanted bias and flaw.

Another reason for the low regard for case study research may come from the use of qualitative data, which are presumed to be based on less robust measures than those used in collecting quantitative data. Qualitative data usually consist of narrative, not numeric, information, and many people may feel uncomfortable with such data because of a lack of understanding the procedures for collecting and assessing narrative data, such as discussed in Chapter 5 of the main text of this book.

Yet another discomfort with case study research comes from the perceived inability to generalize the findings from a case study to any broader level. The challenge of generalizing from case studies also has been discussed throughout the main text of this book, with the critical insight being the need to distinguish *analytic generalization* from *statistical generalization* (see Chapter 2 of this book).

When case studies are done poorly, all of the preceding caveats can come together in a negative way, potentially re-creating the prejudices against case study research. In contrast, more systematic and careful use of case study research can begin to overcome, if not dissipate, the concerns. For instance, and as has been suggested in Chapter 4 of this book, case studies should rely on multiple sources of evidence in a triangulating fashion that attempts to overcome the deficiencies and measures associated with any given source (see pp. 134–139). Chapter 4 also discusses other techniques—such as creating a case study database and establishing a chain of evidence—that will help to increase the reliability of such data.

The preceding recommendations have been just a few examples of the ways in which case study research practices can address the general concerns with the method. The procedures covered by the six chapters of this book, covering research design, data collection, data analysis, and the role of theory in conducting case studies, all have been intended to buttress the use of case studies in psychology and to minimize the threats posed by the caveats.

△   Note to Appendix A

1. In comparative psychology, the large number of variables also can characterize single-subject research studies. For instance, independent variables may be deliberately manipulated at different ages of an animal's life cycle (Denenberg, 1982). The significant findings then often lie with the interaction among the independent variables, producing yet more variables, challenging the independence of the variables, and therefore also requiring "a more complicated model than causality as a framework for interpreting [the] findings" (Denenberg, 1982, p. 22).

Appendix B

A Note on the Uses of Case Study Research in Evaluations

Evaluation textbooks have given case study evaluations mixed attention. One longstanding textbook has, over the course of its seven editions, consistently ignored the topic (Rossi, Lipsey, & Freeman, 2004). The textbook makes no mention of case study evaluations or of case study research, and *case study* does not appear in its glossary or index. A second well-received textbook (Mertens, 2010) omits case study evaluations from its initial review of a large number of evaluation models and processes (pp. 47–87). The textbook does recognize the case study but relegates it to a minor status—serving as but one of seven types under the qualitative research model (p. 230) and one of six types of data collection methods (Table 12.1, p. 352).

In contrast to the preceding two treatments, a third textbook, whose first author also is a leading evaluation scholar, gives considerable attention to the role of case study evaluations (Stufflebeam & Shinkfield, 2007). First, the textbook recognizes case study evaluations among 26 choices of evaluation methods (pp. 181–184). Then, after formally rating all the methods according to the standards of the American Evaluation Association, the textbook ranks case study evaluations as the fifth among the 8 best approaches for designing and conducting evaluations (pp. 242–243).

Despite its spotty recognition by existing evaluation textbooks, case study research has a functional and legitimate role in doing evaluations. Three major applications have frequently appeared in published evaluations. First, one or more case studies may serve as part of a larger evaluation (e.g., Cronbach & Associates, 1980, pp. 222–223; Datta, 1997, pp. 348–351). Second, case study research may serve as the primary evaluation method (e.g., Yin, 2000a). Third, case study research can be part of dual-level evaluation arrangements. The first application has been the most common and has been used for a long time, but the second and third have been the more challenging.

The purpose of the following note is to restate briefly the role of case study research in doing evaluations and then to describe the three applications in greater detail.

Case Study Research as an Evaluation Method

The use of case study research in doing evaluations emanates from the defining feature of case study research highlighted in Chapter 1 of this book (see p. 18): to gain an in-depth (and up-close) examination of a "case" within its real-world context. Compared to other evaluation methods such as surveys, experiments, and quasi-experiments, case study evaluations can (1) capture the complexity of a case, including relevant changes over time, and (2) attend fully to contextual conditions, including those that potentially interact with the case. Despite these advantages, earlier references to case study research as an evaluation method received highly misleading recognition, including an initial confusion with the "posttest-only" design in quasi-experiments—an inappropriate connection to case study research that was later retracted by the original author (see Chapter 2, p. 50 of this book).

When applied to evaluations, case study research shares the other features relevant in doing any other form of case study research. These features are covered in detail in the main body of this book and are summarized briefly as follows.

First, to cover the complexity of a case and its context, a case study evaluation should rely on multiple sources of evidence, which may include interviews, documents, field observations, archival records, physical artifacts, and participant-observation. A case study evaluation should deliberately triangulate the evidence from these multiple sources, to confirm and corroborate the findings. Second, the variety of evidence can include quantitative or qualitative data (or both) and can cover *realist* or *relativist* (or *interpretivist*) perspectives. For example, the quantitative part of a case study evaluation might assume a *realist* orientation (e.g., presenting the researcher's questions and interpretations about the case being studied), whereas the qualitative part might assume a contrasting, *relativist* (or *interpretivist*) orientation (e.g., presenting the case from participants' multiple perspectives and meanings—including the possibility of challenging the researcher's original assumptions).

Third, a case study evaluation also can benefit by having an initial though tentative theory about the case. The initial theory may be descriptive (e.g., hypothesizing about the expected characteristics of the case) or explanatory (e.g., conjecturing about the "how's" and "why's" of a case). When explanatory, a case study evaluation should explicitly entertain rival explanations as an integral part of the design and data collection procedures (see Donald Campbell's foreword to this book and Chapter 2, p. 70 of this book).

All these features of case study research will be relevant in doing case study evaluations, represented by the three applications discussed next.

Case Study Research as Part of a Larger Evaluation

In the first application, one or more case studies will be part of a larger evaluation. The larger evaluation will focus on an initiative—either a planned intervention or an ongoing operation—possibly assessing the effectiveness of the initiative by using an experimental or quasi-experimental design. As part of the design, some evaluations even may randomly assign entities to *treatment* and *control* conditions.

As part of the larger evaluation, the case studies will examine more closely one or more of the entities within these treatment and control conditions. The case studies will complement the larger evaluation method in the following way: Whereas the experimental or quasi-experimental portion will assess effectiveness by determining the *strength* of a relationship between an initiative and its outcomes, the case study portion will offer an *explanation* of the relationship, indicating how the initiative actually worked (or not) to produce the relevant outcomes. As noted in one authoritative review of numerous evaluations of K–12 mathematics curricula and their student achievement outcomes (National Research Council, 2004, p. 167),

> Case studies provide insight into mechanisms at play that are hidden from a comparison of [outcomes, such as] student achievement, . . . as the actual treatment in a large-scale [experimental] study is often ill-defined.

For example, the larger evaluation might cover an innovative curriculum involving many classrooms. The experimental design for the larger evaluation might assign groups of classrooms to different treatment and control conditions, and the analysis would compare the outcomes of these conditions on some common measure—such as student achievement scores. A series of case studies might then deliberately focus on a few of the classrooms, selected from each of the experimental conditions, to examine the specific teaching and learning processes in this smaller number of classrooms. In this manner, the case studies could shed important light on the way that the innovative curriculum had worked (or not).

The findings from the case study portion of a larger evaluation may be presented for each case separately or consolidated into a cross-case synthesis. However, the reporting of the case study results will likely be subordinate to the reporting of the findings from the larger evaluation—in the preceding example, the analysis of the student achievement scores across the different groups of classrooms.

You can imagine many other examples like the preceding one. In public health, the evaluation of a new health program might present clinical outcome data about the treatment results at many clinics and then use case study research to capture the experiences at a few individual clinics. In community development, the evaluation of a housing program might involve an economic study examining the relationship between a new initiative and the prices of the housing units, with the case study research covering a small group of households living in these units. In business research, an evaluation might be about an executive management program aimed at developing rising leaders: The larger evaluation might compare groups of participants and nonparticipants through a survey, with the case study research focusing on a select but small number of people in both groups.

The diversity of the examples readily illustrates why this first application of case study research has been so common to evaluations and is likely to remain so. The combination of the larger evaluation design and the component case study or case studies also may be considered an example of a mixed method study (Datta, 1997; Yin, 2006b).

At the same time, this application also comes with some caveats. One early caveat expressed about case study evaluations was that the case studies were likely to incur a high cost because of their labor intensiveness and lengthy time doing fieldwork (e.g., U.S. Government Accountability Office, 1990, p. 10). However, contemporary evaluations using strong experimental designs have by now shown that their costs can readily exceed those of doing case studies. Similarly, the amount of effort devoted to a case study need not be exorbitant.

Another caveat arises out of the nature of the evaluation team and teamwork. Because the case study research is a subsidiary and not the main part of an evaluation, the research may receive inadequate attention with regard to its design and conduct. The person(s) doing the case studies also may be inexperienced in case study research, producing rather mundane case studies with few insights. Conversely, the person(s) may be too experienced, producing case studies that may assume a unique character that does not suit the larger evaluation. In yet other situations, the person(s) doing the case studies may not communicate closely enough with those doing the larger evaluation, and the case studies may be (undesirably) treated as if part of a separate evaluation.

Case Study Research as the Primary Evaluation Method

In the second application, the initiative being evaluated becomes the main case in a case study evaluation. The research on the main case may be supplemented with data from subordinate case studies of some lesser units of analyses (e.g., individual persons or groups), or with the use of other methods, quantitative or qualitative. This second application can pertain to at least three different situations—focusing on (1) the initiative being evaluated, (2) the outcomes of the initiative, or (3) both an initiative and its outcomes.

1. Focus on the initiative. Because of the strength of case study research in capturing the complexity of a case as well as changes in the case over time, case study research is the conventional way for doing *process* or *implementation* evaluations. A case study evaluation would follow the course of events in putting an initiative into place, especially being helpful when the initiative has complex coordinating or organizational features. In contrast, initiatives such as the testing of a new drug may only involve the one-time administration of a drug to a patient; in such situations, implementation would be considered rather straightforward, and a case study of the process would not be informative.

The case study evaluation can track the implementation process with fieldwork conducted throughout the implementation period. Alternatively, the evaluation data can come from open-ended queries of interviewees and the retrieval of documents that retrospectively cover earlier time periods, so that the case study can cover a calendar period that exceeds the elapsed time devoted to any fieldwork.

The case study evaluation would start by capturing the complexity of the initiative, noting the main and any subordinate units of analysis as well as the individuals, groups, or organizations carrying out the initiative. The case study would then proceed to examine and explain the "how" and "why" of the implementation process—tracking the actions that occur over time as well as providing insights into the likely strength, timing, and fidelity of the initiative.

Such a case study evaluation may be the entirety of an evaluation when the tracking of outcomes is premature. In such a circumstance, the case study evaluation can play a *formative* role, with the findings from the evaluation helping to refine or redirect the initiative. For example, a major initiative might take one or more years to implement. A case study evaluation that is completed during the first year could provide useful formative feedback.

Alternatively, a case study evaluation may be the entirety of an evaluation when its main purpose is to clarify whether several like-named initiatives are in fact examples of the same intervention or are merely related types (see BOX B-1). Such an evaluation could lay the foundation for subsequent evaluations by pressing them to clarify explicitly the type of initiative being evaluated.

BOX B.1
Using a Case Study Evaluation as a Prelude to Subsequent Evaluations

A common evaluation problem arises when interventions having similar labels or closely resembling each other in fact differ and should not be unknowingly confused in the same evaluation. For instance, residents in many communities have organized themselves to operate formal citizen patrols, aimed at preventing crime. Understanding how such volunteer patrols work and whether they might create their own problems, such as becoming "vigilante groups," was the topic of an evaluation covering many such patrols in a variety of community settings (also see BOX 27, Chapter 5, p. 137).

Case studies of 32 of these patrols revealed that, although they were like-named, there were actually three distinguishable types of patrols: patrols limited to buildings or residential compounds (*building patrols*), patrols of neighborhood streets more generally (*neighborhood patrols*), and patrols offering escort, delivery, or other community services (*service patrols*). Of the three, the neighborhood patrols were the most prone to accusations of vigilantism because patrol members cannot readily distinguish the residents who live in the neighborhood from those who do not (see Yin, 2012, pp. 59–66). The findings laid important groundwork for later patrols' evaluations, forewarning evaluators of the need to clarify the type of patrol when selecting those to be evaluated.

2. Focus on outcomes. In a second situation, a case study evaluation can focus entirely on an initiative's presumed outcomes. The case study evaluation may be tasked with uncovering the full panoply of outcomes, as in defining the relevant performance measures and indicators for assessing a particular public agency's services (Wholey, 1997, pp. 131–132).

Case study outcome evaluations also can be useful when the outcomes of interest already have been identified. Now, the more challenging task would be to collect the outcome data and to draw conclusions about the direction or magnitude of the outcome trends (e.g., Schwandt, 2009, p. 202). For instance, an evaluation of *public school choice*— an initiative that permits students to choose their own schools rather than being assigned to them—assessed two sets of outcomes: student achievement trends and whether the initiative had indeed expanded the range of educational opportunities for all parents and students, not just a select group of them (Teske, Schneider, Roch, & Marschall, 2000)[1]— see BOX B-2.

BOX B.2
Conducting a Quantitative Outcome Analysis as a Part of a Case Study Evaluation

An evaluation of a public school choice initiative (the "case") relied heavily on a statistical analysis that examined annual 10th-grade student achievement scores in a single school district over a 22-year period (Teske et al., 2000). The analysis compared the district's scores with those from the city's other 32 districts, finding that the district's scores rose significantly, compared to the citywide averages, in both mathematics and reading.

None of the other districts had implemented a choice initiative. The full evaluation therefore went beyond the analysis of the student achievement data, with important data also coming from interviews of the district's officials and the retrieval of documentary evidence. These data supported a detailed description of the initiative, including the timing of its full implementation, to define the years when the 10th-grade scores could most readily have been expected to have improved in comparison to the district's scores.

In addition to either uncovering the outcomes or collecting and interpreting data on trends of previously identified outcomes, case study evaluations can try to explain the outcomes. For example, in another education evaluation, an important outcome finding was that parents did not sufficiently collaborate with their children on school assignments designed to take place in the home (Yin, 2011, pp. 188–192). An initial explanation for this outcome was that the parents were too preoccupied or distracted, whether because they were working parents, had to attend to other siblings, or were overly burdened with housework. However, intensive analysis of field-based case study data suggested an alternative explanation. It derived from an appreciation of the fuller context surrounding the families—which happened to be a rural setting with a decades-long declining economy, population, and employment opportunities: The parents feared that if their children excelled in school, the children would be more likely to gain the social mobility to leave the community after completing their schooling. The parents therefore did not want to help their children with their school assignments.

3. Focus on initiative and outcomes. In the third situation, case study evaluations can attempt to explain the links between an initiative and its outcomes (Mark, 2008, p. 125; Shavelson & Towne, 2002, pp. 99–110).

In this respect, the role of a case study contrasts with that of evaluations using experimental designs—including those with randomized controlled trials (RCTs). The main strength of an RCT is to make a causal inference about the effectiveness of an initiative (e.g., Bickman & Reich, 2009). However, the RCT still remains a "black box" evaluation (Labin, 2008, p. 101) because it does not uncover the processes or mechanisms whereby an initiative might have produced its outcomes (e.g., Julnes & Rog, 2009, pp. 102–103). A case study evaluation would address this void.

In such a situation, the use of logic models (see Chapter 5, p. 174 of this book) can assume a key role in designing the needed case study evaluation. At the outset of the evaluation, a logic model can be specified in hypothetical terms—that is, by defining the conceptually linked relationships whereby some initiative (*input*) is assumed to precede an immediate outcome of interest (*output*) that in turn is assumed to precede a desired later outcome (*impact*). Although logic models have largely been portrayed in a linear fashion, the reality of the relevant inputs, outputs, and impacts is that they can involve more complex and interactive relationships over time. Thus, a recursive and more dynamic rather than linear model may need to be rendered and become the subject of data collection and data analysis (e.g., see Dyehouse, Bennett, Harbor, Childress, & Dark, 2009; also see Tutorial 5-2 in this book).

The relevant logic models should operationalize the links—that is, specify "how" the actions might produce the immediate outcome of interest, and so on, not just name them as correlates.[2] Even stronger logic models would contain rival explanations to compete with the initially hypothesized links. Such rivals can be especially critical because "the greater the latency between the onset of an intervention and changes in measured outcomes, the more difficult it is to rule out alternative causal explanations" (Julnes & Rog, 2009, p. 110).

Although case study evaluations trying to explain how initiatives produce their outcomes are difficult to conduct, good examples of such evaluations can be cited, including:

- the impact created by the closing of a military base in a small community (Bradshaw, 1999);

- the outcomes from a single revitalization initiative in a neighborhood (Galster et al., 2006);
- the outcomes from implementing a comprehensive mental health system for children (Bickman & Mulvaney, 2005); and
- student achievement trends associated with an education reform initiative in a large urban school district (Supovitz & Taylor, 2005).[3]

Additional examples are found in Chapters 13 to 15 of Yin (2012), covering a community coalition's drug prevention actions, a law enforcement initiative, and an HIV/AIDS technical assistance initiative.

Case Study Research as Part of Dual-Level Evaluation Arrangements

Either of the first two applications of case study research can appear in dual-level evaluation arrangements—those in which a single evaluation consists of one or more subevaluations. Most commonly, a broad but single programmatic initiative (in some policy or practice area such as health promotion, education, mental health services, neighborhood revitalization, or coordinated social services) may consist of a group of separately funded projects, each operating in a different locale. Moreover, each project even may be conducted by two or more collaborating organizations, working as a partnership that operates several of its own initiatives, thereby creating a multifaceted initiative.

The broad programmatic initiative could call for a single *program evaluation,* whereas the narrower but related projects could call for multiple *project evaluations.* The combined program and project evaluations typically represent a dual-level or multitiered arrangement (e.g., Chaskin, 2003). In this arrangement, the single program evaluation is likely to be a case study. In one form, it might review and synthesize the work of the multiple project evaluations (see BOX B-3). In other forms, the case study evaluation might draw conclusions about the program as a whole by aggregating and analyzing a sample of the data from the project evaluations, with each project evaluation still attending to and analyzing its own full set of data by following its own method of choice—case studies or otherwise. Alternatively, the program evaluation could collaborate with the project evaluations, together defining the data collection and instruments to be used by the project evaluations.

An even more complicated version of the dual-level or multitiered arrangement can follow a phased approach, with the first phase consisting of a group of project evaluations assessing the implementation processes and a second phase consisting of an outcome-oriented program evaluation (e.g., Rog & Randolph, 2002). In this arrangement, only the program evaluation would collect outcome data, and only about those projects that had satisfactorily implemented their initiatives. The single program evaluation would

---

BOX B.3
A Dual-Level Evaluation

The United Kingdom started a large new initiative, Sure Start, in 1999 (see Allen & Black, 2006). This complex community initiative called for a coordinated change in local services—to provide greater speech, health, and social support to families with children under age 4, to benefit the children, the families, and communities. From an evaluation standpoint, an important characteristic of the initiative was that it eventually involved about 500 Sure Start projects across England. As a result, a case study evaluation at the "national" level reviewed the design and findings by 56 of the "local" evaluations. Among its other findings, the national-level evaluation showed that, although the local evaluations had drawn conclusions about the success of the local initiatives, only about half of the local evaluations had collected any outcome data, and fewer had collected any comparison data.

---

therefore bear the brunt of assessing the effectiveness and long-term impact of the entire program. Examples of this last arrangement especially appeared under the auspices of the Substance Abuse and Mental Health Services Administration in the U.S. Department of Health and Human Services in the 1980s and 1990s.

Summary

The preceding applications show how case study evaluations can apply to a variety of situations. In fact, the diversity of situations means that judgments about the usefulness, relevance, and quality of case study evaluations need to distinguish carefully among the situations. For instance, case study evaluations may be underappreciated when the only application is in serving as a minor part of a larger evaluation. In contrast, when case study research represents the primary evaluation method, it is likely to provide useful and usable information. Thus, despite the disparate recognition given to case study evaluations by various evaluation textbooks, case study research remains an integral part of the broader portfolio of evaluation methods.

Notes to Appendix B   △

1. A lengthy excerpt of the original article appears in an anthology of case studies in education (Yin, 2005, pp. 277–304).

2. Logic models are usually presented graphically as a series of boxes, with arrows connecting the boxes. Although evaluators typically define the contents of the boxes (usually a set of

variables), they rarely operationalize the arrows—which are the explanatory links (see Yin, 2000a). Thus, the arrows represent the *mechanisms* or *processes* whereby different inputs produce the outputs, the outputs produce the outcomes, and so on. The challenge to case study evaluations is therefore to define these mechanisms and processes (also see Chapter 5, Figure 5.5, in the main text of the present book).

3. The authors of neither the neighborhood revitalization nor children's mental health evaluations identified their studies as case study evaluations. However, in both studies, as well as with the two other cited examples, the evaluations collected field data about the main initiative (essentially treating it as the main "case" of interest), and all four of the studies drew their main conclusions at that level. Because all four studies engaged in extensive quantitative analyses at a lower, subunit level (economic indicators in the military base study, housing parcels in the neighborhood revitalization study, client behavior in the mental health services study, and student achievement in the education reform study), the methods used at these lesser levels consumed the bulk of the authors' reports.

APPENDIX C

INDEX OF INDIVIDUAL CASE STUDIES
(cited in BOXES or from Expanded
Case Study Materials)

This appendix enables readers to use a 14-category index to find specific case studies related to the reader's topic of interest. The specific case studies are those cited in the BOXES as well as certain case materials cited in the book's main text. The appendix therefore contains: (1) the index, (2) a complete list of the case studies in the BOXES, and (3) a list of citations in the main text that refer to the expanded case materials to be found in two companion volumes to this book.

INDEX TO CASE STUDIES △

(Either contained in BOXES or in the expanded materials found in two companion volumes, *Applications of Case Study Research* and *Case Study Anthology*)

△   LIST OF **BOXES**

Chapter 1

Chapter 2

Chapter 3

Chapter 4

Chapter 6

Appendix A (all are NEW to the fifth edition)

Appendix B (all are NEW to the fifth edition)

B.1. Using a case study evaluation as a prelude to subsequent evaluations (*crime prevention*)—same as BOX 27   **223**

B.2. Conducting a quantitative outcome analysis as a part of a case study evaluation (*education*)   **224**

B.3. A dual-level evaluation (*health and social services*)   **227**

△   REFERENCES TO EXPANDED CASE STUDY MATERIALS

Location of Citation	Area of Interest of Illustrative Case Study	Reference to Expanded Material (see key)
CHAPTER 1: Getting Started		
BOX 1, p. 7	International Affairs	CSA-2
text, p. 7	Education	ACSR-7
text, p. 7	Health and Social Services	ACSR-8
text, p. 7	Business and Industry	ACSR-9
text, p. 7	Education	ACSR-4
text, p. 7	Crime Prevention	ACSR-5
text, p. 7	Community Organizations	ACSR-6
BOX 2B, p. 8	Health and Social Services	CSA-1
CHAPTER 2: Designing Case Studies		
BOX 6B, p. 33	Business and Industry	CSA-6
text, p. 39	Five different case studies	ACSR-3
BOX 7B, p. 43	Cities and Towns	CSA-4
BOX 8, p. 51	Education	CSA-9
text, p. 52	Business and Industry	ACSR-9
BOX 10, pp. 54–55	Business and Industry	CSA-10
text, p. 58	Education	ACSR-11
text, p. 58	Business and Industry	ACSR-12

Location of Citation	Area of Interest of Illustrative Case Study	Reference to Expanded Material (see key)
text, p. 58	Health and Social Services	ACSR-15
CHAPTER 3: Preparing to Collect Case Study Evidence		
BOX 14, p. 80	Cities and Towns	CSA-3
text, p. 95	Business and Industry	ACSR-3 (pp.32-39)
text, p. 97	Computers and Technology	ACSR-3 (pp.29-32)
CHAPTER 4: Collecting Case Study Evidence		
BOX 17, p. 107	Education	CSA-19
BOX 18, pp. 108	Crime Prevention	CSA-13
text, p. 109	Education	ACSR-11
BOX 20A, p. 114	Computers and Technology	CSA-12
BOX 20B, p. 114	Education	CSA-9
BOX 23, p. 119	Health and Social Services	CSA-15
BOX 25, p. 125	Government Agencies	ACSR-2
text, p. 127	Community Organizations	ACSR-6
CHAPTER 5: Analyzing Case Study Evidence		
text, p. 137	Cities and Towns	CSA-3
text, p. 142	Business and Industry	ACSR-10
BOX 29, p. 144	Business and Industry	ACSR-10
BOX 30, p. 145	Environment	ACSR-3 (pp. 45-48)
BOX 31, p. 148	Business and Industry	ACSR-10
BOX 32A, pp. 148–149	Government Agencies	CSA-8
BOX 33, p. 151	Crime Prevention	CSA-17
text, p. 155	Education	CSA-11
text, p. 159	Health and Social Services	ACSR-15
BOX 35, p. 164	Business and Industry	CSA-7

(Continued)

(Continued)

Location of Citation	Area of Interest of Illustrative Case Study	Reference to Expanded Material (see key)
BOX 38, p. 169	Business and Industry	CSA-6
CHAPTER 6: Reporting Case Studies		
text, p. 185	Community Organizations	ACSR-2
BOX 50, p. 204	Business and Industry	ACSR-10
APPENDIX A: A Note on the Uses of Case Study Research in Psychology		
none		
APPENDIX B: A Note on the Uses of Case Study Research in Evaluations		
BOX B.1, p. 223	Crime Prevention	ACSR-5
text, p. 226	Community Organizations	ACSR-13
text, p. 226	Crime Prevention	ACSR-14
text, p. 226	Health and Social Services	ACSR-15

CSA = *Case Study Anthology*, Yin, 2004 (the number denotes the chapter number in this book).

ACSR = *Applications of Case Study Research*, Yin, 2012 (ditto the chapter number).

Brief Glossary of Terms Directly Related to Case Study Research

analytic generalization: the logic whereby case study findings can extend to situations outside of the original case study, based on the relevance of similar theoretical concepts or principles. Also see *external validity.* Contrast with *statistical generalization.*

case: the main subject of study in a case study—usually a concrete entity (e.g., a person, organization, community, program, process, policy, practice, or institution, or an occurrence such as a decision); totally abstract "cases" (e.g., arguments, claims, or propositions) can pertain to all social science methods and may be less distinctive as cases for case studies.

case boundaries: the time period, social groups, organizations, geographic locations, or other conditions that fall within (as opposed to outside of) the case in a case study, understanding that the boundaries can be fuzzy.

case record: an administrative file, usually maintained in medicine, social work, law, and other practices but not in itself a case study.

case study: a study that investigates a contemporary phenomenon in depth and in its real-world context.

case study database: see *database.*

case study designs: four types of case studies, falling within a 2 × 2 typology (whether a case study is a single- or multiple-case study and whether it is holistic or consists of embedded units of analyses).

case study interview: see *interview.*

case study protocol: see *protocol.*

chain of evidence: the links—showing how findings come from the data that were collected and in turn from the guidelines in the case study protocol and from the original research questions—that strengthen the reliability of a case study's research procedures.

computer-assisted qualitative data analysis (CAQDAS) tools: computer software designed to support the coding and analysis of qualitative (e.g., narrative) data, including case study data.

construct validity: the accuracy with which a case study's measures reflect the concepts being studied.

cross-case synthesis: a compiling of data for a multiple-case study, by examining the results for each individual case and then observing the pattern of results across the cases; stronger syntheses would have sufficient data to entertain plausible rival cross-case patterns.

database: the systematic archive of all the data (field notes, documents, archival records, etc.) from a case study, assembled to enable the later retrieval of specific pieces of evidence, if needed, and sufficiently organized so that the entire archive can be reviewed by an outside reader, if desired. Also see *field notes*.

descriptive case study: a case study whose purpose is to describe a phenomenon (the "case") in its real-world context. Also see *explanatory case study* and *exploratory case study*.

embedded unit of analysis: a unit lesser than the main unit of analysis, from which case study data also are collected (e.g., household data within a neighborhood case, individual employee data within an organization case, or project data within a program case). Also see *unit of analysis*.

explanation building: analysis of case study data by using the data to develop an explanation about the occurrences in a case; stronger analyses would have sufficient data to entertain plausible rival explanations.

explanatory case study: a case study whose purpose is to explain how or why some condition came to be (e.g., how or why some sequence of events occurred or did not occur). Also see *descriptive case study* and *exploratory case study*.

exploratory case study: a case study whose purpose is to identify the research questions or procedures to be used in a subsequent research study, which might or might not be a case study. Also see *descriptive case study* and *explanatory case study*.

external validity: the extent to which the findings from a case study can be analytically generalized to other situations that were not part of the original study. Also see *analytic generalization*.

field notes: the researcher's notes resulting from doing fieldwork; the notes may vary in formality from jottings to formal narratives and can include drawings and other nonverbal material produced by the researcher. Also see *database* and *fieldwork.*

fieldwork: a common mode of data collection in a case study, whereby interviews, documentary evidence, and direct observations all are gathered in the real-world setting of the case being studied. Also see *field notes.*

informant: a case study participant is a subject of study but who also provides critical information or interpretations about the case and who may suggest other sources of evidence for the researcher to check. Also see *participant.*

internal validity: the strength of a cause-effect link made by a case study, in part determined by showing the absence of spurious relationships and the rejection of rival hypotheses.

interview: the mode of data collection involving verbal information from a case study participant; the interview is usually conversational in nature and guided by the researcher's mental agenda, as the interview questions do not follow the exact same verbalization with every participant interviewed. Also known as "intensive interviews," "in-depth interviews," or "unstructured interviews." Also see *mental line of inquiry* and *verbal line of inquiry.*

literal replication: the selection of two (or more) cases within a multiple-case study because the cases are predicted to produce similar findings. Also see *replication logic.* Contrast with *theoretical replication.*

logic models: analysis of case study data by comparing the empirically based conceptual scheme (that is, logic model) with the conceptual scheme specified prior to data collection; stronger analyses would have sufficient data to entertain plausible rival conceptual schemes.

mental line of inquiry: the protocol questions and topics that drive a researcher's thinking (or "mental agenda") in doing a case study. Contrast with *verbal line of inquiry.*

mixed methods study: a single study embracing both qualitative and quantitative components, with a case study potentially being one of the components.

multiple-case study: a case study organized around two or more cases. Also see *single-case study.*

multiple sources of evidence: data that come from different data collection sources (e.g., interviews, documents, direct observations, archives, and participant-observation), with the aim being to strengthen findings through the convergence or triangulation of the data.

participant: a person from whom case study data are collected, usually through interviews; one or more participants may later be asked to review the draft case study report. Also see *informant*.

participant-observation: the mode of data collection whereby a case study researcher becomes involved in the activities of the case being studied.

pattern matching: analysis of case study data by comparing or matching the pattern within the collected data with a pattern defined prior to data collection; stronger analyses would have sufficient data to entertain plausible rival matches.

pilot case study: a preliminary case study aimed at developing, testing, or refining the planned research questions and procedures that will later be used in the formal case study; the data from the pilot case study should not be reused in the formal case study.

protocol: the procedural guide for collecting the data for a case study, including a set of field questions to be addressed by the researcher, representing the researcher's "mental agenda." Also see *mental line of inquiry*.

reliability: the consistency and repeatability of the research procedures used in a case study.

replication logic: the logic for selecting the two or more cases in a multiple-case study. Also see *literal replication* and *theoretical replication*.

research design: a plan that logically links the research questions with the evidence to be collected and analyzed in a case study, ultimately circumscribing the types of findings that can emerge.

research question: the driving force for most empirical studies; for case studies, the most appropriate research questions will likely start with a "how" or "why" query.

rival explanation: a plausible alternative—different from a study's originally stipulated propositions—for interpreting the data or findings in a case study.

single-case study: a case study organized around a single case; the case might have been chosen because it was a critical, common, unusual, revelatory, or longitudinal case. Also see *multiple-case study*.

statistical generalization: the logic whereby the findings from a sample are claimed to apply to its universe, usually involving some statistical inference; not usually relevant for generalizing from case studies. Contrast with *analytic generalization*.

table shell: the layout for a table, with the rows and columns defined but with (numeric or narrative) data not yet placed in the cells; useful as a tool for identifying the data to be collected in a case study.

teaching case study: a case study used for pedagogical purposes and not to be confused with a case study conducted for research purposes.

theoretical replication: the selection of two (or more) cases in a multiple-case study because the cases are predicted to have contrasting findings, but for anticipatable reasons. Also see *replication logic*. Contrast with *literal replication*.

time-series analysis: analysis of case study data by arraying the data according to time markers and comparing the trends against those originally stipulated prior to data collection; stronger analyses would have sufficient data to entertain plausible rival trends.

training (to do a case study): preparation for understanding the key concepts and methodology for doing a planned case study—attaining a level of expertise sufficient to deal with the discretionary choices that may arise during data collection and the other phases of the research.

triangulation: the convergence of data collected from different sources, to determine the consistency of a finding.

unit of analysis: the case in a case study. Also see *embedded unit of analysis*.

verbal line of inquiry: the actual words used in querying a person during a case study interview. Contrast with *mental line of inquiry*.

REFERENCES

Abercrombie, N., Hill, S., & Turner, B. S. (2006). *The Penguin dictionary of sociology* (5th ed.). London: Penguin.

Agranoff, R., & Radin, B. A. (1991). The comparative case study approach in public administration. *Research in Public Administration, 1,* 203–231.

Alkin, M., Daillak, R., & White, P. (1979). *Using evaluations: Does evaluation make a difference?* Beverly Hills, CA: Sage.

Allen, M., & Black, M. (2006). Dual level evaluation and complex community initiatives: The local evaluation of Sure Start. *Evaluation, 12,* 237–249.

Allison, G. T. (1971). *Essence of decision: Explaining the Cuban missile crisis.* Boston: Little, Brown.

Allison, G. T., & Zelikow, P. (1999). *Essence of decision: Explaining the Cuban missile crisis* (2nd ed.). New York: Addison Wesley Longman.

American Anthropological Association. (1998). *Code of ethics of the American Anthropological Association.* Washington, DC: Author.

American Association of University Professors. (2006). *Research on human subjects: Academic freedom and the institutional review board.* Washington, DC: Author.

American Educational Research Association. (2000). *Ethical standards of the American Educational Research Association.* Washington, DC: Author.

American Evaluation Association. (2004). *Guiding principles for evaluators.* Washington, DC: Author.

American Political Science Association Committee on Professional Ethics, Rights, and Freedom. (2008). *A guide to professional ethics in political science* (2nd ed.). Washington, DC: Author.

American Psychological Association. (2010). *Ethical principles of psychologists and code of conduct.* Washington, DC: Author.

American Sociological Association. (1999). *Code of ethics and policies and procedures of the ASA committee on professional ethics.* Washington, DC: Author.

Anaf, S., Drummon, C., & Sheppard, L. A. (2007). Combining case study research and systems theory as a heuristic model. *Qualitative Health Research, 17,* 1309–1315.

Anderson, R., Crabtree, B. F., Steele, D. J., & McDaniel, R. R., Jr. (2005). Case study research: The view from complexity science. *Qualitative Health Research, 15,* 669–685.

Auerbach, C. F., & Silverstein, L. B. (2003). *Qualitative data: An introduction to coding and analysis.* New York: New York University Press.

Bachor, D. G. (2002). Increasing the believability of case study reports. *The Alberta Journal of Educational Research, XLVIII,* 20–29.

Barlow, D. H., & Nock, M. (2009). Why can't we be more idiographic in our research? *Perspectives on Psychological Science, 4,* 19–21.

Barzun, J., & Graff, H. (1985). *The modern researcher* (4th ed.). New York: Harcourt Brace Jovanovich.

Basu, O. N., Dirsmith, M. W., & Gupta, P. P. (1999). The coupling of the symbolic and the technical in an institutionalized context. *American Sociological Review, 64,* 506–526.

Baxter, P., & Jack, S. (2008). Qualitative case study methodology: Study design and implementation for novice researchers. *The Qualitative Report, 13,* 544–559.

Becker, H. S. (1958). Problems of inference and proof in participant observation. *American Sociological Review, 23,* 652–660.

Becker, H. S. (1967). Whose side are we on? *Social Problems, 14,* 239–247.

Becker, H. S. (1986). *Writing for social scientists: How to start and finish your thesis, book, or article.* Chicago: University of Chicago Press.

Becker, H. S. (1998). *Tricks of the trade: How to think about your research while you're doing it.* Chicago: University of Chicago Press.

Bennett, A. (2010). Process tracing and causal inference. In H. Brady & D. Collier (Eds.), *Rethinking social inquiry: Diverse tools, shared standards* (2nd ed., pp. 207–219). Lanham, MD: Rowman & Littlefield.

Berends, M., & Garet, M. S. (2002). In (re)search of evidence-based school practices: Possibilities for integrating nationally representative surveys and randomized field trials to inform educational policy. *Peabody Journal of Education, 77*(4), 28–58.

Berman, P., & McLaughlin, M. (1974–1978). *Federal programs supporting educational change* (8 vols.). Santa Monica, CA: RAND.

Beverland, M., & Lindgreen, A. (2010). What makes a good case study? A positivist review of qualitative case research published in *Industrial Marketing Management,* 1971–2006. *Industrial Marketing Management, 39*(1), 59–63.

Bickman, L. (1987). The functions of program theory. In L. Bickman (Ed.), *Using program theory in evaluation* (pp. 5–18). San Francisco: Jossey-Bass.

Bickman, L., & Mulvaney, S. (2005). Large scale evaluation of children's mental health services: The Ft. Bragg and Stark County studies. In R. Steele & M. Roberts (Eds.), *Handbook of mental health services for children, adolescents, and families* (pp. 371–386). New York: Kluwer Academic/Plenum.

Bickman, L., & Rog, D. J. (Eds.). (2009). *The Sage handbook of applied research methods.* (2nd ed.). Thousand Oaks, CA: Sage.

Blau, P. M. (1955). *The dynamics of bureaucracy.* Chicago: University of Chicago Press.

Boruch, R. (2007, October 12). *The flight of error: Scientific questions, evidential answers, and STEM education research.* Presentation at workshop on STEM Education Research Designs: Conceptual and Practical Considerations for Planning Experimental Studies, Arlington, VA, sponsored by the University of California, Irvine.

Boruch, R., & Foley, E. (2000). The honestly experimental society. In L. Bickman (Ed.), *Validity & social experimentation: Donald Campbell's legacy* (pp. 193–238). Thousand Oaks, CA: Sage.

Bouchard, T. J., Jr. (1976). Field research methods. In M. D. Dunnette (Ed.), *Industrial and organizational psychology* (pp. 363–413). Chicago: Rand McNally.

Bourgois, P. (2003). *In search of respect: Selling crack in El Barrio* (2nd ed.). Cambridge, England: Cambridge University Press.

Bradshaw, T. K. (1999). Communities not fazed: Why military base closures may not be catastrophic. *Journal of the American Planning Association, 65,* 193–206.

Brinton, C. (1938). *The anatomy of a revolution*. Englewood Cliffs, NJ: Prentice Hall.

Bromley, D. B. (1986). *The case-study method in psychology and related disciplines*. Chichester, England: Wiley.

Bruns, W. J., Jr. (1989). A review of Robert K. Yin's 'Case Study Research: Design and Methods.' *Journal of Management Accounting Research, 1,* 157–163.

Bryk, A. S., Bebring, P. B., Kerbow, D., Rollow, S., & Easton, J. Q. (1998). *Charting Chicago school reform: Democratic localism as a lever for change*. Boulder, CO: Westview.

Burawoy, M. (1991). The extended case method. In M. Burawoy, A. Burton, A. A. Ferguson, K. J. Fox, J. Gamson, N. Gartrell, et al. (Eds.), *Ethnography unbound: Power and resistance in the modern metropolis* (pp. 271–287). Berkeley: University of California Press.

Burke, W. W. (2007). *Organizational change: Theory and practice* (3rd ed.). Thousand Oaks, CA: Sage.

Busigny, T., Graf, M., Mayer, E., & Rossion, B. (2010). Acquired prosopagnosia as a face-specific disorder: Ruling out the general visual similarity account. *Neuropsychologia, 48,* 2051–2067.

Busigny, T., & Rossion, B. (2011). Holistic processing impairment can be restricted to faces in acquired prosopagnosia: Evidence from the global/local Navon effect. *Journal of Neuropsychology, 5,* 1–14.

Camic, P., Rhodes, J. E., & Yardley, L. (Eds.). (2003). *Qualitative research in psychology: Expanding perspectives in methodology and design*. Washington, DC: American Psychological Association.

Campbell, D. T. (1969). Reforms as experiments. *American Psychologist, 24,* 409–429.

Campbell, D. T. (1975). Degrees of freedom and the case study. *Comparative Political Studies, 8,* 178–193.

Campbell, D. T., & Stanley, J. (1966). *Experimental and quasi-experimental designs for research*. Chicago: Rand McNally.

Campbell, J. P., Daft, R. L., & Hulin, C. L. (1982). *What to study: Generating and developing research questions*. Beverly Hills, CA: Sage.

Carroll, J., & Johnson, E. (1992). Decision research: A field guide. *Journal of the Operational Research Society, 43,* 71–72.

Caulley, D. N. (2008). Making qualitative research reports less boring: The techniques of writing creative nonfiction. *Qualitative Inquiry, 14,* 424–449.

Caulley, D. N., & Dowdy, I. (1987). Evaluation case histories as a parallel to legal case histories. *Evaluation and Program Planning, 10,* 359–372.

Chaskin, R. J. (2001). Building community capacity: A definitional framework and case studies from a comprehensive community initiative. *Urban Affairs Review, 36,* 291–323.

Chaskin, R. J. (2003). The challenge of two-tiered evaluation in community initiatives. *Journal of Community Practices, 11,* 61–83.

Chassan, J. B. (1960). Statistical inference and the single case in clinical design. *Psychiatry, 23,* 173–184.

Cochran, W. G., & Cox, G. M. (1957). *Experimental designs* (2nd ed.). New York: John Wiley.

Cook, T. D., & Campbell, D. T. (1979). *Quasi-experimentation: Design and analysis issues for field settings*. Chicago: Rand McNally.

Cook, T. D., & Foray, D. (2007). Building the capacity to experiment in schools: A case study of the Institute of Educational Sciences in the US Department of Education. *Economics of Innovation and New Technology, 16*(5), 385–402.

Cook, T. D., & Payne, M. R. (2002). Objecting to the objections to using random assignment in educational research. In F. Mosteller & R. Boruch (Eds.), *Evidence matters: Randomized trials in education research* (pp. 150–178). Washington, DC: Brookings Institution Press.

Cooper, C. A., McCord, D. M., & Socha, A. (2011). Evaluating the college sophomore problem: The case of personality and politics. *Journal of Psychology, 145,* 23–37.

Cooper, H. M. (1984). *The integrative research review.* Beverly Hills, CA: Sage.

Cooper, H. M., & Hedges, L. V. (Eds.). (1994). *The handbook of research synthesis.* New York: Russell Sage Foundation.

Corbin, J., & Strauss, A. (2007). *Basics of qualitative research: Techniques and procedures for developing grounded theory* (3rd ed.). Thousand Oaks, CA: Sage.

COSMOS Corporation. (1983). *Case studies and organizational innovation: Strengthening the connection.* Bethesda, MD: Author.

COSMOS Corporation. (1998). *Evaluation of MEP-SBDC partnerships: Final report.* Report prepared for the National Institute of Standards and Technology, U.S. Department of Commerce, Gaithersburg, MD.

Crabtree, B. F., & Miller, W. L. (Eds.). (1999). *Doing qualitative research* (2nd ed.). Thousand Oaks, CA: Sage.

Crane, J. (Ed.). (1998). *Social programs that work.* New York: Russell Sage Foundation.

Creswell, J. W. (2007). *Qualitative inquiry & research design: Choosing among five approaches* (2nd ed.). Thousand Oaks, CA: Sage.

Creswell, J. W. (2012). *Qualitative inquiry & research design: Choosing among five approaches* (3rd ed.). Thousand Oaks, CA: Sage.

Crewe, K. (2001). The quality of participatory design: The effects of citizen input on the design of the Boston Southwest Corridor. *APA Journal, 67,* 437–455.

Cronbach, L. J. (1975). Beyond the two disciplines of scientific psychology. *American Psychologist, 30,* 116–127.

Cronbach, L. J., & Associates. (1980). *Toward reform of program evaluation: Aims, methods, and institutional arrangements.* San Francisco: Jossey-Bass.

Dabbs, J. M., Jr. (1982). Making things visible. In J. Van Maanen, J. M. Dabbs Jr., & R. R. Faulkner (Eds.), *Varieties of qualitative research* (pp. 31–63). Beverly Hills, CA: Sage.

Datta, L. (1997). Multimethod evaluations. In E. Chelimsky & W. R. Shadish (Eds.), *Evaluation for the 21st century* (pp. 344–359). Thousand Oaks, CA: Sage.

David, M. (Ed.). (2006a). *Case study research* (4 vols.). London: Sage.

David, M. (2006b). Editor's introduction. In M. David (Ed.), *Case study research* (pp. xxiii–xlii). London: Sage.

Denenberg, V. H. (1982). Comparative psychology and single-subject research. In A. E. Kazdin & A. H. Tuma (Eds.), *Single-case research designs* (No. 13, pp. 19–31). San Francisco: Jossey-Bass.

Denzin, N. K. (1978). The logic of naturalistic inquiry. In N. K. Denzin (Ed.), *Sociological methods: A sourcebook.* New York: McGraw-Hill.

Derthick, M. (1972). *New towns in-town: Why a federal program failed.* Washington, DC: The Urban Institute.

DeWalt, K. M., & DeWalt, B. (2011). *Participant observation: A guide for fieldworkers* (2nd ed.). Lanham, MD: Alamira Press.

Dion, D. (1998). Evidence and inference in the comparative case study. *Comparative Politics, 30,* 127–145.

Donmoyer, R. (1990). Generalizability and the single-case study. In E. W. Eisner & A. Peshkin (Eds.), *Qualitative inquiry in education: The continuing debate* (pp. 175–200). New York: Teachers College Press.

Drucker, P. F. (1986). The changed world economy. In P. F. Drucker (Ed.), *The frontiers of management* (pp. 21–49). New York: Dutton.

Dubois, A., & Gadde, L.-E. (2002). Systematic combining: An abductive approach to case research. *Journal of Business Research, 55,* 553–560.

Duff, P. A. (2008). *Case study research in applied linguistics.* New York: Routledge.

Dul, J., & Hak, T. (2008). *Case study methodology in business research.* Oxford, England: Butterworth-Heinemann.

Dunbar, G. (2005). *Evaluating research methods in psychology: A case study approach.* Malden, MA: Blackwell.

Duneier, M. (1999). *Sidewalk.* New York: Farrar, Straus, & Giroux.

Dyehouse, M., Bennett, D., Harbor, J., Childress, A., & Dark, M. (2009). A comparison of linear and systems thinking approaches for program evaluation illustrated using the Indiana Interdisciplinary GK-12. *Evaluation and Program Planning, 32,* 187–196.

Eckstein, H. (1975). Case study and theory in political science. In F. I. Greenstein & N. W. Polsby (Eds.), *Strategies of inquiry* (pp. 79–137). Reading, MA: Addison-Wesley.

Eilbert, K. W., & Lafronza, V. (2005). Working together for community health—a model and case studies. *Evaluation and Program Planning, 28,* 185–199.

Eisenhardt, K. M. (1989). Building theories from case study research. *Academy of Management Review, 14,* 532–550.

Ellet, W. (2007). *The case study handbook: How to read, discuss, and write persuasively about cases.* Boston: Harvard Business School Press.

Elmore, R. F., Abelmann, C. H., & Fuhrman, S. H. (1997). The new accountability in state education reform: From process to performance. In H. F. Ladd (Ed.), *Holding schools accountable* (pp. 65–98). Washington, DC: Brookings Institution.

Ericksen, J., & Dyer, L. (2004). Right from the start: Exploring the effects of early team events on subsequent project team development and performance. *Administrative Science Quarterly, 49,* 438–471.

Eriksson, P., & Kovalainen, A. (2008). *Qualitative methods in business research.* London: Sage.

Feagin, J. R., Orum, A. M., & Sjoberg, G. (Eds.). (1991). *A case for the case study.* Chapel Hill: University of North Carolina Press.

Fiedler, J. (1978). *Field research: A manual for logistics and management of scientific studies in natural settings.* San Francisco: Jossey-Bass.

Fielding, N., & Warnes, R. (2009). Computer-based qualitative methods in case study research. In D. Byrne & C. C. Ragin (Eds.), *The Sage handbook of case-based methods* (pp. 270–288). London: Sage.

Fielding, N. G., & Lee, R. M. (1998). *Computer analysis and qualitative research.* Thousand Oaks, CA: Sage.

Flyvberg, B. (2006). Five misunderstandings about case-study research. *Qualitative Inquiry, 12,* 219–245.

Forrester, M. (2010). Introduction. In M. Forrester (Ed.), *Doing qualitative research in psychology: A practical guide*. London: Sage.

Fowler, F. J., Jr. (1988). *Survey research methods* (Rev. ed.). Newbury Park, CA: Sage.

Friese, S. (2012). *Qualitative data analysis with ATLAS.ti*. London: Sage.

Funnell, S. C., & Rogers, P. J. (2011). *Purposeful program theory: Effective use of theories of change and logic models*. San Francisco: Jossey-Bass.

Galster, G., Tatian, P., & Accordino, J. (2006). Targeting investments for neighborhood revitalization. *Journal of the American Planning Association, 72*, 457–474.

Gans, H. J. (1962). *The urban villagers: Group and class in the life of Italian-Americans*. New York: Free Press.

Garmezy, N. (1982). The case for the single case in research. In A. E. Kazdin & A. H. Tuma (Eds.), *Single-case research designs* (No. 13, pp. 5–17). San Francisco: Jossey-Bass.

Garvin, D.A. (2003, September–October). Making the case: Professional education for the world of practice. *Harvard Magazine, 106*(1), 56–107.

Geertz, C. (1973). *The interpretation of cultures*. New York: Basic Books.

George, A. L., & Bennett, A. (2004). *Case studies and theory development in the social sciences*. Cambridge: MIT Press.

Gerring, J. (2004). What is a case study and what is it good for? *American Political Science Review, 98*, 341–354.

Gibbert, M., Ruigrok, W., & Wicki, B. (2008). What passes as a rigorous case study? *Strategic Management Journal, 29*, 1465–1474.

Gilgun, J. F. (1994). A case for case studies in social work research. *Social Work, 39*, 371–380.

Glaser, B., & Strauss, A. (1967). *The discovery of grounded theory: Strategies for qualitative research*. Chicago: Aldine.

Golden, L. B. (2004). *Case studies in marriage and family therapy* (2nd ed.). Upper Saddle River, NJ: Pearson.

Gomm, R., Hammersley, M., & Foster, P. (2000). Case study and generalization. In R. Gomm, M. Hammersley, & P. Foster (Eds.), *Case study method* (pp. 98–115). London: Sage.

Gordon, M. E., Slade, L. A., & Schmitt, N. (1986). The 'science of the sophomore' revisited: From conjecture to empiricism. *Academy of Management Review, 11*, 191–207.

Gottschalk, L. (1968). *Understanding history: A primer of historical method*. New York: Knopf.

Grinnell, R. M., & Unrau, Y. A. (Eds.). (2008). *Social work research and evaluation: Foundations of evidence-based practice*. New York: Oxford University Press.

Gross, N., Bernstein, M., & Giacquinta, J. B. (1971). *Implementing organizational innovations: A sociological analysis of planned educational change*. New York: Basic Books.

Hahn, C. (2008). *Doing qualitative research using your computer: A practical guide*. Thousand Oaks, CA: Sage.

Hamel, J. (Ed.). (1992). The case study method in sociology [Whole issue]. *Current Sociology, 40*.

Hammond, P. E. (1968). *Sociologists at work: Essays on the craft of social research*. Garden City, NY: Doubleday.

Hanna, K. S. (2000). The paradox of participation and the hidden role of information. *Journal of the American Planning Association, 66*, 398–410.

Hanna, K. S. (2005). Planning for sustainability. *Journal of the American Planning Association, 71*, 27–40.

Hedrick, T., Bickman, L., & Rog, D. J. (1993). *Applied research design.* Newbury Park, CA: Sage.

Henrich, J., Heine, S. J., & Norenzayan, A. (2010). The weirdest people in the world? *Behavioral and Brain Sciences, 33,* 61–83.

Herriott, R. E., & Firestone, W. A. (1983). Multisite qualitative policy research: Optimizing description and generalizability. *Educational Researcher, 12,* 14–19.

Hersen, M., & Barlow, D. H. (1976). *Single-case experimental designs: Strategies for studying behavior.* New York: Pergamon.

Hipp, J. R. (2007). Block, tract, and levels of aggregation: Neighborhood structure and crime and disorder as a case in point. *American Sociological Review, 72,* 659–680.

Hoaglin, D. C., Light, R. J., McPeek, B., Mosteller, F., & Stoto, M. A. (1982). *Data for decisions: Information strategies for policymakers.* Cambridge, MA: Abt Books.

Hooks, G. (1990). The rise of the Pentagon and U.S. state building: The defense program as industrial policy. *American Journal of Sociology, 96,* 358–404.

Jacobs, J. (1961). *The death and life of great American cities.* New York: Random House.

Jacobs, R. N. (1996). Civil society and crisis: Culture, discourse, and the Rodney King beating. *American Journal of Sociology, 101,* 1238–1272.

Jadad, A. (1998). *Randomised controlled trials.* London: BMJ Books.

Janesick, V. J. (2010). *Oral history for the qualitative researcher: Choreographing the story.* New York: Guilford.

Johnson, R. B., & Onwuegbuzie, A. J. (2004). Mixed methods research: A research paradigm whose time has come. *Educational Researcher, 33,* 14–26.

Johnston, W. J., Leach, M. P., & Liu, A. H. (2000). Using case studies for theory testing in business-to-business research: The development of a more rigorous case study methodology. *Advances in Business Marketing and Purchasing, 9,* 215–241.

Joint Committee on Standards for Educational Evaluation. (1981). *Standards for evaluations of educational programs, projects, and materials.* New York: McGraw-Hill.

Jorgensen, D. (1989). *Participant observation: A methodology for human studies.* Newbury Park, CA: Sage.

Julnes, G., & Rog, D. (2009). Evaluation methods for producing actionable evidence: Contextual influences on adequacy and appropriateness of method choice. In S. I. Donaldson, C. A. Christie, & M. M. Mark (Eds.), *What counts as credible evidence in applied research and evaluation practice?* (pp. 96–131). Thousand Oaks, CA: Sage.

Kates, N. (2008). Integrating mental health services into primary care: The Hamilton FHT mental health program. In R. Kessler & D. Stafford (Eds.), *Collaborative medicine case studies: Evidence in practice* (pp. 71–82). New York: Springer.

Kaufman, H. (1981). *The administrative behavior of federal bureau chiefs.* Washington, DC: Brookings Institution.

Kazdin, A. E. (1982). *Single-case research designs: Methods for clinical and applied settings.* New York: Oxford University Press.

Kazdin, A. E. (2003). Drawing valid inferences from case studies. In A. E. Kazdin (Ed.), *Methodological issues and strategies in clinical research* (3rd ed., pp. 655–669). Washington, DC: American Psychological Association.

Keating, W. D., & Krumholz, N. (Eds.). (1999). *Rebuilding urban neighborhoods: Achievements, opportunities, and limits.* Thousand Oaks, CA: Sage.

Kelling, G. L., & Coles, C. M. (1997). *Fixing broken windows: Restoring order and reducing crime in our communities.* New York: Simon & Schuster.

Kelly, A. E., & Yin, R. K. (2007). Strengthening structured abstracts for education research: The need for claim-based structured abstracts. *Educational Researcher, 36,* 133–138.

Kennedy, M. M. (1976). Generalizing from single case studies. *Evaluation Quarterly, 3,* 661–678.

Kessler, R., & Stafford, D. (Eds.). (2008). *Collaborative medicine case studies: Evidence in practice.* New York: Springer.

Kidder, L., & Judd, C. M. (1986). *Research methods in social relations* (5th ed.). New York: Holt, Rinehart & Winston.

Kidder, T. (1981). *The soul of a new machine.* Boston: Little, Brown.

Knowlton, L. W., & Phillips, C. C. (2009). *The logic model guidebook: Better strategies for great results.* Thousand Oaks, CA: Sage.

Kratochwill, T. R. (1978). *Single subject research.* New York: Academic Press.

Krueger, R. A., & Casey, M. A. (2009). *Focus groups: A practical guide for applied research* (4th ed.). Thousand Oaks, CA: Sage.

Labin, S. N. (2008). Research syntheses: Toward broad-based evidence. In N. L. Smith & P. R. Brandon (Eds.), *Fundamental issues in evaluation* (pp. 89–110). New York: Guilford.

Lavrakas, P. J. (1987). *Telephone survey methods.* Newbury Park, CA: Sage.

Lawrence-Lightfoot, S., & Davis, J. H. (1997). *The art and science of portraiture.* San Francisco: Jossey-Bass.

Lee, E., Mishna, F., & Brennenstuhl, S. (2010). How to critically evaluate case studies in social work. *Research on Social Work Practice, 20,* 682–689.

Lempert, L. B. (2011). Asking questions of the data: Memo writing in the grounded theory tradition. In A. Bryant & K. Charmaz (Eds.), *The Sage handbook of grounded theory* (pp. 245–264). Thousand Oaks, CA: Sage.

Leopold, D. A., Bondar, I. V., & Giese, M. A. (2006). Norm-based face encoding by single neurons in the monkey inferotemporal cortex. *Nature, 442,* 572–575.

Lewins, A., & Silver, C. (2007). *Using software in qualitative research: A step-by-step guide.* London: Sage.

Liebow, E. (1967). *Tally's corner.* Boston: Little, Brown.

Lijphart, A. (1975). The comparable-cases strategy in comparative research. *Comparative Political Studies, 8,* 158–177.

Lincoln, Y. S., & Guba, E. G. (1985). But is it rigorous? Trustworthiness and authenticity in naturalistic evaluation. In D. D. Williams (Ed.), *Naturalistic evaluation* (pp. 73–84). San Francisco: Jossey-Bass.

Lipset, S. M., Trow, M., & Coleman, J. (1956). *Union democracy: The inside politics of the International Typographical Union.* New York: Free Press.

Lipsey, M. W. (1990). *Design sensitivity: Statistical power for experimental research.* Thousand Oaks, CA: Sage.

Lipsey, M. W. (1992). Meta-analysis in evaluation research: Moving from description to explanation. In H. T. Chen & P. Rossi (Eds.), *Using theory to improve program and policy evaluations* (pp. 229–241). New York: Greenwood.

Llewellyn, K. N. (1948). Case method. In E. Seligman & A. Johnson (Eds.), *Encyclopedia of the social sciences.* New York: Macmillan.

Lynd, R. S., & Lynd, H. M. (1929). *Middletown: A study in modern American culture.* New York: Harcourt Brace Jovanovich.

Lynd, R. S., & Lynd, H. M. (1937). *Middletown in transition: A study in cultural conflicts.* New York: Harcourt Brace Jovanovich.

Magaziner, I. C., & Patinkin, M. (1989). *The silent war: Inside the global business battles shaping America's future.* New York: Random House.

Mark, M. M. (2008). Building a better evidence base for evaluation theory. In N. L. Smith & P. R. Brandon (Eds.), *Fundamental issues in evaluation* (pp. 111–134). New York: Guilford.

Markus, M. L. (1983). Power, politics, and MIS implementation. *Communications of the ACM, 26,* 430–444.

Marshall, C., & Rossman, G. B. (2011). *Designing qualitative research* (5th ed.). Newbury Park, CA: Sage.

Marwell, N. P. (2007). *Bargaining for Brooklyn: Community organizations in the entrepreneurial city.* Chicago: University of Chicago Press.

McAdams, D. R. (2000). *Fighting to save our urban schools . . . and winning! Lessons from Houston.* New York: Teachers College Press.

McClintock, C. (1985). Process sampling: A method for case study research on administrative behavior. *Educational Administration Quarterly, 21,* 205–222.

McKone, E., Kanwisher, N., & Duchaine, B. C. (2007). Can generic expertise explain special processing for faces? *Trends in Cognitive Science, 11,* 8–15.

McNemar, Q. (1946). Opinion-attitude methodology. *Psychological Bulletin, 43,* 289–374.

Mertens, D. (2010). *Research and evaluation in education and psychology* (3rd ed.). Thousand Oaks, CA: Sage.

Merton, R. K., Fiske, M., & Kendall, P. L. (1990). *The focused interview: A manual of problems and procedures* (2nd ed.). New York: Free Press.

Meyer, C. B. (2001). A case in case study methodology. *Field Methods, 13,* 329–352.

Michel, J.-B., Shen, Y. K., Aiden, A. P., Veres, A., Gray, M. K., The Google Books Team, et al. (2010). Quantitative analysis of culture using millions of digitized books. *Science, 331,* 176–182.

Miles, M. B., & Huberman, A. M. (1994). *Qualitative data analysis: An expanded sourcebook.* Thousand Oaks, CA: Sage.

Mills, A. J., Durepos, G., & Wiebe, E. (Eds.). (2010a). *Encyclopedia of case study research* (2 vols.). Los Angeles: Sage.

Mills, A. J., Durepos, G., & Wiebe, E. (2010b). Introduction. In A. J. Mills, G. Durepos, & E. Wiebe (Eds.), *Encyclopedia of case study research* (pp. xxxi–xxxvi). Thousand Oaks, CA: Sage.

Mitchell, J. C. (1983). Case and situation analysis. *Sociological Review, 31,* 187–211.

Miyahara, M., & Wafer, A. (2004). Clinical intervention for children with developmental coordination disorder: A multiple case study. *Adapted Physical Activity Quarterly, 21,* 281–300.

Moore, B., Jr. (1966). *Social origins of dictatorship and democracy: Lord and peasant in the making of the modern world.* Boston: Beacon.

Morgan, D. L., & Morgan, R. K. (2009). *Single-case research methods for the behavioral and health sciences.* Thousand Oaks, CA: Sage.

Morris, L. L., Fitz-Gibbon, C. T., & Freeman, M. E. (1987). *How to communicate evaluation findings.* Beverly Hills, CA: Sage.

Mosteller, F., & Wallace, D. L. (1984). *Applied Bayesian and classical inference: The case of "The Federalist" papers* (2nd ed.). New York: Springer Verlag.

Mulroy, E. A., & Lauber, H. (2004). A user-friendly approach to program evaluation and effective community interventions for families at risk of homelessness. *Social Work, 49,* 573–586.

Murphy, J. T. (1980). *Getting the facts: A fieldwork guide for evaluators and policy analysts.* Santa Monica, CA: Goodyear.

Murray, D. M. (1998). *Design and analysis of group-randomized trials.* New York: Oxford University Press.

Nachmias, D., & Nachmias, C. (1992). *Research methods in the social sciences.* New York: St. Martin's.

Nathan, I., Lund, J. F., Gausset, Q., & Andersen, S. K. (2007). On the promise of devolution: Overcoming the constraints of natural resource management in a village in Tanzania. *Journal of Transdisciplinary Environmental Studies, 6,* 1–20.

National Research Council. (2003). *Protecting participants and facilitating social and behavioral sciences research.* Washington, DC: National Academies Press.

National Research Council. (2004). *On evaluating curricular effectiveness: Judging the quality of K–12 mathematics evaluations.* Washington, DC: National Academies Press.

Naumes, W., & Naumes, M. J. (1999). *The art & craft of case writing.* Thousand Oaks, CA: Sage.

Nesman, T. M., Batsche, C., & Hernandez, M. (2007). Theory-based evaluation of a comprehensive Latino education initiative: An interactive evaluation approach. *Evaluation and Program Planning, 30,* 267–281.

Neuman, S. B., & Celano, D. (2001). Access to print in low-income and middle-income communities: An ecological study of four neighborhoods. *Reading Research Quarterly, 36,* 8–26.

Neustadt, R. E., & Fineberg, H. (1983). *The epidemic that never was: Policy-making and the swine flu affair.* New York: Vintage.

O'Reilly, K. (2005). *Ethnographic methods.* London: Routledge.

Patton, M. Q. (2002). *Qualitative research and evaluation methods* (3rd ed.). Thousand Oaks, CA: Sage.

Peters, T. J., & Waterman, R. H., Jr. (1982). *In search of excellence.* New York: Harper & Row.

Peterson, K. A., & Bickman, L. (1992). Using program theory in quality assessments of children's mental health services. In H. T. Chen & P. Rossi (Eds.), *Using theory to improve program and policy evaluations* (pp. 165–176). New York: Greenwood.

Peterson, R. K. (2001). On the use of college students in social science research: Insights from a second-order meta-analysis. *Journal of Consumer Research, 28,* 450–461.

Philliber, S. G., Schwab, M. R., & Samsloss, G. (1980). *Social research: Guides to a decision-making process.* Itasca, IL: Peacock.

Phillips, R., & Pittman, R. H. (2009). A framework for community and economic development. In R. Phillips & R. H. Pittman (Eds.), *An introduction to community development* (pp. 3–19). Abingdon, England: Routledge.

Piekkari, R., Welch, C., & Paavilainen, E. (2009). The case study as disciplinary convention: Evidence from international business journals. *Organizational Research Methods, 12,* 567–589.

Platt, J. (1992). "Case study" in American methodological thought. *Current Sociology, 40,* 17–48.

Prescott, H. M. (2002). Using the student body: College and university students as research subjects in the United States during the twentieth century. *Journal of the History of Medicine, 57,* 3–38.

Pressman, J. L., & Wildavsky, A. (1973). *Implementation: How great expectations in Washington are dashed in Oakland.* Berkeley: University of California Press.

Ragin, C. C. (1987). *The comparative method: Moving beyond qualitative and quantitative strategies*. Berkeley: University of California Press.

Ragin, C. C., & Becker, H. S. (Eds.). (1992). *What is a case? Exploring the foundations of social inquiry*. New York: Cambridge University Press.

Raizen, S. A., & Britton, E. D. (Eds.). (1997). *Bold ventures* (3 vols.). Dordrecht, The Netherlands: Kluwer Academic.

Randolph, J. J., & Eronen, P. J. (2007). Developing the Learner Door: A case study in youth participatory program planning. *Evaluation and Program Planning, 30,* 55–65.

Redman, E. (1973). *The dance of legislation*. New York: Simon & Schuster.

Rihoux, B., & Lobe, B. (2009). The case for qualitative comparative analysis (QCA): Adding leverage for thick cross-case comparison. In D. Byrne & C. C. Ragin (Eds.), *The Sage handbook of case-based methods* (pp. 222–242). London: Sage.

Rivera, L. A. (2008). Managing "spoiled" national identity: War, tourism, and memory in Croatia. *American Sociological Review, 73,* 613–634.

Robben, A. C. G. M., & Sluka, J. A. (Eds.). (2007). *Ethnographic fieldwork: An anthropological reader*. Malden, MA: Blackwell.

Robertson, L. C., Knight, R. T., Rafal, R., & Shimamura, A. P. (1993). Cognitive psychology is more than single-case studies. *Journal of Experimental Psychology, 19,* 710–717.

Rog, D. J., & Huebner, R. B. (1992). Using research and theory in developing innovative programs for homeless individuals. In H. T. Chen & P. Rossi (Eds.), *Using theory to improve program and policy evaluations* (pp. 129–144). New York: Greenwood.

Rog, D. J., & Randolph, F. I. (2002). A multisite evaluation of supported housing: Lessons from cross-site collaboration. *New Directions for Evaluation, 94,* 61–72.

Rogers, E. M., & Larsen, J. K. (1984). *Silicon Valley fever: Growth of high-technology culture*. New York: Basic Books.

Rogers, P. J. (2000). Program theory: Not whether programs work but how they work. In D. L. Stufflebeam, G. F. Madaus, & T. Kelleghan (Eds.), *Evaluation models: Viewpoints on educational and human services evaluation* (2nd ed., pp. 209–232). Boston: Kluwer.

Rogowski, R. (2010). How inference in the social (but not the physical) sciences neglects theoretical anomaly. In H. Brady & D. Collier (Eds.), *Rethinking social inquiry: Diverse tools, shared standards* (2nd ed., pp. 89–97). Lanham, MD: Rowman & Littlefield.

Rolls, G. (2005). *Classic case studies in psychology*. Abingdon, England: Hodder Education.

Rosenbaum, D. P. (Ed.). (1986). *Community crime prevention: Does it work?* Thousand Oaks, CA: Sage.

Rosenbaum, P. R. (2002). *Observational studies* (2nd ed.). New York: Springer.

Rosenthal, R. (1966). *Experimenter effects in behavioral research*. New York: Appleton-Century-Crofts.

Rossi, P., Lipsey, M. W., & Freeman, H. E. (2004). *Evaluation: A systematic approach* (7th ed.). Thousand Oaks, CA: Sage.

Rubin, A., & Babbie, E. (1993). *Research methods for social work*. Pacific Grove, CA: Brooks/Cole.

Rubin, H. J., & Rubin, I. S. (2011). *Qualitative interviewing: The art of hearing data* (3rd ed.). Thousand Oaks, CA: Sage.

Ruddin, L. P. (2006). You can generalize stupid! Social scientists, Bent Flyvbjerg, and case study methodology. *Qualitative Inquiry, 12,* 797–812.

Saldaña, J. (2009). *The coding manual for qualitative researchers*. London: Sage.

Schatzman, L., & Strauss, A. (1973). *Field research*. Englewood Cliffs, NJ: Prentice Hall.

Schein, E. (2003). *DEC is dead, long live DEC: Lessons on innovation, technology, and the business gene*. San Francisco: Berrett-Koehler.

Schlesselman, J. J. (1982). *Case-control studies: Design, conduct, analysis*. New York: Oxford University Press.

Schorr, L. B. (1997). *Common purpose: Strengthening families and neighborhoods to rebuild America*. New York: Anchor.

Schramm, W. (1971, December). *Notes on case studies of instructional media projects*. Working paper for the Academy for Educational Development, Washington, DC.

Schwandt, T. A. (2007). *The Sage dictionary of qualitative inquiry* (3rd ed.). Los Angeles: Sage.

Schwandt, T. A. (2009). Toward a practical theory of evidence for evaluation. In S. I. Donaldson, C. A. Christie, & M. M. Mark (Eds.), *What counts as credible evidence in applied research and evaluation practice?* (pp. 197–212). Thousand Oaks, CA: Sage.

Scoville, W. B., & Milner, B. (1957). Loss of recent memory in bilateral hippocampal lesions. *Journal of Neurology, Neurosurgery, and Psychiatry, 20,* 11–22.

Scriven, M. (2009). Demythologizing causation and evidence. In S. I. Donaldson, C. A. Christie, & M. M. Mark (Eds.), *What counts as credible evidence in applied research and evaluation practice?* (pp. 134–152). Thousand Oaks, CA: Sage.

Sears, D. O. (1986). College sophomores in the laboratory: Influences of a narrow database on social psychology's view of human nature. *Journal of Personality and Social Psychology, 51,* 515–530.

Selznick, P. (1980). *TVA and the grass roots: A study of politics and organization*. Berkeley: University of California Press. (Original work published 1949)

Shavelson, R., & Towne, L. (Eds.). (2002). *Scientific research in education*. Washington, DC: National Academies Press.

Sidman, M., Soddard, L. T., & Mohr, J. P. (1968). Some additional quantitative observations of immediate memory in a patient with bilateral hippocampal lesions. *Neuropsychologia, 6,* 245–254.

Sidowski, J. B. (Ed.). (1966). *Experimental methods and instrumentation in psychology*. New York: Holt, Rinehart & Winston.

Silverman, D. (2010). *Doing qualitative research: A practical handbook* (3rd ed.). Thousand Oaks, CA: Sage.

Small, M. L. (2004). *Villa Victoria: The transformation of social capital in a Boston barrio*. Chicago: University of Chicago Press.

Small, M. L. (2009). "How many cases do I need?" On science and the logic of case selection in field-based research. *Ethnography, 10,* 5–38.

Smith, J. (Ed.). (2008). *Qualitative psychology: A practical guide to research methods* (2nd ed.). London: Sage.

Speiglman, R., & Spear, P. (2009). The role of institutional review boards: Ethics: Now you see them, now you don't. In D. M. Mertens & P. E. Ginsberg (Eds.), *The handbook of social research ethics* (pp. 121–134). Thousand Oaks, CA: Sage.

Spilerman, S. (1971). The causes of racial disturbances: Tests of an explanation. *American Sociological Review, 36,* 427–442.

Stake, R. E. (2005). Qualitative case studies. In N. K. Denzin & Y. S. Lincoln (Eds.), *The Sage handbook of qualitative research* (3rd ed., pp. 443–466). Thousand Oaks, CA: Sage.

Stake, R. E. (2006). *Multiple case study analysis*. New York: Guilford.

Standerfer, N. R., & Rider, J. (1983). The politics of automating a planning office. *Planning, 49,* 18–21.

Stein, H. (1952). Case method and the analysis of public administration. In H. Stein (Ed.), *Public administration and policy development* (pp. xx–xxx). New York: Harcourt Brace Jovanovich.

Stoecker, R. (1991). Evaluating and rethinking the case study. *The Sociological Review, 39,* 88–112.

Stufflebeam, D. L., & Shinkfield, A. J. (2007). *Evaluation theory, models, and applications*. San Francisco: Jossey-Bass.

Sudman, S., & Bradburn, N. M. (1982). *Asking questions: A practical guide to questionnaire design*. San Francisco: Jossey-Bass.

Supovitz, J. A., & Taylor, B. S. (2005). Systemic education evaluation: Evaluating the impact of systemwide reform in education. *American Journal of Evaluation, 26,* 204–230.

Sutton, R. I., & Staw, B. M. (1995). What theory is *not*. *Administrative Science Quarterly, 40,* 371–384.

Szanton, P. (1981). *Not well advised*. New York: Russell Sage Foundation and The Ford Foundation.

Tawney, J. W., & Gast, D. L. (1984). *Single subject research in special education*. Columbus, OH: Merrill.

Teske, P., Schneider, M., Roch, C., & Marschall, M. (2000). Public school choice: A status report. In D. Ravitch & J. P. Viteritti (Eds.), *Lessons from New York City schools* (pp. 313–338). Baltimore: Johns Hopkins University Press.

Thacher, D. (2006). The normative case study. *American Journal of Sociology, 111,* 1631–1676.

Towl, A. R. (1969). *To study administrations by cases*. Boston: Harvard University Business School.

Trochim, W. (1989). Outcome pattern matching and program theory. *Evaluation and Program Planning, 12,* 355–366.

United Nations Development Programme. (2010). *Evaluation of UNDP contribution to strengthening national capacities*. New York: Evaluation Office.

U.S. Government Accountability Office, Program Evaluation and Methodology Division. (1990). *Case study evaluations*. Washington, DC: Government Printing Office.

U.S. National Commission on Neighborhoods. (1979). *People, building neighborhoods*. Washington, DC: Government Printing Office.

U.S. Office of Technology Assessment. (1980–1981). *The implications of cost-effectiveness analysis of medical technology: Case studies of medical technologies*. Washington, DC: Government Printing Office.

Van Maanen, J. (1988). *Tales of the field: On writing ethnography*. Chicago: University of Chicago Press.

Vaughan, D. (1992). Theory elaboration: The heuristics of case analysis. In C. C. Ragin & H. D. Becker (Eds.), *What is a case? Exploring the foundations of social inquiry* (pp. 173–202). Cambridge, England: Cambridge University Press.

Vaughan, D. (1996). *The* Challenger *launch decision: Risky technology, culture, and deviance at NASA*. Chicago: University of Chicago Press.

Veerman, J. W., & van Yperen, T. A. (2007). Degrees of freedom and degrees of certainty: A developmental model for the establishment of evidence-based youth care. *Evaluation and Program Planning, 30,* 212–221.

Vertue, F. M. (2011). Applying case study methodology to child custody evaluations. *Family Court Review, 49,* 336–347.

Vissak, T. (2010). Recommendations for using the case study method in international business research. *The Qualitative Report, 15,* 370–388.

Warner, W. L., & Lunt, P. S. (1941). *The social life of a modern community.* New Haven, CT: Yale University Press.

Wax, R. (1971). *Doing field work.* Chicago: University of Chicago Press.

Weiss, R. S. (1994). *Learning from strangers: The art and method of qualitative interview studies.* New York: The Free Press.

Wertz, F. J., Charmaz, K., McMullen, L. M., Josselson, R., Anderson, R., & McSpadden, E. (2011). *Five ways of doing qualitative analysis: Phenomenological psychology, grounded theory, discourse analysis, narrative research, and intuitive inquiry.* New York: Guilford.

Wholey, J. (1979). *Evaluation: Performance and promise.* Washington, DC: The Urban Institute.

Whyte, W. F. (1993). *Street corner society: The social structure of an Italian slum* (4th ed.). Chicago: University of Chicago Press. (Original work published 1943)

Wilford, J. N. (1992). *The mysterious history of Columbus.* New York: Vintage.

Wilson, R. F. (Ed.). (1982). *Designing academic program reviews* (New Directions for Higher Education, No. 37). San Francisco: Jossey-Bass.

Windsor, D., & Greanias, G. (1983). The public policy and management program for case/course development. *Public Administration Review, 26,* 370–378.

Wolcott, H. F. (2009). *Writing up qualitative research* (3rd ed.). Thousand Oaks, CA: Sage.

Wolf, P. (1997). Why must we reinvent the federal government? Putting historical developmental claims to the test. *Journal of Public Administration Research and Theory, 3,* 358–388.

Yardley, L. (2009). Demonstrating validity in qualitative psychology. In J. A. Smith (Ed.), *Qualitative psychology: A practical guide to research method* (pp. 235–251). Los Angeles: Sage.

Yin, R. K. (1978). Face perception: A review of experiments with infants, normal adults, and brain-injured persons. In R. Held, H. Liebowitz, & H.-L. Teuber (Eds.), *Handbook of sensory physiology: Vol. VIII. Perception* (pp. 593–608). New York: Springer-Verlag.

Yin, R. K. (1980). Creeping federalism: The federal impact on the structure and function of local government. In N. J. Glickman (Ed.), *The urban impacts of federal policies* (pp. 595–618). Baltimore: Johns Hopkins University Press.

Yin, R. K. (1981a). The case study as a serious research strategy. *Knowledge: Creation, Diffusion, Utilization, 3,* 97–114.

Yin, R. K. (1981b). The case study crisis: Some answers. *Administrative Science Quarterly, 26,* 58–65.

Yin, R. K. (1981c). Life histories of innovations: How new practices become routinized. *Public Administration Review, 41,* 21–28.

Yin, R. K. (1982a). *Conserving America's neighborhoods.* New York: Plenum.

Yin, R. K. (1982b). Studying the implementation of public programs. In W. Williams, R. F. Elmore, J. S. Hall, R. Jung, M. Kirst, S. A. MacManus, et al. (Eds.), *Studying implementation: Methodological and administrative issues* (pp. 36–72). Chatham, NJ: Chatham House.

Yin, R. K. (1986). Community crime prevention: A synthesis of eleven evaluations. In D. P. Rosenbaum (Ed.), *Community crime prevention: Does it work?* (pp. 294–308). Thousand Oaks, CA: Sage.

Yin, R. K. (1994a). Discovering the future of the case study method in evaluation research. *Evaluation Practice, 15,* 283–290.

Yin, R. K. (1994b). Evaluation: A singular craft. In C. Reichardt & S. Rallis (Eds.), *New directions in program evaluation* (pp. 71–84). San Francisco: Jossey-Bass.

Yin, R. K. (1997). Case study evaluations: A decade of progress? *New Directions for Evaluation, 76,* 69–78.

Yin, R. K. (1999). Enhancing the quality of case studies in health services research. *Health Services Research, 34,* 1209–1224.

Yin, R. K. (2000a). Case study evaluations: A decade of progress? In D. L. Stufflebeam, G. F. Madaus, & T. Kelleghan (Eds.), *Evaluation models: Viewpoints on educational and human services evaluation* (2nd ed., pp. 185–193). Boston: Kluwer.

Yin, R. K. (2000b). Rival explanations as an alternative to "reforms as experiments." In L. Bickman (Ed.), *Validity & social experimentation: Donald Campbell's legacy* (pp. 239–266). Thousand Oaks, CA: Sage.

Yin, R. K. (2003). *Applications of case study research* (2nd ed.). Thousand Oaks, CA: Sage.

Yin, R. K. (Ed.). (2004). *The case study anthology.* Thousand Oaks, CA: Sage.

Yin, R. K. (Ed.). (2005). *Introducing the world of education: A case study reader.* Thousand Oaks, CA: Sage.

Yin, R. K. (2006a). Case study methods. In J. Green, G. Camilli, & P. Elmore (Eds.), *Handbook of complementary methods in education research* (3rd ed., pp. 111–122). Washington, DC: American Educational Research Association.

Yin, R. K. (2006b). Mixed methods research: Are the methods genuinely integrated or merely parallcl? *Research in the Schools, 13,* 41–47.

Yin, R. K. (2011). *Qualitative research from start to finish.* New York: Guilford.

Yin, R. K. (2012). *Applications of case study research* (3rd ed.). Thousand Oaks, CA: Sage.

Yin, R. K., Bingham, E., & Heald, K. (1976). The difference that quality makes. *Sociological Methods and Research, 5,* 139–156.

Yin, R. K., & Davis, D. (2006). State-level education reform: Putting all the pieces together. In K. Wong & S. Rutledge (Eds.), *Systemwide efforts to improve student achievement* (pp. 1–33). Greenwich, CT: Information Age Publishing.

Yin, R. K., & Davis, D. (2007). Adding new dimensions to case study evaluations: The case of evaluating comprehensive reforms. In G. Julnes & D. J. Rog (Eds.), *Informing federal policies for evaluation methodology* (New Directions in Program Evaluation, No. 113, pp. 75–93). San Francisco: Jossey-Bass.

Yin, R. K., & Heald, K. (1975). Using the case survey method to analyze policy studies. *Administrative Science Quarterly, 20,* 371–381.

Yin, R. K., & Oldsman, E. (1995). *Logic model for evaluating changes in manufacturing firms.* Unpublished paper prepared for the National Institute of Standards and Technology, U.S. Department of Commerce, Gaithersburg, MD.

Yin, R. K., Schmidt, R. J., & Besag, F. (2006). Aggregating student achievement trends across states with different tests: Using standardized slopes as effect sizes. *Peabody Journal of Education, 81*(2), 47–61.

Yin, R. K., & Yates, D. T. (1975). *Street-level governments: Assessing decentralization and urban services.* Lexington, MA: Lexington Books.

Zigler, E., & Muenchow, S. (1992). *Head Start: The inside story of America's most successful educational experiment.* New York: Basic Books.

Author Index

Subject Index

Note: In page references, b indicates boxes, e indicates exercises and f indicates figures.

SAGE researchmethods

The essential online tool for researchers from the world's leading methods publisher

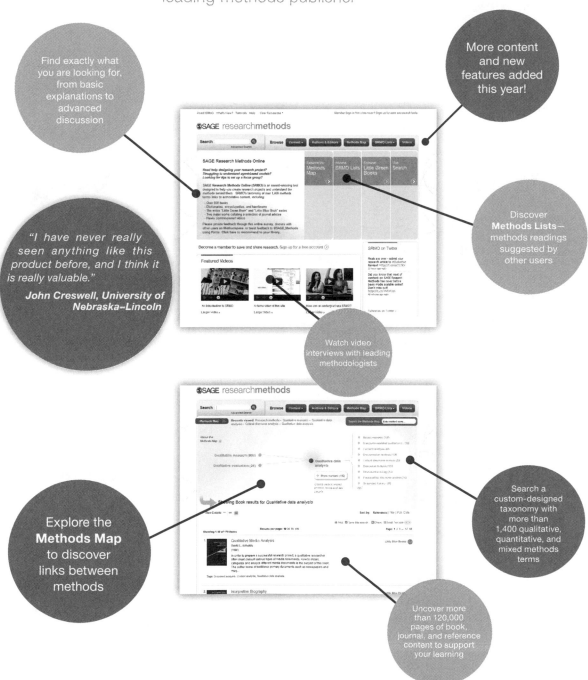

Find exactly what you are looking for, from basic explanations to advanced discussion

More content and new features added this year!

"I have never really seen anything like this product before, and I think it is really valuable."

John Creswell, University of Nebraska–Lincoln

Discover **Methods Lists**— methods readings suggested by other users

Watch video interviews with leading methodologists

Explore the **Methods Map** to discover links between methods

Search a custom-designed taxonomy with more than 1,400 qualitative, quantitative, and mixed methods terms

Uncover more than 120,000 pages of book, journal, and reference content to support your learning

Find out more at
www.sageresearchmethods.com